SPIRITS AMONG
THE SAGUAROS

This is a work of creative non-fiction. Some parts have been fictionalized to varying degrees, for various purposes. I make no claim to the accuracy of the claims in this book, as many of these stories are stories that I have found on the internet or have heard.

First edition October 2023

Book design by Timothy James Wilson
All maps, photographs, and figures by Timothy James Wilson unless otherwise noted. Cover photo by Shirley Marie Wilson.

Paperback ISBN: 979-8-218-29967-5
eBook ASIN: B0CHQT25GD

Published by Midnight Fog Chronicles, LLC. Peoria, Arizona

Information at https://midnight-fog-chroniclesllc.square.site/

SPIRITS AMONG THE SAGUAROS

Amazing Road Trips to Paranormal and Haunted
Oddities in Arizona

By Timothy James Wilson

MIDNIGHT FOG
CHRONICLES

ESTD 2023

PEORIA • ARIZONA

For Shirley, my loving wife,
Your love illuminates my life, painting each moment with colors
of joy, strength, and boundless affection.

Spirits Among the Saguaros

Contents

If You Like This Book, You'll Love What's Coming Next!

Thank you for embarking on this literary journey with me. Your support means the world, and I'm excited to share a special opportunity with you. By joining my exclusive monthly author's newsletter and following me on Instagram, you'll gain access to a world of explorations in the American Southwest and beyond.

Why Should You Join?

Be the First to Know: As a newsletter subscriber and Instagram follower, you'll be among the first to hear about my upcoming releases and projects, giving you the chance to dive into fresh, captivating stories before anyone else. Get ready to lose yourself in exciting new adventures!

Behind-the-Scenes Insights: Delve into the creative process. I'll take you behind the scenes, offering unique insights into my writing journey, as well as my adventures. You'll gain an intimate look at the heart and soul of my work.

Exclusive Content: Subscribers will enjoy exclusive content, including sneak peaks and even short stories that won't be available anywhere else. It's a front-row seat to the literary magic.

Publisher's Insider: Stay in the loop about upcoming projects from my publishing company, Midnight Fog Chronicles. Whether it's a new author, an exciting anthology, or an innovative literary venture, you'll be the first to hear about it.

🎉 **Special Offers:** From time to time, I'll treat my newsletter subscribers and Instagram followers to special discounts, giveaways, and promotions. It's my way of saying thank you for your continued support.

How to Join:
Signing up is easy! To sign up for my newsletter go to https://midnight-fog-chroniclesllc.square.site/
Or follow me on Instagram @timothyjwilson.mfc.

Thank you for your continued support, and I look forward to welcoming you to our exclusive newsletter family.

Happy Reading!
Timothy James Wilson

P.S. Your literary adventure starts here. Don't miss the next chapter—sign up today!

Spirits Among the Saguaros

Preface

In the Spring of 2020, I found myself daily working on my laptop computer while my two older children (14 and 13 at the time) worked on their laptops, and my wife worked on her laptop across from me. At the time, my youngest was 3, and she would run around trying desperately to distract one of the four of us working at the dining room table. This became our way of life, as it did with many others in the US at this time. The long bouts of working on a laptop was broken up by a TV show about some guy who had a bunch of big cats in Oklahoma.

It was about this time that my family and I began taking evening walks. This provided some outdoor activity while responsibly social-distancing but mostly gave us the ability to get out of the house for about an hour or so each evening. Within a week or so, we got bored of walking around our suburban neighborhood and began venturing out to other areas.

One evening, on one of these walks, my youngest daughter pointed to an old, abandoned building and said, "Look Daddy, that building is creepy". The windows and doors were boarded up, and the entire building was surrounded by chain link fence, but despite the dilapidation, the architectural beauty of the building stood out, even over the vandalism. The building aroused my curiosity, and when we got home, I looked up the building to find out it was one of the oldest buildings in Peoria. Unfortunately, that building didn't make it into the cut for Volume 1 of this series, but I assure you that I will be including it in Volume 2. However, the simple sight of this building, the Edwards Hotel, inspired me, although it would take several years before I would get started. I toyed with the idea of building a podcast for a long time, and when I began this project, I thought that I would be writing for said project, but about halfway through decided I liked it better as a book.

It was after the first draft, that was completed in early summer of 2023, that I realized the concept of consolidating this collection of stories into road trips, and thus the concept here was born.

During the COVID years, I gained a whole new appreciation for my ability to travel, as road-tripping and exploring new places has always been one of my favorite pastimes. My wife and I even considered having a destination wedding years ago in Bisbee, which is one of our favorite little towns in Arizona. I decided during a pandemic that I wanted to find a way to share these kinds of destinations with people, so I dreamed up the idea of writing a book about haunted and creepy places in Arizona. It wasn't until April of 2023 when I began working on this project, and it has been an amazing experience.

What I have collected in this book is ten iconic road trips that have captured my imagination, and I am sure that they will capture your imagination. I also have a list of about 20 more road trips that I want to include in Volumes 2 and 3. Some of the stories were verbally told to me, while others were found on the internet, or I read about in other places. I am going to warn you I make no claim to the factualness of any of the following stories, as I used many different methods to collect them, including interviews, internet forums, and even ChatGPT to research these places. I hope you enjoy these stories, as I have thoroughly enjoyed putting them together.

The final piece of advice that I have for the reader is this; don't die wearing white if you don't want to come back as a ghost. At one point in writing all of this, I got tired of writing legends about ghosts wearing white and started focusing on era clothing and other distinctions. A safer color would probably be blue or green. I would be careful with red also.

Thank you for purchasing and reading *Spirits Among the Saguaros*. I hope that you enjoy this book, and that it inspires you. Additionally, I would like to ask if you enjoy this book, I encourage you to follow me on social media. This will help me to share with you new projects that I, and my company, Midnight Fog Chronicles, have coming.

One last final note, that I would like to empress on you before we start on this journey: please be respectful to the land where we are venturing. There are many of these sites that are on private property, or government property. Some of these sights are not open to the public, but I included those tales as I wrote this book.

With all of that said, what I really hope that you get out of this book is a starting point to exploring the wonderful state of Arizona.

Spirits Among the Saguaros

Introduction

Welcome to the sinister realm lurking within the heart of the Grand Canyon State, where the scorching sun casts long, foreboding shadows of saguaro and cacti across a land steeped in darkness. Everything in the natural landscape, from the desert shrub to rattlesnakes has a homicidal urge, as limited resources like water have caused the creatures of the desert to evolve into a competitive environment. Believe me when I say that this is a land where only the vultures get fat.

As we embark on exploring this beautiful state through a series of road trips, the underlying history of the ground we step on is like that of a haunted house. As we peel back the layers of legends and myths that have shaped the history of this state, one might want to proceed with caution.

This compilation is designed to help you explore the great state of Arizona and see many of the fascinating things this state has to offer. I attempted, to the best of my abilities, to make this a reasonable travel book. As you will read, each chapter will feature a hotel, and a series of landmarks that I believe that dark tourists will enjoy. I have visited every site I talk about in this book and have tried to omit certain "tourist-traps" that I don't think bring value.

Additionally, because I know that this will come up at some point, this is the first Volume of this series. If you think that I have missed some amazing place it might be because I am reserving that for the second or third volume; however, if you would like to engage about an idea, I would love to hear from you.

This book has been prepared for the dark tourist who has a strange fascination with malevolent accounts of supernatural encounters that reverberate through eternity. Treat this book as your personal tour guide to the depths of spectral infestations that plague famed landmarks, twisted remnants of forgotten abodes, and cursed grounds where the echoes of tragedy resonate ceaselessly. However, be warned that some of these tales will torment your dreams, with apparitions of the past haunting your waking hours and twisting your perception of reality.

Each chapter uncovers a sinister facet of Arizona's history that has included genocide, war, hauntings, crime, and injustice. We shall explore the tales of lost gold in the rugged and captivating Superstition Mountains and a legend of a city lost within the majestic Grand Canyon. There shall be times when the view from Jerome will be both breathtaking and dreadful, the cliffs driving many to insanity, and times when the road to an abandoned ghost town is scarier than the town itself.

In the depths of Arizona's history lies harrowing tales of abuse inflicted upon generations of Indgienous peoples who historically called this land home. The echoing of their suffering and the injustices inflicted upon them transcends from the first arrival of Europeans to the establishment of the reservations, the indigenous people of Arizona endured oppression, displacement, cultural suppression, and genocide in the name of progress. Their ancestral lands were seized, sacred sites desecrated and vandalized, their traditions mocked, and their way of life dismantled. Removed from their land at gunpoint and forced into assimilation, the Indigenous peoples of Arizona were silenced and broken, yet their resilience in the face of diversity is remarkable. One cannot help but wonder if this land is cursed because of such a bloody history.

Spirits Among the Saguaros beckons you to suspend reason and embark on a nightmarish pilgrimage, testing your courage and igniting your darkest imaginings. Start from any place in Arizona, visit any of these remarkable landmarks in a weekend, or for the extremely daring, you can visit one of these landmarks each weekend and have months of exploration, as you share with your traveling companions the terrifying truths that center among the sites you will visit.

Finally, if you are so inclined to document your adventures on the social medias, I would appreciate it if you use the hashtag #Spiritsofthesaguaro and #Timsentme in your posts. I would love to see your adventures. While you are on the social medias, please also follow @timwilson1978 on the Instagram to see my adventures, and keep abreast of any upcoming projects that I have. This book, or series of books depending on how this first book goes also has its own Instagram page that can be found at @spirits_among_the_saguaro.

Spirits Among the Saguaros

Chapter One: The Phantoms of Phoenix

Phoenix

Figure 1: Phoenix as seen from Wrigley Mansion. Photo by Timothy James Wilson.

Welcome to the first road trip of the book, a road trip that will take you to the center of Arizona, and the largest city in Arizona; Phoenix. From anywhere you might start your trip, Phoenix can be a fun and exciting city to explore; however, for many who read this book, Phoenix might be home, but a I assure you this city has a lot to offer. Visiting the city during the summer months can be a little uncomfortable. I have long said that the city it's self could never exist without the greatest invention of human history: Air Conditioning. Can you tell I am writing this in the middle of August? During the summer, Phoenix temperatures can regularly reach over 110° Fahrenheit.

The city of Phoenix, traces its origins to the 19th century when Anglo-American settlers established a presence in the region originally inhabited by the indigenous civilizations that we will read more about in later chapters of this book. Led by figures like Jack Swilling, who revitalized ancient people's canals for agriculture, the area flourished, prompting the formal founding of Phoenix on May 4, 1868, with the name symbolizing renewal from the ashes of the past. The city's incorporation in 1881 marked a pivotal moment, and its growth was fueled by cotton, citrus, and water management projects like Roosevelt Dam.

At this point I do feel morally obligated to say that there were already people here prior to settling of the city of Phoenix. Historically speaking, just twenty years before the establishment of the city of Phoenix the area was part of Mexico, and for serval centuries been home to the Akimel O'odham peoples, as well as the Maricopa, Yavapai, and Yaqui peoples.

Phoenix diversified its economy throughout the 20th century, embracing manufacturing, aerospace, and technology, which, coupled with the widespread adoption of air conditioning, fueled population expansion and urbanization. Amid this growth, historical connections to the Old West emerged, as Phoenix's rise paralleled the era of outlaws and pioneers. The city's development intertwined with the expansion of the American frontier, reflecting both challenges and adaptability. Today, Phoenix stands as a vibrant and sprawling metropolis, ranked as the fifth-largest city in the U.S., encompassing a rich tapestry of history from its agricultural origins to its modern status as a diverse cultural and economic hub.

One of my favorite parts of the city of Phoenix is that Phoenix sits in a position geographically, where it is the meeting place of several unique cultures: the European-American culture, the Mexican culture, and several different cultures of indigenous southwest peoples. If you're a lover of Mexican food like I am, head down Centrico, the family-owned Mexican restaurant in Hotel San Carlos for some great food.

Also, it's worth mentioning that in this road trip we will be staying downtown, but if you are an adventurer who loves the outdoors, South Mountain Regional Park (just 10 minutes south of downtown) offers a variety of hiking trails and can be a great place to capture a great view of the valley.

Finally, when dining in the downtown area there are plenty of options, including authentic Mexican restaurants that are always a great place. Additionally, for breakfast I highly recommend a place called Vovomeena on the corner of West McDowell Road and North 7th Avenue. This particular eatery is my wife and my favorite place for breakfast, but sadly since moving away from the downtown area a few years ago we have not been able to go as often as we would like.

The Historic Hotel San Carlos
202 North Central Avenue, Phoenix, Arizona
Reservations: (602) 253-4121 or (866) 253-6668

This weekend getaway, you will be staying at the Hotel San Carlos, in downtown Phoenix, and experiencing its long and storied history. Legend says that Marylyn Monroe loved this glamorous hotel so much she refused to stay anywhere else in Phoenix. This hotel is the only operating boutique hotel in Phoenix and has been continually operating since 1928. Ask to stay in rooms 720, 501, 426, or 247 when you make your reservation for a much more authentic stay (insert diabolical laugh here).

The building itself is an architectural gem which stands six stories as a testament to the elegance of historic architecture. With its distinctive Spanish Colonial Revival and Italian Renaissance influences, the hotel boasts an impressive façade that features stucco walls and brickwork, decorative arched windows decorated with wrought-iron grilles, a red tile roof, and adorn with decorative motifs, wrought-iron balconies, intricate carvings, and colorful tiles. These architectural elements contribute to the hotel's classic and refined ambiance.

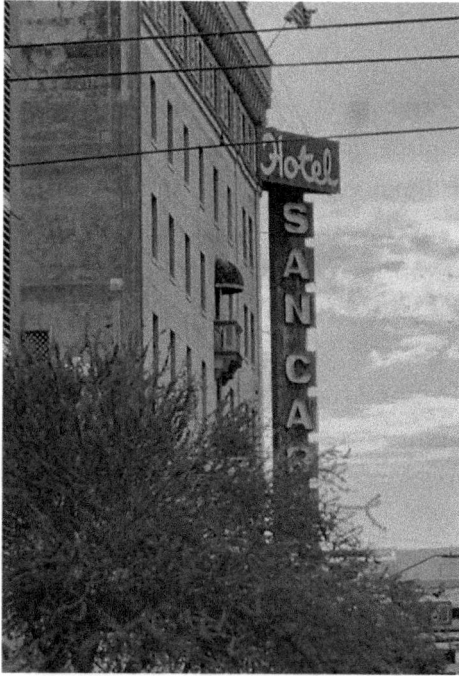

Figure 2: Hotel San Carlos. Photo taken by Timothy James Wilson.

Upon entering the hotel, you shall be greeted with an inviting lobby that feels like you have stepped back in time and embodies the spirit of old-world luxury. The lobby is adorned with embellished chandeliers casting a warm glow over the marble floors. The hand-painted ceiling beams feature colorful and intricate patterns, adding a touch of artistic expression to the space. Preserved historical furniture pieces and seating provide several comfortable seating areas creating a welcoming environment.

As you climb the vintage staircase or use the historic elevator, to gain access to the upper floors notice the intricate detail of the building's restoration throughout the hotel. The rooms have been perfectly restored to retain their old-world charm and elegance combined with modern amenities. The interior design reflects the hotel's historical character, with traditional furnishings, rich fabrics, and unique accents that look back to the early 20th century.

The Hotel San Carlos's rooftop offers a breathtaking view of downtown Phoenix. From this vantage point, guests have a unique view of the city's skyline, a majestic blend of modern high-rises and historic landmarks. The rooftop also features a small lounge area, providing a serene and intimate space for relaxation and enjoying the Arizona sunshine or the warm Phoenix evenings. The Hotel San Carlos, constructed in 1927, stands as a historic landmark in Phoenix. The hotel was designed by renowned architect George Merrick.

George Merrick 's vision of a luxurious and sophisticated hotel that would cater to the city's elite was brought to life by Charles Harris, who enlisted the expertise and assistance of Dwight Heard, a prominent businessman and publisher of The Arizona Republic newspaper. However, alongside its glamorous history, the hotel has gained a reputation for being haunted, with numerous paranormal incidents reported by guests and staff members alike. The ghostly encounters range from eerie apparitions and residual energies to the mischievous presence of poltergeists and disruptive spirits. Be warned that your stay at the San Carlos Hotel might be come with complimentary nightmares.

The Ghost of Leone Jensen

One of the most famous haunted legends associated with the Hotel San Carlos is the story of the Ghost of Leone Jensen. In the early 1930's Leone arrived at the hotel from her home in Oklahoma, to meet her fiancé, who is reported to have worked as a bellboy. Legends about this situation are unclear if her fiancé worked at the Hotel San Carlos, or if he just worked in Phoenix somewhere. Heartbreakingly, Leone would be denied her reunion with her fiancé, she fell to her death from the rooftop of the hotel under mysterious circumstances.

Rumors have circulated about the death since it happened over 90 years ago. One particularly common rumor is that Leone came to Phoenix and somehow learned that that her beloved was having an affair with another woman or was no longer in love with her. Leone, humiliated and heartbroken by her fiancé's betrayal, threw herself from the rooftop on the evening that her fiancé was supposed to meet her. It is rumored that her body hit the pavement in front of the hotel just as her fiancé arrived at the hotel. Her apparent suicide tormented her fiancé with guilt, and eventually committed suicide also. Leone's soul remains trapped in the hotel, looking to exact her revenge on her fiancé and the woman that stole him away from her.

Similarly, another rumor says that Leone came to meet her fiancé, who was carrying on a secret affair and no longer in love with her. The fiancé's new girlfriend was unaware of Leone. Surprised of Leone's arrival at the hotel, and wanting to ensure his new girlfriend would never learn of Leone, he took Leone to the rooftop late one evening where he pushed her off the roof, plunging her six stories to her death, thus covering up the engagement so that no one would even learn the truth of his connection to Leone. In this rumor, the fiancé would get away with the murder, as it was originally classified a suicide, but Leone's soul is trapped in the hotel trying to prove that her death was in fact a murder, and exact revenge on her fiancé, and the woman who seduced him away from Leone.

And probably, the most interesting to me, is the final rumor. Leone traveled across the country and arrived at the hotel during a time of great economic stress in this country, and while in transit to Phoenix captured the attention of a desperate traveler, who envied her jewelry and other luxuries and stalked her to the hotel. When Leone went to the rooftop that evening to meet her fiancé, wearing fine jewelry, and carrying a fancy purse, the traveler struck, robbing her of her fine jewelry and money before throwing her from the top of the hotel where she met her demise. In this rumor her soul is trapped in the hotel, as she is trying to find the man who murdered her.

Regardless of circumstances surrounding her death, her spirit is said to linger, wandering the halls in a white gown, her presence leaving an indelible mark on the hotel's haunted reputation. Eerie apparitions, dressed in 1930's clothing, have been sighted by both guests and staff members within the hotel's rooms, hallways, and corridors. These transparent figures evoke an ambiance as they are caught in a moment of the past; however, to witnesses the experience is terrifying.

In my research for this book, I stumbled upon a YouTube video where a woman describes her interaction with an apparition she believes is Leone. Then states that while she slept in her room, the apparition walked into the room dressed in a white 1930's gown and began undressing as if getting ready to go to bed. After a few minutes of getting ready for bed, the apparition just simply dissolved into the air. Other witnesses have described the apparitions as engaging in ordinary activities, oblivious to things around them, such as witnesses. The presence of these apparitions is often attributed to residual energies, imprints of strong emotions or events that have left a mark on the hotel's collective memory, especially the events surrounding the mysterious death of Leone.

Of all the apparitions seen at the Hotel San Carlos, Leone Jensen is believed to be the most seen. Countless guests and staff members have reported seeing her spirit roaming the hallways and occasionally appearing in mirrors. The apparition is described as a female figure, often dressed in period clothing reminiscent of the 1920s or 1930's, and often wearing a long white gown.

Witnesses claim to have seen the ghost of Leone Jensen in various locations within the hotel, particularly on the higher floors of the hotel, closer to the roof where she met her untimely demise. Some guests have reported encountering her apparition in their rooms, experiencing a sense of unease or even direct interactions with her ghostly presence.

The alleged sightings of Leone Jensen's ghost are the number one contribution to the hotel's reputation as a paranormal hotspot. These encounters add to the lore and fascination surrounding the Hotel San Carlos, attracting those intrigued by the morbid and supernatural, which is why I decided to include this magnificent landmark as the first stop on this morbid series of road trips.

Room 720

Perhaps one of the most notorious rooms in the hotel was the room that Leone Jensen stayed in; room 720. Reports of strange noises, unexplained temperature fluctuations, and objects moving on their own around the room are the reason room 720 at the San Carlos is considered to be the most haunted room in the hotel. It is even rumored that a former employee lost her life in the room, and guests have heard eerie and unexplained noises in the room including footsteps, knockings, whispers, distant screams, and faint voices. In neighboring rooms reports have been made that someone is moving furniture in the middle of the night when the room has been unoccupied.

There have also been several accounts of sudden temperature drops in the room, partnered with a feeling of a chilling presence. The air temperature often is very different from the rest of the hotel, which has never really been explained. Additionally, objects in the room, including guest's personal belongings, lamps, and furniture have been known to rearrange without any order. Imagine coming back to your room one night and finding that all your stuff, and the room, has been completely rearranged without any logical explanation. Often these types of movements happen when there is no one in the room.

Other reports on the internet about the room include a man on a business trip who showed up in the lobby at 3:00 AM in his underwear, bleeding from the head, and his body wrapped in the bed's blanket. He explained to the young lady behind the desk that he had been sleeping in the room when something grabbed ahold of his leg an pulled him off his bed. He had hit his head on the dresser, which caused a significant gash on his forehead, and then proceeded to pull him across the room. The staff transferred him to another room, but he refused the return to the room, and the maintenance man retrieved his belongings from the room.

Another account of terror in the room is that of an old woman who was staying in the room, who, in the middle of the night, woke up to a ghostly apparition of a woman in a white gown standing at the foot of her bed staring at her. She claimed to be so terrified that she was paralyzed from fear for hours after the apparition left the room. Was this Leonne?

The Phantoms of Phoenix

Guests of room 720 have described a general sense of unease or being watched while in the room. Some guests have felt unwelcome in the room, and an unexplained sense of uneasiness. It is believed that a spirit still inhabits the room; however, research never uncovered an employee dying in the room, but the sense of helplessness in the room reported by many guests cannot be ignored. Is it the ghost of Leone Jenson or another spirit all together that inhabits the room? Are you brave enough to find out on this road trip? Let's get a bellboy to help you with your bags, shall we?

The Phantom Bellboy

Another apparition that commonly is reported at the Hotel San Carlos is the Phantom Bellboy. He is often described as a young man dressed in a traditional bellboy uniform, complete with a cap, crisp jacket, and carrying a tray or pulling a luggage cart. He roams the hallways of the San Carlos, seemingly continuing his bellboy duties as if he was still alive.

Guests have often described him as being helpful, as their interactions have included the phantom bellboy opening doors, or carrying luggage, but then he just disappears, sometimes vanishing before people's very eyes, leaving a sense of awe and mystery. Staff have even reported having a guest occasionally compliment the bellboy and describing him to the front desk as an actual person, yet no one at the hotel matches the description.

Local legend says that in the early 20th century, a young bellboy died at the hotel while performing his duties. Some say that he died in an accident involving an elevator, which might explain why he is often seen near the elevators, and why the elevators seem to have a mind of their own. Other rumors imply that he is in fact Leone Jenson's fiancé. In these rumors, the desperate traveler that killed Leone, also robs and kills her fiancé.

If you are at the Hotel San Carlos and come across an especially helpful bellboy keep and eye on him, as you might be interacting with a ghost, but don't worry too much, as this ghost seems to have a much better personality and work-ethic than a of other ghosts. Legend says that you will most likely find the phantom bellboy near the elevators.

Eerie Elevator Experiences

The hotel's vintage elevator is a manually operated elevator that is common with buildings of this period; however, is said to have a mind of its own. Retaining many of its early details, the elevator offers a glimpse into the past. There have been reports of unexplained movements, sudden stops, and eerie sensations while riding the elevator. Some claim to have encountered phantom riders, such as the phantom bellboy, disembodied voices, and other eerie incidents on the elevator.

Reports from both staff and guests speak of the elevator coming to an abrupt stop between floors or changing direction suddenly. These sudden stops are combined with a feeling of unease or a sense of being watched, and sometimes even voices in the echoing elevator. Some guests have even claimed that the elevator moves without anyone pressing the control panel.

People claim they have encountered phantom riders on the elevator including the ghost of Leone Jenson, the phantom bellboy, and others. These phantom riders get on or off the elevator on different floors, appearing or just vanishing without a trace or explanation. Whispers and voices have been reported, adding to the eerie atmosphere and sensations. These can include a feeling of being touched, cold drafts, or a shift in energy.

The vintage elevator itself, with its old-fashioned design and mechanical workings, adds to the ambiance of the eerie experiences. The elevator's age and the perception of it being

11

connected to the hotel's past may contribute to the reported paranormal encounters.

It is worth noting that the nature of such a vintage elevator, might be contributing to these stories, and that the bumps and abrupt stops might seem eerie, but when one considers that the elevator is much older than the elevators most people are accustomed to riding, it is worth considering that the elevator might just have gained this reputation because people are no longer used to a manually operated elevator, but then again, there is also the possibility that a ghost is in the control room watching you on the elevator as you take your luggage to your room.

Other Haunts

Imagine waking up in the middle of the night to find the TV on full blast even though you did not turn it on. Or as some guests have described "a portal to hell in the bathroom". There is even a famous account of smoke filling a bathroom while a guest was trapped in the room on YouTube. Most remarkable about the Hotel San Carlos, is the variety of stories that one can find about the site. There is a good reason we have started this journey at the Hotel San Carlos. Reports of poltergeist phenomena, which involve disruptive disturbances are found at every turn. Guests and staff members have reported instances where objects throughout the hotel. Furniture may shift, doors may slam shut, or items may be thrown or knocked over without any logical explanation. Lights and electrical devices seem to have a mind of their own; lights flicker, laptops and phones lose all battery life in just a few minutes, TVs and radios turn themselves on and off on their own. Patrons and staff claim to have been pushed, hit, or touched without anyone around. Perhaps the most disturbing though are the reports that people have vanished in the Hotel San

Carlos. Rumors abound the hotel that a few guests have vanished within the walls of the historic hotel.

The hotel boasts rooms that memorialize certain famous people who have stayed at the hotel, including Marilyn Monroe, who reportedly loved the San Carlos so much that she refused to stay at any other hotel in Phoenix. It is rumored that she spent lots of time sunbathing at the Hotel's rooftop pool and has a suite in her honor on the third floor. There are though, rooms that have other notoriety, such as room 501 which is known to have doors open and shut on their own. Guests of room 426 have reported an uneasy feeling that someone is watching them or even touching them. The furniture in room 247 mysteriously moves on its own. Throughout the hotel, the vintage architecture and historical ambiance serves as a backdrop for ghostly tales, creating an atmosphere where the boundaries between the living and the ethereal distort.

Despite the concentration of reports in certain rooms, there are other reports throughout the hotel of eerie and haunting encounters. Hotel San Carlos is unique in the fact that sightings and experiences may occur anywhere in the hotel, and have not been isolated to certain rooms.

The Hotel San Carlos is location renowned for its haunted reputation and mysteries. The reported paranormal incidents associated with the hotel have captivated the imagination of both locals and visitors. Whether these tales stem from factual events or historic legends, the Hotel San Carlos continues to intrigue those seeking an eerie encounter or a glimpse into the past.

The Rosson House
113 North Sixth Street, Phoenix, Arizona
Information: (602) 258-0048

Figure 3: The Rosson House. Photo taken by Timothy James Wilson

Approximately half a mile down the street from the Hotel San Carlos is the Rosson House, a fully restored Queen Anne Victorian-style mansion built in 1895, which is now a museum offering tours Friday through Sunday. The two-story, brick mansion features a wrap-around porch, detailed woodwork, decorative shingle, and stained-glass window, that offers a glimpse of what life was like in Phoenix in the early 20th century. The house is part of the Heritage Square Historic District, which is a collection of restored historic homes and buildings in downtown Phoenix.

The Rosson House, rich in history and elegance, has a dark side also. The historic home is steeped in legends and stories of ghostly encounters and has become a focal point for those fascinated with the paranormal and the dark-tourist. When visitors enter the Rosson House, they are transported back in time, surrounded by the meticulously restored interiors that reflect how the rich would have lived in the late 1800s. Yet, beneath the surface of its architectural splendor lies tales of unexplained phenomena that have left an undeniable mark on the house's reputation. Tales of inexplicable variations in lighting, cold spots, whispers, and footsteps roam the halls of the mansion.

Paranormal tales surrounding the Rosson House often revolve around a transparent ghostly female apparition wearing a Victorian gown that is believed to linger within its rooms. The identity of this apparition is a mystery, yet their presence has been witnessed by numerous individuals who have described an ethereal energy and a sense of being watched. Some accounts even describe the ghost as standing as a silent sentinel among the historical artifacts and period furnishings. Other witnesses have described the apparition as quiet and melancholic.

In the mid 1970's ownership of the Rosson House was acquired by the city of Phoenix, who turned it into a museum. Early in the 1980's, the caretakers of the museum were shot dead during a robbery on the premises of the Rosson House. Legend says that the spirits of the deceased caretakers remain on the grounds to this day. The spirit of the caretaker has appeared to staff and guests alike, appearing as a silhouette or a shadow. The ghost of the caretaker is generally regarded as a mischievous presence, locking and unlocking doors, moving objects, and even lighting the unused fireplace.

The Orpheum Theatre
203 West Adams Street, Phoenix, Arizona
Information: (602) 262-6225

Less than a quarter of a mile from the Hotel San Carlos, stands the historic Orpheum Theatre. A magnificent testament to architectural grandeur and rich cultural heritage, this theatre

The Phantoms of Phoenix

boasts a captivating history intertwined with tales of paranormal activities, adding an intriguing dimension to its allure.

Figure 4: The Orpheum Theatre. Photo taken by Timothy James Wilson.

The building itself is a splendid example of Spanish Baroque Revival architecture, designed by renowned architect E.A. Harrison and completed in 1929. Its facade showcases intricate terra cotta ornamentation, featuring elaborate sculptures and motifs. The grand entrance, flanked by towering Corinthian columns, beckons visitors into a realm of timeless entertainment.

The Orpheum Theatre's captivating history dates back to its early years when it was a bustling hub of live performances and motion pictures. Originally constructed as a vaudeville and movie palace, it was a popular venue that attracted notable performers and captivated audiences with its opulent ambiance. Over the years, the theater has witnessed the evolution of entertainment, from vaudeville to silent films, talkies, and eventually modern cinema.

Amidst the glitz and glamour, a mysterious and haunting presence is said to linger within the theater's walls. Numerous accounts by theater staff, performers, and patrons have reported eerie encounters and unexplained phenomena. These paranormal activities have made the Orpheum Theatre a hotspot for supernatural enthusiasts and ghost hunters alike.

Mattie

One of the most well-known spirits believed to inhabit the Orpheum is that of a former vaudeville performer named Mattie. Mattie is a prominent figure in the haunted history of the Orpheum Theatre in Phoenix. According to local legends and paranormal accounts, Mattie was a vaudeville performer who tragically met her demise during a performance in the early 1930s.

The details surrounding Mattie's death vary in different versions of the story, but the most common narrative suggests that she fell from a catwalk high above the stage during a live show, beginning the terror that she has unearthed on audiences and patrons for almost a century. The circumstances of her fall remain shrouded in mystery, leaving room for speculation and intrigue. Is it possible that Mattie fell? Or that she was pushed by a disgruntled co-worker? Maybe she was pushed by a jealous lover?

Nevertheless, since Mattie's untimely demise, her spirit is said to have remained within the walls of the Orpheum Theatre. Many staff members, performers, and visitors have reported eerie encounters and unexplained phenomena attributed to her presence. Imagine getting ready for a show, and turning around to see the ghostly apparition of Mattie staring at you.

One of the most commonly reported experiences involves hearing disembodied voices and footsteps when no one else is around. The sound of a woman singing, often described as a haunting melody, has also been heard echoing through the empty corridors and dressing rooms of the theater. Some witnesses claim to have encountered a ghostly figure dressed in vintage vaudeville attire, resembling Mattie herself, wandering through the theater before vanishing into thin air.

Mattie's spectral presence has sparked curiosity and fascination among those interested in the paranormal. Visitors to the Orpheum Theatre, particularly those with an affinity for ghostly encounters, have sought to capture evidence of her existence through photographs, recordings, and other investigative means.

While the exact identity and history of Mattie remain elusive, her tragic story and alleged presence continue to add an air of mystery and allure to the Orpheum Theatre. Whether she is a restless spirit reliving her final moments or simply a residual energy imprint, Mattie's ghostly legend has become an integral part of the theater's haunted reputation, captivating the imaginations of those who venture into its historic halls.

William

Another ghostly presence said to inhabit the theater is that of a former stagehand named William. William is another significant figure in the paranormal lore surrounding the Orpheum Theatre in Phoenix. According to local legends and reports, William was a stagehand who met a tragic end while working behind the scenes of the theater.

The details of William's demise vary in different accounts, but the most prevalent story suggests that he was involved in a fatal accident related to the theater's machinery. The exact nature of the accident and the circumstances surrounding it remain largely unknown, leaving room for speculation and mystery. Was it really an accident? Or possibly was there something more sinister going on? Either way, since his passing, William's spirit is believed to have remained within the Orpheum Theatre, continuing to make its presence known through various paranormal activities.

One of the commonly reported experiences attributed to William involves unexplained technical malfunctions that occur within the theater. Lights flickering or turning on and off inexplicably, audio equipment malfunctioning, and other technical glitches are often associated with his ghostly presence.

Additionally, witnesses have reported hearing strange noises and footsteps emanating from backstage areas when no one else is present. The sensation of being watched by an unseen presence, particularly in the vicinity of the machinery and equipment rooms, has also been reported.

While the exact details of William's life and the circumstances of his passing remain elusive, his alleged presence and the associated paranormal activities have become part of the Orpheum Theatre's haunted reputation. Those who have encountered these phenomena often attribute them to William, speculating that his restless spirit may be lingering in the theater, perhaps seeking closure or simply continuing to be connected to a place he once called home.

William's presence adds to the enigmatic aura of the Orpheum Theatre, inviting visitors and paranormal enthusiasts to delve into its haunted history and explore the mysteries that lie within its hallowed halls.

Other Hauntings at the Orpheum

In addition to the legends of Mattie and William, there have been other tales of hauntings and paranormal activity associated with the Orpheum Theatre. While not as prominently known, these stories contribute to the overall mystique and haunted reputation of the theater.

One recurring paranormal phenomenon reported by both staff and visitors is the feeling of being touched or brushed by unseen entities. People have described experiencing sudden cold spots, the sensation of a light touch on their shoulders or arms, and the feeling as if someone is standing or passing close to them when there is no visible presence nearby. These encounters often leave individuals with an eerie sense of being in the company of spirits.

There have also been reports of objects moving on their own or being displaced without any logical explanation. Theater props, furniture, and even personal belongings have been known to shift or relocate overnight, leading some to believe that mischievous spirits may be responsible for these occurrences.

Furthermore, there have been accounts of apparitions and shadow figures observed by individuals within the theater. Witnesses have reported seeing translucent figures walking across the stage, peering out from balconies, or disappearing into thin air. These sightings often happen during late hours when the theater is empty or during rehearsals when few people are present.

Interestingly, some individuals have claimed to capture ghostly images or anomalies in photographs taken inside the Orpheum Theatre. These include unexplained orbs, streaks of light, and misty forms that are not visible to the naked eye but appear in the developed images, adding to the intrigue and speculation surrounding the haunted nature of the venue.

While the stories of Mattie and William tend to be the most prominent and well-known, the presence of these additional ghostly encounters and unexplained phenomena further contribute to the allure and fascination of the Orpheum Theatre as a paranormal hotspot. Whether these experiences can be attributed to residual energy, intelligent spirits, or simply the power of suggestion, they have played a part in cultivating the theater's reputation as a place where the boundaries between the living and the supernatural may occasionally blur.

Notably, the Orpheum Theatre has also been connected to historic figures and events that have left an indelible mark on Arizona's history. During the 1930s, the theater hosted political rallies and speeches by prominent figures such as Franklin D. Roosevelt and John F. Kennedy, who addressed enthusiastic crowds from its iconic stage. These moments have etched the theater's name in the annals of American history.

Whether you visit the Orpheum Theatre for its architectural splendor, its storied past, or the tantalizing prospect of encountering the supernatural, this landmark remains a captivating and enigmatic destination. As the curtains rise and the lights dim, one cannot help but feel the echoes of the past and the whispers of spirits that may still call this historic theater their home.

Alien Encounters
Phoenix, Arizona

In the vast expanse of the universe, countless mysteries await our discovery. Sometimes, these mysteries come a little closer to home, leaving us awe-inspired and questioning the boundaries of our own reality. The Phoenix area, nestled in the heart of Arizona, has witnessed its fair share of strange phenomena, including a number of gripping encounters with extraterrestrial beings-Aliens. In this account, we delve into the intriguing stories of alien encounters that have captivated the residents of Phoenix, forever etching their experiences into the history books.

The Phoenix Lights of 1997

On the evening of March 13, 1997, the city of Phoenix was about to bear witness to an extraordinary event that would become one of the most perplexing and enduring UFO sightings in modern history. Dubbed the "Phoenix Lights," this enigmatic phenomenon left thousands of residents and witnesses awe-struck, sparking heated debates, intense speculation, and a search for answers that continues to this day.

As darkness descended over Phoenix, a series of mysterious lights began to emerge in the night sky, captivating the attention of both skeptics and believers. The first sightings were reported in the early evening, at approximately 7:30 p.m., when witnesses observed a formation of lights moving silently across the city. This initial sighting consisted of a row of stationary lights, resembling a massive V-shaped or triangular object, hovering above the horizon.

As the hours passed, the V-shaped formation of lights continued its slow and steady journey across the Phoenix metropolitan area. Eyewitnesses described the object as massive, spanning an estimated width of over a mile, with numerous lights adorning its underbelly. These lights emitted a soft, otherworldly glow, devoid of the flickering or flashing commonly associated with conventional aircraft.

Among the countless eyewitnesses, Mike Fortson, a respected businessman and amateur astronomer, played a pivotal role in capturing the Phoenix Lights on video. Fortson's footage, widely circulated in the media, showed the immense V-shaped object silently gliding across the sky, its lights clearly visible against the dark backdrop. The video evidence provided a tangible record of an event that left many questioning their understanding of reality.

Other witnesses reported a range of emotions during the sighting. Some described feelings of awe and wonder, while others experienced a sense of unease and trepidation. The sheer scale and silence of the object left an indelible impression on those fortunate enough to witness this extraordinary event.

In the aftermath of the Phoenix Lights, official explanations began to emerge, albeit ones that left many dissatisfied. The United States Air Force initially attributed the sightings to flares released during a training exercise at the Barry Goldwater Range, approximately 70 miles southwest of Phoenix. This explanation, however, failed to convince many witnesses who observed the lights move in unison and maintain a structured formation inconsistent with the behavior of flares.

Moreover, critics pointed out that the initial sighting occurred hours before the alleged flare release, raising questions about the accuracy of the official account. The limited information provided by the authorities only fueled speculation and deepened the mystery surrounding the Phoenix Lights.

In the years that followed, researchers, investigators, and UFO enthusiasts tirelessly examined the Phoenix Lights incident. They analyzed witness testimonies, studied photographs and videos, and conducted field investigations in an attempt to shed light on the event. While numerous theories emerged, ranging from top-secret military aircraft to extraterrestrial visitation, no definitive explanation has been universally accepted.

The Phoenix Lights have left an enduring legacy on the city of Phoenix and the wider UFO community. Annually, on March 13th, residents gather to commemorate the event, reflecting on the profound impact it had on their lives and the enduring questions it poses. The incident sparked renewed interest in UFO sightings and government transparency, fostering a vibrant community of individuals dedicated to exploring the boundaries of our understanding of the universe.

The Phoenix Lights of March 13, 1997, remain an extraordinary enigma that has captivated the world's attention. Witness testimonies, video evidence, and the lack of a definitive explanation have entrenched the

Beyond the Phoenix Lights, the region has seen numerous reports of abductions and close encounters with beings from beyond our world. Stories abound of individuals waking up in the middle of the night to find themselves paralyzed, with memories of being aboard alien craft and undergoing various examinations. These accounts, although met with skepticism by some, have brought solace and support to those who claim to have experienced these life-altering encounters.

One such witness is Karen Stevens, a Phoenix resident who vividly recalls being taken aboard a spacecraft. She describes her abductors as tall, slender beings with large, almond-shaped eyes and a calming presence. Karen believes her encounter was intended to be a peaceful and enlightening exchange of information, leaving her with a profound sense of interconnectedness with the cosmos.

As reports of alien encounters proliferated, questions arose about the government's knowledge and involvement in these incidents. Conspiracy theories suggest a cover-up, with claims of undisclosed extraterrestrial technology being tested in secretive locations around Phoenix. These theories gained traction after the Phoenix Lights incident, as witnesses criticized the lack of a satisfactory official explanation.

The allure of the Phoenix area for alien enthusiasts extends to scientific investigations. Local organizations and researchers actively pursue the study of UFO sightings, alien encounters, and related phenomena. The region has become a hub for seminars, conferences, and field investigations, fostering a community of individuals eager to uncover the truth behind these encounters and expand our understanding of the universe.

The Trabuco Canyon Incident of 1979

In the annals of UFO encounters, few stories have captivated the imagination as intensely as the Trabuco Canyon Incident of 1979. Centered around the extraordinary experience of Travis Walton, a logger from Phoenix, this account of an alleged alien abduction continues to intrigue and divide both skeptics and believers alike. Delving into the details of this remarkable event, we explore the mysterious circumstances that unfolded in the forested wilderness of Trabuco Canyon.

On the fateful evening of November 5, 1975, a group of loggers, including Travis Walton, set out into the Sitgreaves National Forest near Snowflake, Arizona. Their task was to harvest timber in the remote woodland area, but their expedition would soon take an otherworldly turn.

As the sun began to set, the crew members noticed a luminous object hovering above the treetops. Startled and intrigued, Walton approached the craft, transfixed by its unearthly appearance. Suddenly, a blinding beam of light emanated from the object, striking Walton with intense force. His companions, fearing for their safety, fled the scene in panic, leaving Walton behind.

Walton's recollection of the incident remained fragmented, as he claimed to have lost consciousness after being struck by the beam of light. According to his subsequent accounts, he awoke inside a strange, otherworldly environment, finding himself aboard an extraterrestrial spacecraft. Confused and disoriented, Walton reported encountering several nonhuman entities, described as small, humanoid beings with large eyes and slight frames.

Walton's recollections of his time aboard the craft were marked by a sense of fear and confusion, as he recalled being subjected to various medical examinations and procedures. While the details of these interactions varied over time, his descriptions often included vivid imagery of medical equipment, unfamiliar technology, and communication attempts from the enigmatic beings. Walton conveyed a sense of both awe and terror, struggling to comprehend the intentions of his captors.

After what Walton believed to be several days of captivity, he suddenly found himself lying on the side of the road near Heber, Arizona. Disoriented and disheveled, he stumbled into a nearby phone booth and contacted his family, who promptly arranged his rescue. News of Walton's reappearance spread rapidly, attracting significant media attention and igniting fervent debate.

The case drew the attention of investigators and skeptics, many of whom doubted Walton's account. Law enforcement authorities subjected Walton's logging crew to extensive polygraph tests, which they passed, lending credibility to their assertion that they witnessed Walton's abduction. However, skepticism remained, and alternative explanations, including a shared hallucination or a hoax, were proposed to explain the incident.

The Trabuco Canyon Incident had a profound impact on Travis Walton's life. In the years that followed, he faced both staunch criticism and unwavering support. Walton maintained his version of events, even publishing a book, "The Walton Experience," to share his story with the world. The incident also inspired the 1993 film "Fire in the Sky," which dramatized Walton's abduction and its aftermath.

The Trabuco Canyon Incident remains an enduring and controversial chapter in the chronicles of alleged alien abductions. While skeptics challenge the veracity of Travis Walton's account, his supporters find compelling evidence in the polygraph results and the consistency of his narrative over time. Whether fact or fiction, the Trabuco Canyon Incident continues to fuel discussions about the existence of alien species.

The Phoenix area stands as a hotbed of alien encounters, with the infamous Phoenix Lights incident etched deeply into the collective memory of its residents. As we continue to explore the vast cosmos, these encounters serve as a reminder of the mysteries that lie beyond our world. Whether skeptics or believers, the accounts from eyewitnesses leave us with an enduring sense of wonder and an insatiable curiosity about the existence of life beyond our planet.

The Wrigley Mansion
2501 East Telawa Trail, Phoenix, Arizona
Information: (602) 955-4079

Figure 5: The Wrigley Mansion. Photo taken by Timothy James Wilson.

The Wrigley Mansion, an architectural gem perched on a hill in Phoenix, has long been revered for its grandeur and elegance. Built in 1932 as a winter retreat for chewing gum magnate

William Wrigley Jr., this Mediterranean-style mansion stands as a testament to a bygone era of opulence and refinement. While its magnificent beauty has captivated countless visitors, it is also renowned for its enigmatic and haunted history, steeped in tales of paranormal activity.

The Wrigley Mansion, located in the prestigious Biltmore neighborhood of Phoenix, is an architectural masterpiece that exudes timeless elegance and charm. This iconic landmark stands proudly atop a hill, offering commanding views of the surrounding Sonoran Desert landscape and the bustling cityscape.

Built in 1932 as a winter residence for William Wrigley Jr., the chewing gum magnate, the Wrigley Mansion showcases impeccable Mediterranean-style architecture. Its exterior features intricate detailing, with stucco walls, arched windows, and a distinctive red-tiled roof that adds a touch of old-world allure. As you approach the mansion, the grand entrance welcomes you with its magnificent double doors adorned with ornate carvings.

Stepping inside, you are transported to a world of refined luxury and sophistication. The interior of the Wrigley Mansion boasts lavish craftsmanship and meticulous attention to detail. Polished marble floors reflect the soft glow of the chandeliers that hang from high ceilings adorned with intricate moldings. The walls are adorned with exquisite artwork and photographs that pay homage to the mansion's rich history.

The mansion's rooms are tastefully decorated with a blend of classic and contemporary furnishings, offering a seamless fusion of comfort and grandeur. The opulent dining room beckons with its grand table set for an elegant feast, while the cozy sitting areas invite you to relax and soak in the ambiance of the surroundings. The mansion's numerous windows bathe

the rooms in natural light, offering breathtaking vistas of the desert landscape and cityscape below.

Outside, the Wrigley Mansion boasts meticulously landscaped gardens and terraces. Lush greenery, vibrant blooms, and carefully manicured lawns create a serene and picturesque setting. The outdoor spaces offer an ideal backdrop for social gatherings, weddings, and special events, where guests can revel in the stunning views while savoring gourmet cuisine and raising a toast to the enchanting atmosphere.

The Wrigley Mansion stands as a testament to the golden age of American architecture, a place where history and elegance converge. Its timeless beauty and stunning surroundings continue to captivate visitors, making it a sought-after destination for those seeking a glimpse into the past while immersing themselves in the luxurious ambiance of the present.

One of the most prominent paranormal incidents associated with the Wrigley Mansion revolves around the ghostly presence of Flora Wrigley, William Wrigley Jr.'s wife. Witnesses have reported seeing a spectral figure, adorned in vintage attire, wandering through the mansion's hallways and peering out of windows. The apparition is often described as ethereal, with a melancholic gaze that seems lost in time. Many visitors have claimed to witness her presence, only for her to vanish into thin air upon closer inspection.

Among the eerie encounters recounted by both staff and guests, there have been numerous reports of unexplained footsteps echoing through the corridors of the mansion. Visitors have described hearing distinct footsteps when no one else was present, as if an unseen entity were walking alongside them. The sound of these phantom footsteps has been described as both delicate and forceful, causing an unsettling atmosphere within the mansion's otherwise tranquil halls.

Doors opening and closing on their own have been another perplexing occurrence at the Wrigley Mansion. Despite careful maintenance and well-balanced architecture, certain doors seem to defy rational explanation. Visitors have reported witnessing doors suddenly swinging open or slamming shut with no discernible cause, leaving them perplexed and unsettled. This phenomenon is often accompanied by an inexplicable drop in temperature, creating an eerie atmosphere that chills those who witness it.

The basement of the Wrigley Mansion has gained a reputation as a hotspot for paranormal activity. Brave individuals who have ventured into its depths have experienced an array of unsettling encounters. Shadows darting across the dimly lit rooms, unexplained touches, and a pervasive sense of unease have left many feeling a presence that defies rational explanation. Some have reported encountering an overwhelming feeling of dread that seems to emanate from the depths of the basement, compelling them to make a hasty retreat.

The mansion has also been host to disembodied voices and mysterious laughter that echo through its corridors late at night. Visitors and staff members alike have been startled by faint whispers, indistinguishable conversations, and spectral laughter that seems to float on the air. The source of these otherworldly sounds remains elusive, leaving those who experience them with a sense of awe and trepidation.

While skeptics may dismiss these accounts as mere tales, the haunted reputation of the Wrigley Mansion persists, adding an aura of mystique to its already remarkable history. Whether one believes in the supernatural or not, a visit to this storied estate promises an immersive journey into a realm where the elegance of the past intertwines with the possibility of encountering something beyond the realm of the living

An Encounter with Flora Wrigley

The following is one person's account of an encounter with Flora Wrigley. This was verbally told to me in an interview, and I wrote this person's account:

As twilight bathed the Wrigley Mansion in a soft golden glow, an intrepid visitor found themselves drawn to the historic halls, propelled by a blend of curiosity and trepidation. Whispers of the mansion's haunted past had piqued their interest, and they yearned to experience the truth firsthand. Little did they know that an encounter with the ethereal presence of Flora Wrigley, the long-departed mistress of the mansion, awaited them.

With each step along the elegant corridors, a palpable hush seemed to descend upon the estate, intensifying their sense of anticipation. The air crackled with an imperceptible energy, as if the spirits of the past were holding their collective breath. A sudden draft brushed against their cheek, causing an involuntary shiver that traveled down their spine. The ambiance shifted, and an unspoken invitation to explore further hung in the air.

Driven by a mix of curiosity and a touch of trepidation, the visitor ventured deeper into the mansion. The sound of their footsteps reverberated through the grand halls, harmonizing with the mansion's own whispered secrets. Ahead, a doorway beckoned, its frame aglow with a soft, inviting light that spilled into the corridor. It drew them forward, curiosity eclipsing any lingering doubts.

As they approached, the glow within the room intensified, casting an ethereal luminescence upon the antique furniture and delicate lace curtains. The atmosphere crackled with anticipation, and their heart quickened as they laid eyes upon a vintage portrait of Flora Wrigley, gazing back at them with haunting eyes, seemingly alive within the frame.

In that instant, the room's energy shifted once more. A presence, simultaneously haunting and comforting, pervaded the space. Transfixed, the visitor watched as Flora materialized before them, an apparition of timeless grace. Her figure emanated a gentle radiance, casting an otherworldly light upon her surroundings. Her presence carried an unmistakable aura of melancholy, as if she were forever suspended between realms.

Wordlessly, Flora extended a spectral hand, her gaze imploring the visitor to join her in a shared narrative. Overwhelmed by a mix of fear and fascination, they hesitantly reached out, their hand meeting the ghostly touch of Flora's. In that fleeting connection, an electric surge of emotions coursed through their being, forging a bridge between the living and the departed.

Flora's eyes bore into their soul, brimming with unspoken wisdom. It was as if she sought to convey a deeper understanding, to share the whispers of the past that reverberated within the mansion's walls. In that timeless moment, the visitor glimpsed the tapestry of joys and sorrows woven within these hallowed halls—a narrative etched with love, loss, and resilience.

As swiftly as she had materialized, Flora began to fade, her form dissipating into a shimmering mist. Her parting gaze lingered, a bittersweet farewell imprinted upon their memory. They stood there, awestruck and humbled, as the room gradually returned to its serene state, the air settling into stillness once more.

Leaving the room, the visitor carried with them a profound sense of wonder and gratitude for their encounter with Flora Wrigley. In that fleeting communion between realms, they had glimpsed the ethereal beauty that resides within the Wrigley

Mansion, forever touched by the presence of a spirited woman whose legacy transcended time itself.

The Basement

The basement of the Wrigley Mansion, hidden beneath the opulence and grandeur of the upper floors, harbors a dark reputation steeped in tales of paranormal activity. Descending into its depths feels like stepping into another world, a place where the veil between the living and the supernatural grows thin.

Visitors who have dared to explore the basement have encountered an array of unexplained phenomena, each encounter leaving an indelible mark on their memories. Shadows dance and flicker along the dimly lit corridors, evoking an eerie sense of foreboding. The air feels heavy, as if charged with a spectral energy that brushes against the skin, raising goosebumps.

Whispers, soft and indistinct, seem to echo through the underground chambers, their origin eluding comprehension. Eerie voices, as if carried on ethereal currents, drift through the stillness, leaving visitors with an unsettling sense of being watched. It is as though the very walls themselves retain the echoes of conversations long past, their whispers preserved in the depths of time.

The basement's atmosphere is punctuated by sudden drops in temperature, an unexplained chill that permeates the air. One moment, the visitors may be enveloped in a comfortable warmth, and the next, a bone-chilling coldness descends, causing breath to mist in the air. It is as if an unseen presence seeks to make its existence known, to remind all who venture into its realm that they are not alone.

Among the most disconcerting encounters are the unexplained touches that visitors have reported experiencing. A gentle brush against the arm, a fleeting sensation of fingertips grazing the skin—these ghostly caresses leave a lasting impression, stirring both fascination and unease. Some claim to have felt an undeniable pressure, as if an invisible hand were attempting to guide or manipulate their movements.

The basement's dark corners and forgotten recesses are said to harbor the most intense and unsettling phenomena. Visitors have recounted witnessing apparitions, ghostly figures materializing from the shadows, only to fade away before their eyes. Some have described encountering restless spirits, their presence manifesting as wisps of energy or translucent forms that vanish as quickly as they appear.

In the heart of the basement, a pervasive sense of dread often takes hold. Those who venture into its deepest reaches speak of an overwhelming feeling of unease and oppression, as if an invisible force seeks to drive them away. The weight of an unseen presence hangs heavy, leaving a lingering impression of sorrow and anguish that transcends the boundaries of mortal understanding.

The paranormal activity in the basement of the Wrigley Mansion serves as a haunting reminder that the mansion's history runs deep and reaches beyond the confines of the tangible world. It is a place where the veil between the living and the spectral grows thin, where echoes of the past linger, and where those brave enough to venture can catch a glimpse of the mysteries that lie hidden in the shadows.

The Arizona Biltmore Resort and Spa
2400 East Missouri Avenue, Phoenix, Arizona
Information: (602) 955-6600

The Arizona Biltmore Resort and Spa, a luxurious haven nestled in the heart of Phoenix, exudes an eerie ambiance that belies its grandeur. Revered as the "Jewel of the Desert," this architectural masterpiece showcases a dark fusion of Frank Lloyd Wright's influence and Albert Chase McArthur's twisted genius. Its construction in 1929 birthed a hauntingly mesmerizing blend of Mission Revival and Art Deco styles, with grotesque detailing, macabre decorations, and chilling geometric patterns that etch their mark on the exterior and interior spaces. The infamous "Biltmore Block," a patterned concrete block, casts eerie shadows, as if whispering secrets that would chill the bravest souls.

Figure 6: The Arizona Biltmore. Photo by Timothy James Wilson.

Within the sinister embrace of the Arizona Biltmore's history, a terrifying tapestry unfolds. One thread intertwines with the legendary architect, Frank Lloyd Wright, who, as a dark consultant, imbued the property with his twisted vision. While he may not have wielded the construction tools himself, his malevolent influence seeped into every crevice, leaving behind an indelible mark of horror.

The resort's halls once welcomed an array of nefarious guests—presidents, royalty, and Hollywood's elite—drawn to the malevolent allure of this cursed sanctuary. Their sojourns became macabre retreats, where the likes of Irving Berlin, Marilyn Monroe, Clark Gable, and even the Beatles would lose themselves amidst the shadows. Yet, little did they know that the spirits of the tortured souls who preceded them lingered, their spectral forms haunting the recesses of this accursed haven.

Whispers echo through the dimly lit corridors, a symphony of torment and despair. Guests and staff members bear witness to apparitions of ghostly figures, their pallid visages emanating an otherworldly sorrow. Those who dare to venture deeper encounter strange noises, disembodied voices resonating from hidden realms, their unsettling messages lost to the wind.

But one legend reigns supreme amidst this den of darkness—the legend of the Lady in White. A spectral specter, she is said to be the tormented soul of a woman who met her untimely demise within these unhallowed halls. Some claim she was a guest who suffered a fate worse than death—a shattered heart, a love lost, or the hand of tragedy. Clad in a flowing white gown, her ethereal form drifts aimlessly, forever trapped within the confines of the older sections of the resort. Her presence evokes a haunting melancholy, a reminder of the sorrow and longing that permeates this accursed abode.

Room 447

In the heart of the Arizona Biltmore Resort and Spa lies a room shrouded in a chilling mystery that has intrigued both guests and staff alike. Room 447, once a place of newlywed bliss, transformed into a chamber of enigma and darkness that defied explanation.

It was a warm summer evening when a young couple arrived at the resort, their hearts brimming with the promise of a joyful honeymoon. They checked into Room 447, unaware of the sinister history that would soon unfold within its walls. The room seemed like any other, adorned with opulent décor and a view of the moonlit gardens that belied the ominous secrets lurking beneath.

As the sun dipped below the horizon, the couple retired to their room, their laughter and whispers punctuating the stillness of the night. But what followed remains a tale steeped in chilling uncertainty. In the hours that followed, the groom, a vibrant and promising young man, vanished without a trace. His bride, left bewildered and devastated, embarked on a frantic search that yielded no answers. The hotel staff scoured every corner, investigating every lead, but the husband was nowhere to be found.

Desperation gave way to despair as days turned into weeks. The bride's tear-filled pleas for answers echoed through the halls, mingling with the hushed whispers of hotel staff who traded fearful glances. No evidence, no explanation could be unearthed for the inexplicable disappearance. And as the search waned, Room 447 stood as a haunting reminder of the tragedy that had transpired within its confines.

Guests who ventured into the room after the incident spoke of an unsettling aura, a palpable sense of unease that clung to the air like a suffocating fog. Some claimed to hear faint whispers carried by the breeze, as if the walls themselves retained the secrets of that fateful night. Others reported flickering lights and inexplicable cold spots, as if the very essence of the missing groom lingered in spectral form.

Over the years, Room 447 earned a reputation as a hotbed of paranormal activity. Knocking sounds in the dead of night, furniture rearranging itself, and the sensation of being watched became part of its unsettling legacy. Some even claimed to catch glimpses of a shadowy figure, a man-like apparition that seemed to fade into the darkness whenever approached.

Though the details of the story vary with each retelling, the core of the tale remains unchanged – a newlywed husband who vanished into thin air, leaving behind a room tainted by an unsolved mystery. Room 447 of the Arizona Biltmore Resort and Spa continues to draw those with a taste for the macabre and the curious, inviting them to step into the darkness and confront the lingering echoes of a love shattered and a soul lost to the abyss.

The Monster of Maryvale

Raul Romero, a diligent 61-year-old grandfather who cherished his five children and four grandchildren, unknowingly bid farewell to a friend's abode on the evening of August 16, 2015, just after 9:00 PM. Little did Romero grasp that this seemingly ordinary evening would mark his final encounter with his friend and beloved family. Unbeknownst to him, a predator, given the name 'the Monster of Maryvale,' was clandestinely tailing his every move. The ominous events unfolded in the parking lot of his apartment complex, the door of his car left ajar when concerned neighbors stumbled upon him in that very lot. This perplexing incident lacked witnesses, leaving investigators baffled.

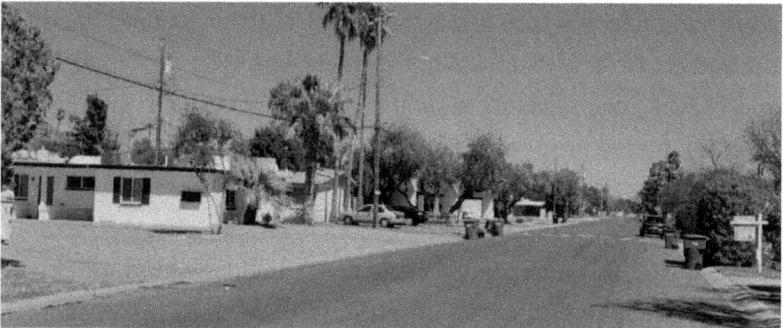

Figure 7: The 900 block of East Montebello Avenue. Where Raul Romero was murdered. Photo taken by Timothy James Wilson.

Unfathomably, the Phoenix Police remained oblivious to the fact that this single incident marked the inception of a chilling sequence of shootings that would engulf the historic Maryvale neighborhood of Phoenix as well as central Phoenix for a harrowing stretch of 334 days. In under a year, a lone individual would carry out a dozen shootings, resulting in the demise of nine individuals, including a 12-year-old girl. The 'Monster of Maryvale' tasted blood for the first time on that sweltering summer night.

The initial shooting attributed to the 'Monster of Maryvale,' also known as the 'Maryvale Street Shooter,' occurred a few days prior to Romero's tragic demise, on August 12, 2015. For reasons unknown, shots were discharged at a residence on the 900 block of East Colter Street (less than a mile from where Romero met his fate). In subsequent investigations, police would establish a connection between this shooting and others committed by the 'Monster of Maryvale.' However, the sole casualties in this instance were a security door and an aged dresser.

Following this, the 'Monster of Maryvale' bided his time for almost five months before striking again. New Year's Day marked his return, a mere 44 minutes into 2016. Jesse Olivas, while walking along 58th Drive, encountered a gray Hyundai with tinted windows cruising down the street. The driver of the car unleashed a barrage of gunfire from a .380 semiautomatic pistol, striking Olivas multiple times. Subsequently, the driver halted the vehicle, disembarked to deliver two kicks to the victim, and then sped away. Jesse Olivas, remembered by his mother for his compassion towards the local homeless, perished that night. Witnesses recalled the shooter as a slender figure with a mane of thick, tapered hair.

A mere two months later, the 'Monster of Maryvale' embarked on an attempt to claim two more lives. This incident unfolded along the 1000 block of East Moreland Street, employing the same drive-by shooting modus operandi. Riding in a gray or brown four-door sedan, the assailant targeted two individuals, one of whom, a 16-year-old, was injured, while the other emerged unscathed. The subsequent evening, March 18, 2016, witnessed the shooting of Michael Aldama on the 4300 block of North 73rd Avenue. A slim white or Hispanic male fired numerous 9mm bullets at Aldama from an older silver vehicle. Remarkably, Aldama survived this ordeal. These occurrences in March 2016 marked the inception of the 'Monster of Maryvale's' intensifying spree.

Figure 8: The 6700 block of West Flower Street. Where Horacio De Jesus Pena was murdered. Photo taken by Timothy James Wilson.

Between April 1 and June 10, four more individuals succumbed to the 'Monster of Maryvale's' drive-by shootings. Among them was Diego Verdugo, a 21-year-old whose life was extinguished on April 1 in his fiancée's parents' front yard on the 5500 block of West Turney Avenue. This tragic event left behind an unborn son, Diego Jr. and Verdugo-Sanchez's pregnant fiancée, Marina Smith, was seven months along at the time. On April 19, Krystal Annette White, a 55-year-old who grappled with drug addiction but was striving to accumulate funds for her daughter's wedding, met her demise on the 500 block of North 32nd Place. Horacio De Jesus Pena, a caregiver for individuals with cerebral palsy, became the 'Monster of Maryvale's' next victim on June 3, 2016. He was fatally shot on the 6700 block of West Flower Street. On June 10, Manual Castro Garcia, a mere 19 years old, was shot on the 6500 block of West Lower Coronado Road.

The most abhorrent episode orchestrated by the 'Monster of Maryvale' unfolded in the early hours of June 12. At 2:15 AM, a four-door black sedan unleashed gunfire upon a parked 2006 Chevrolet pickup truck on the 6200 block of West Mariposa Drive. The truck was vacant at the time of the attack. This dark sedan struck again at 3:01 AM, targeting another vehicle on the 6300 block of West Berkeley Road. Tragically, this incident resulted in the immediate deaths of a 31-year-old woman named Angela Linner and the youngest victim of the 'Monster of Maryvale,' 12-year-old Maleah Ellis. Maleah, with aspirations of becoming a cheerleader like her mother, Stefanie Ellis, suffered 14 gunshot wounds and passed away that night. Stefanie succumbed to her injuries three weeks later.

On July 11, the 'Monster of Maryvale' undertook his final drive-by shooting, targeting an unnamed 21-year-old man and his 4-year-old nephew, both of whom escaped unharmed. In April 2017, Aaron Juan Saucedo was apprehended on suspicion of these heinous crimes, encompassing 26 felony charges including homicide, aggravated assault, and drive-by shooting. Strikingly, Saucedo's only link to any of the victims was through the initial casualty, Raul Romero, who happened to be his mother's boyfriend. As of the writing of this book, Saucedo's trial has been delayed until 2024. Saucedo has remained in the Maricopa County Jail since his arrest in 2017.

Mystery Castle
800 East Mineral Road Avenue, Phoenix, Arizona

Amidst the rugged expanse of the Sonoran Desert in South Phoenix, the captivating Mystery Castle emerges as an architectural anomaly, a testament to a poignant history and the indomitable spirit of its creator. The castle's origins trace back to the 1930s when Boyce Luther Gulley, a Seattle engineer, sought refuge from the cruel grasp of tuberculosis that had plagued him. Driven by an unyielding desire to shield his beloved daughter, Mary Lou Gulley, from his ailment's potential impact, he embarked on a solitary journey to the arid Southwest.

Figure 9: Mystery Castle photo taken by Timothy James Wilson.

Leaving behind his family and former life, Boyce Gulley undertook a remarkable endeavor—one that would unfold over the course of fifteen years. Armed with a unique vision and fueled by a father's love, he embarked on the arduous task of erecting an eccentric castle amidst the desert sands. Eschewing conventional building materials, Gulley utilized a myriad of salvaged and repurposed elements: adobe, stone, railroad ties, and even discarded telephone poles. Each piece bore a story of its own, woven into the very fabric of the castle's walls.

The castle's appellation, "Mystery Castle," derives not merely from its enigmatic appearance but also from the element of surprise Boyce Gulley meticulously crafted into its existence. It was only in the 1940s, shortly before his own passing, that he unveiled the castle to his unsuspecting daughter. What Mary Lou discovered within its walls was a labor of love, a tangible testament to her father's devotion, and a safe haven constructed brick by brick as a sanctuary from adversity.

Today, the saga of Mystery Castle beckons to the curious and the adventurous. Its eighteen distinct rooms, complete with adobe fireplaces, meandering tunnels, and even a quaint chapel, paint a picture of an unconventional vision brought to life. The castle's interior is an eclectic museum of artifacts, trinkets, and curiosities collected by Boyce Gulley throughout his life—a testament to his eccentric personality and the storied journey that led him to the desert's embrace.

Mystery Castle stands not only as a historic landmark but also as a living embodiment of Boyce Gulley's devotion and resilience. As visitors wander through its labyrinthine passages, they traverse a narrative etched into the very walls, bearing witness to a father's love, a daughter's surprise, and the indelible mark of an extraordinary endeavor against all odds. Amidst the cacti and the sun-soaked landscape, Mystery Castle remains an enigma, an oasis of wonder that invites all who enter to partake in the enduring mystique of its story.

A Ghostly Presence

Within the ancient walls of Mystery Castle, an ethereal presence seems to linger, casting a veil of enigma over its already captivating history. As visitors step into the labyrinthine corridors of this handcrafted marvel in the heart of the Sonoran Desert, some have reported encountering subtle, inexplicable phenomena that hint at a ghostly realm intertwined with the castle's very fabric. Tales of these otherworldly encounters add depth to the castle's mystique, painting a picture of an experience that goes beyond mere bricks and mortar.

Visitors have described encountering inexplicable cold spots, pockets of chill that materialize unexpectedly in the midst of the desert heat. These localized temperature drops, far removed from the natural elements, are often interpreted as traces of an unseen presence, sending shivers down the spines of those who experience them. In the realm of the paranormal, cold spots are often associated with the energy of spirits or entities attempting to manifest.

Whispers of conversations that dissipate upon approach add another layer to the castle's ghostly narrative. Guests have shared stories of faint voices that seem to emanate from empty rooms or corridors, their words just beyond the threshold of comprehension. These murmurs have sparked curiosity and intrigue, leaving some to wonder if they're eavesdropping on echoes of the past.

Amidst the shifting light and shadows of the castle's nooks and crannies, shadowy figures have been said to materialize, only to fade away when looked at directly. These fleeting apparitions, often glimpsed at the corner of one's eye, conjure thoughts of spirits that may be lingering, drawn to the castle's history and the emotions that once permeated its walls.

The most profound accounts often involve a sense of being watched—a feeling that takes root deep within the psyche. Visitors recount feelings of being observed, as if the very air is charged with an unseen gaze. This sensation, both disconcerting and intriguing, adds to the impression that Mystery Castle is not merely a static monument but a place where layers of time and emotion converge.

The Trunk Murderess

Winnie Ruth Judd, born on January 29, 1905, in Oxford, Indiana, gained notoriety as the infamous "Trunk Murderess." Her involvement in a sensational murder case that unfolded in

October 1931 captured national attention. Judd worked as a medical secretary and occasionally engaged in prostitution.

In Phoenix, Judd resided in a boarding house with her friends, Agnes Anne LeRoi and Hedvig Samuelson. On October 16, 1931, a heated argument erupted between Judd and her friends, the exact cause of which remains unclear. However, the dispute escalated to a point of extreme violence, culminating in Judd shooting both LeRoi and Samuelson with a .25 caliber pistol.

Realizing the severity of her actions and the consequences that would follow, Judd made a chilling decision. She opted to dismember the bodies and conceal the evidence by packing them into trunks. With a disturbing attention to detail, Judd meticulously cut the corpses into pieces and carefully wrapped them in blankets. To delay decomposition, she used boric acid as a preservative.

Judd enlisted the help of a man named Jack Halloran, whom she had recently met at a nearby hotel. Together, they transported the trunks containing the dismembered remains to the train station, intending to ship them to Los Angeles. However, the putrid odor emanating from the trunks raised suspicions among railway workers, prompting them to inspect the contents.

To their horror, the workers discovered the gruesome sight—the dismembered remains of Agnes Anne LeRoi and Hedvig Samuelson.. The shocking discovery led to immediate police intervention and Judd's subsequent arrest. The media, captivated by the gruesome details, quickly dubbed her the "Trunk Murderess," and the case became a nationwide sensation.

During the investigation and subsequent trial, the exact weapons used in the murders, apart from the .25 caliber pistol, were not extensively detailed. The focus of the case primarily revolved around the shocking manner in which Judd had dismembered the bodies and attempted to conceal the evidence.

Agnes Anne LeRoi, a divorcee in her early twenties, worked as a medical secretary. Hedvig Samuelson, also in her early twenties, was a medical student from Sweden and had been a close friend of Judd. While financial disputes and jealousy over relationships were suspected factors in the fatal argument, the exact motives behind the crime remained somewhat murky.

Judd's trial attracted significant public attention. Her defense team claimed that she suffered from paranoid schizophrenia, leading to questions about her mental state and competency to stand trial. Despite the defense's plea of insanity, Judd was ultimately found guilty of murder. Initially, she was sentenced to death, but her sentence was later commuted to life imprisonment due to her diagnosed mental condition.

For over three decades, Judd spent time in various psychiatric institutions, where she received treatment for her mental illness. In 1971, after more than 30 years of confinement, she was released on parole. Following her release, Judd largely disappeared from the public eye, choosing to live a quiet and secluded life.

Winnie Ruth Judd passed away on October 23, 1998, in Phoenix, at the age of 93. Her death marked the end of a life overshadowed by the notoriety of a sensational and shocking murder case that continues to captivate the interest of those fascinated by true crime in American history.

Chapter Two: The Historic Horrors of Bisbee

Bisbee

Figure 10: Bisbee. Looking down Tombstone Canyon. Photo by Timothy James Wilson.

Bisbee is among one of the most beautiful and charming towns in southern Arizona, in my opinion. The city does, however, have a slightly concerning past. Bisbee is a realm where history, mystery, and supernatural converge to weave a tapestry of tales and encounters. When I married my wife, we toyed with the idea of having a destination wedding in Bisbee, but eventually settled on having our wedding in Phoenix due to the travel distance to an airport.

Located among the rugged hills of southern Arizona, and just 11 miles north of the Mexican border, this town stands as a testament to both the resilience of human endeavor and the lingering specters that often accompany it. Within these historic streets, you'll encounter a quartet of sites that bear witness to the town's ghostly heritage.

As you prepare for this trip, be prepared for encounters with the paranormal and the inexplicable. From phantom footsteps echoing along dimly lit corridors to the lingering presence of those who once walked these very grounds, Bisbee's haunted sites offer a unique portal into the unknown. This chapter is your guide to not only the historical significance of these sites but also the spine-tingling tales of apparitions, mysteries, and legends that continue to captivate those who dare to delve into the realm of the supernatural.

Bisbee's origins trace back to the late 19th century when prospectors, drawn by the promise of copper riches, flocked to the Mule Mountains. In 1880, a substantial copper lode was discovered, igniting a mining boom that birthed the town. The Copper Queen Mine, with its vast mineral wealth, became the lifeblood of Bisbee, fueling not only economic prosperity but also a vibrant community.

As the town's population swelled, a distinctive urban landscape emerged, characterized by charming Victorian architecture and a thriving downtown district. However, prosperity came at a price in these mountains, with grueling working conditions and periodic labor unrest. This tumultuous backdrop sets the stage for the haunting tales that have woven themselves into Bisbee's fabric.

Amidst the tales of mining magnates and labor strife, Bisbee's historic outlaws also add a layer of intrigue. The infamous Clanton Gang, known for their association with the Gunfight at the O.K. Corral in nearby Tombstone, had connections to Bisbee. These outlaws, with their storied escapades, imbue the town with a sense of the Wild West spirit that permeated the region during its frontier days, but we will save these particular tales for a later chapter.

Today, Bisbee is renowned not only for its rich history but also for the paranormal mysteries that shroud its past. Whether you're exploring the Oliver House, a historic abode rumored to be inhabited by restless spirits, or wandering the Muheim Heritage House, where echoes of a bygone era seem to linger, the town's haunting tales beckon intrepid souls to uncover the secrets that lie beneath its charming exterior. In Bisbee, the past and the paranormal converge, inviting you to step back in time and embrace the enigmatic allure of this captivating Arizona gem.

So, arm yourself with curiosity and courage as we set forth into the heart of Bisbee's haunted history. Amidst the creaking timbers, faded portraits, and flickering shadows, the past and the paranormal merge, beckoning you to uncover the secrets that lie just beyond the veil. Welcome to a chapter where the line between the living and the spectral blurs, and every step you take unearths a deeper layer of mystery, inviting you to experience the haunting allure of Bisbee like never before.

The Copper Queen Hotel
11 Howell Avenue, Bisbee, Arizona
Reservations: (520) 432-2216

The Copper Queen Hotel is a historic landmark that exudes both elegance and mystery. The building itself stands as a testament to the rich history of the area, while its stories and legends have captured the imagination of visitors and locals alike, which is why the Copper Queen Hotel is the perfect place to stay on this road trip. Make sure to check out the Bisbee Table for a nice meal at a local veteran-owned business.

Figure 11: The Copper Queen Hotel. Photo by Timothy James Wilson

Constructed in 1902, the Copper Queen Hotel was built to accommodate the influx of miners and businessmen drawn to Bisbee during the height of the mining boom in the early 20th century. Designed in the Victorian style, the hotel boasts a distinctive red brick facade with ornate detailing, showcasing the architectural aesthetics of the time. The interior of the hotel features polished woodwork, elegant furnishings, and a grand staircase that leads guests to their rooms.

Throughout its history, the Copper Queen Hotel has witnessed numerous significant events. One notable incident occurred in 1917 when a fire broke out in the hotel's basement. The fire, which was fueled by the presence of large oil tanks, threatened to engulf the entire building. However, the quick response of the fire department and the efforts of the townspeople saved the hotel from complete destruction.

The hotel also holds associations with notable figures from the past. John Wayne, the renowned Hollywood cowboy, stayed at the Copper Queen Hotel while filming the movie "Red River" in the late 1940s. Additionally, several U.S. presidents, including Theodore Roosevelt and Franklin D. Roosevelt, are said to have visited the hotel during their respective terms.

One aspect that adds to the allure of the Copper Queen Hotel is its reputation for paranormal activity. Over the years, guests and staff have reported numerous eerie occurrences, leading to the hotel being regarded as one of the most haunted places in Arizona. Some claim to have seen the ghostly figure of a woman wandering the halls, believed to be Julia Lowell, a former sex-worker who was tragically murdered in one of the hotel rooms. Others have reported hearing unexplained footsteps, disembodied voices, and doors opening and closing on their own accord. These supernatural tales have fueled the hotel's mystique, attracting paranormal enthusiasts from all over the world.

Julia Lowell

Julia Lowell is a prominent figure in the lore and legends surrounding the Copper Queen Hotel in Bisbee. According to local tales, Julia Lowell was a young woman who worked as a sex-worker in the late 19th century. She is said to have met a tragic end within the confines of the hotel.

The exact details of Julia Lowell's life and demise are shrouded in mystery, and historical records provide limited information about her existence. However, the story that has been passed down through generations suggests that Julia was a beautiful and sought-after woman in her time.

According to the legend, Julia was involved in a passionate love affair with a powerful man, whose identity remains unknown. Their clandestine relationship was discovered, and out of fear that their affai would be exposed, the man allegedly murdered Julia in one of the hotel rooms. The exact room where the tragedy took place varies depending on the version of the story, adding an aura of ambiguity to the tale.

51

Since her untimely demise, Julia Lowell is believed to haunt the Copper Queen Hotel. Many guests and staff members have reported encountering a ghostly woman, believed to be Julia, wandering the hotel's corridors and rooms. She is often described as wearing a flowing white dress, exuding an ethereal and melancholic presence. Witnesses have claimed to see her apparition vanish into thin air or observed objects moving seemingly on their own when in her presence.

The story of Julia Lowell's tragic fate has become deeply intertwined with the hotel's reputation for paranormal activity. Her ghostly presence is often cited as one of the most notable supernatural occurrences experienced by those who have visited the Copper Queen Hotel.

While the historical accuracy of Julia Lowell's existence and her association with the hotel may be difficult to ascertain, her legend has undeniably added to the allure and mystique of the Copper Queen Hotel. Whether true or not, the story of Julia Lowell has become an integral part of the hotel's haunted history, captivating the imagination of visitors and perpetuating the ongoing fascination with the paranormal in Bisbee.

Room 315

Room 315 at the Copper Queen Hotel is an infamous chamber that has become a focal point of paranormal activity and ghostly encounters. This room, nestled on the third floor of the historic hotel, holds a reputation for being one of the most haunted spaces within its hallowed walls.

Guests who have dared to spend the night in Room 315 have often found themselves immersed in an atmosphere thick with eerie energy. As the door creaks open, a sense of anticipation and trepidation fills the air, as if the room itself is brimming with untold stories and lingering spirits.

Upon entering, visitors may immediately notice a distinct change in temperature. Cold spots materialize, seemingly out of thin air, enveloping certain areas of the room. The chill permeates the air, sending shivers down the spine and creating an unsettling sensation that defies logical explanation.

As the night progresses, guests have reported a myriad of unexplained phenomena that defy rationality. Shadows dance along the walls, seemingly animated by unseen forces. Whispers and disembodied voices echo within the room, causing one's hair to stand on end. Some have even claimed to witness apparitions manifesting in their presence, ethereal figures that seem to flicker between dimensions, leaving lingering imprints on the psyche of those who dare to witness their spectral forms.

Many have spoken of the overwhelming feeling of being watched, an uncanny sensation that settles deep in the core of one's being. Some have awakened in the dead of night, their hearts pounding, only to find a shadowy figure standing at the foot of their bed, its presence exuding an otherworldly aura. Others have described encountering a ghostly apparition hovering near the window, its ethereal form bathed in an otherworldly glow.

Doors within Room 315 have been known to open and close of their own accord, their hinges creaking as if manipulated by unseen hands. Lights flicker inexplicably, casting eerie shadows across the room, while the sound of knocking reverberates through the walls, reminiscent of a long-forgotten secret trying to break free from the confines of time.

The origins of the haunting in Room 315 remain shrouded in mystery, leaving guests and paranormal enthusiasts to speculate on the stories that may have unfolded within its confines. Some theorize that a tragic event occurred within the room—a love affair turned sour, a life cut short prematurely, or a soul forever trapped between the realms of the living and the dead.

Regardless of the precise origins, Room 315 continues to captivate those who seek an encounter with the supernatural. Its reputation as a hotbed of unexplained phenomena draws visitors from far and wide, each hoping to catch a glimpse into the unknown, to experience firsthand the eerie sensations and ghostly manifestations that have made this room infamous.

For those who dare to spend a night in Room 315 at the Copper Queen Hotel, it is an invitation to step into a realm where the boundaries between the living and the spirit world blur. It is an opportunity to witness the inexplicable, to feel the weight of history pressing upon one's soul, and to become a part of the enduring tapestry of paranormal legends that have made the Copper Queen Hotel an icon of haunted lore.

Organized Crime

Throughout its history, the Copper Queen Hotel, has been the subject of persistent rumors and speculation linking it to organized crime. These rumors stem from the hotel's proximity to the mining industry, which often attracted a mix of powerful figures, including both legitimate businessmen and individuals involved in less savory activities.

During the early 20th century, when the Copper Queen Hotel was at its peak, Bisbee was a bustling mining town with a thriving economy. The mining industry attracted wealth, and with wealth often came the potential for illicit activities and organized crime. The hotel's central location and reputation as a hub for social gatherings and events made it an ideal setting for clandestine meetings and deals.

While concrete evidence connecting the Copper Queen Hotel to specific criminal organizations or gruesome crimes is scarce, the hotel's association with organized crime has persisted in local lore and oral accounts. The lack of verifiable records and specific details surrounding these rumors has allowed the legends to flourish, leading to tales of secret tunnels, hidden compartments, and covert operations taking place within the hotel's walls.

These rumors have likely been fueled by the historical context of the era, as organized crime was prevalent in many parts of the United States during the early 20th century. Bisbee's proximity to the Mexican border and its position within the mining industry would have made it an attractive location for criminal enterprises looking to profit from the booming economy.

The Copper Queen Hotel's association with organized crime remains speculative and lacks substantial evidence. While rumors persist, the hotel's primary historical significance lies in its connection to the mining industry, famous guests, and paranormal legends rather than its potential links to criminal activities.

Nevertheless, the enduring rumors surrounding organized crime contribute to the hotel's mystique, adding another layer to its rich tapestry of stories and attracting those fascinated by the intersection of history, crime, and the supernatural. The rumors serve as a reminder of the allure and intrigue that often surround historic establishments with a complex past, leaving room for speculation and imagination to fill in the gaps of the hotel's history.

Today, the Copper Queen Hotel stands as a testament to Bisbee's storied past. It continues to welcome guests from all walks of life, offering them a unique blend of historical charm, modern amenities, and the opportunity to explore the mysteries and legends that have become intertwined with its very existence.

Whether you seek a glimpse into the past, a taste of the paranormal, or simply a memorable stay, the Copper Queen Hotel promises an unforgettable experience.

The Oliver House
26 Sowles Avenue, Bisbee, Arizona
Reservations: (520) 227-7837

Figure 12: The Oliver House. Photo by Timothy James Wilson

The Oliver House is a historic building that exudes character and carries a rich tapestry of history within its walls. This stately structure, located at 300 Oliver Street, stands as a testament to the resilience and vibrant past of Bisbee. The Oliver House is a great alternative to staying at the Copper Queen Hotel, or, for the most authentic adventure, one might stay at the Copper Queen Hotel on Friday night and stay at the Oliver House on Saturday night.

Built in 1909, the Oliver House was originally intended as a boarding house for miners working in the nearby Copper Queen Mine. Designed in the Queen Anne architectural style, the building boasts an impressive three-story facade adorned with ornate details, including bay windows, decorative woodwork, and a welcoming wraparound porch. Its vibrant red exterior further adds to the house's striking allure.

Throughout its existence, the Oliver House has witnessed Bisbee's growth as a bustling mining town, and the house accommodated numerous miners seeking respite after long, arduous days in the mines. This unique connection to the mining industry, which played a pivotal role in the growth and development of Bisbee, adds an intriguing layer to the building's historical significance.

The Oliver House was frequented by several notable figures of the time who visited or resided in Bisbee. The town attracted a diverse array of people, including politicians, businessmen, and entertainers. The house's rich history is intertwined with the stories of these visitors, creating a captivating narrative of Bisbee's past.

Legend has it that the Oliver House is also home to a series of paranormal or supernatural occurrences. Over the years, numerous reports have emerged, detailing inexplicable phenomena experienced by visitors and residents alike. Visitors have claimed to witness apparitions, hear disembodied voices, and feel unexplained cold spots throughout the building. These alleged encounters have sparked intrigue and curiosity among paranormal enthusiasts, making the Oliver House a subject of fascination for those seeking supernatural experiences.

The Legend of the Ghostly Victoria

Legend has it that within the walls of the historic Oliver House in Bisbee, a ghostly woman in Victorian-era attire roams the corridors, forever bound to the building by a tragic tale.

During the peak of Bisbee's mining era, the Oliver House served as a boarding house for the weary miners who toiled in the nearby Copper Queen Mine. Among the residents was a young woman named Victoria, whose grace and beauty captivated the hearts of all who crossed her path.

Victoria was said to be a vivacious spirit, always donning elegant gowns and exuding an air of sophistication. Her laughter echoed through the halls, filling the house with an enchanting energy. She possessed a magnetic charm that drew the attention of many, including a prominent politician named Edward.

Edward, a distinguished gentleman, was immediately taken by Victoria's radiant presence. Their encounters grew more frequent, and soon their connection blossomed into a deep and passionate love. They dreamt of a future together, where they could escape the confines of Bisbee and embark on a life of happiness and prosperity.

However, their bliss was short-lived. Tragedy struck when Edward's political ambitions led him away from Bisbee, leaving Victoria behind. Heartbroken, she waited patiently for his return, clinging to the hope that their love would withstand the test of time.

Months turned into years, and still, Edward did not return. Victoria's heart gradually filled with despair and loneliness. Her once vibrant spirit faded, and she succumbed to illness, never knowing the fate of her beloved Edward.

Since her untimely passing, visitors and residents of the Oliver House claim to have encountered Victoria's ghostly presence. Dressed in exquisitely tailored Victorian-era gowns, she drifts through the hallways and rooms, her ethereal form emanating a sense of longing and melancholy. Witnesses describe her as a wistful figure, her eyes filled with a combination of love and sorrow.

Guests have reported hearing the soft rustling of her gown as she passes by, and a delicate scent of roses often lingers in her wake. Some claim to have witnessed her standing by the window, her gaze fixed on the horizon, as if searching for a long-lost love.

The legend of the Ghostly Victoria has become intertwined with the Oliver House's history, adding a layer of mystery and romance to its walls. Whether Victoria's spirit remains tethered to the house due to her unrequited love or a desire to find closure, her presence continues to captivate those who visit, drawing them into the melancholic tale of a love that was never fulfilled.

While the truth of this legend remains shrouded in the mists of time, the story serves as a reminder of the enduring power of love and the lingering spirits that inhabit the halls of the Oliver House, forever preserving the echoes of Bisbee's past.

The Legend of the Miner

Deep within the shadows of the Oliver House in Bisbee, another spectral presence is said to linger—a ghostly miner, forever bound to the building by a tragic fate that befell him in the depths of the Copper Queen Mine.

The legend tells of a miner named Samuel, a rugged and hardworking man who dedicated his life to the pursuit of copper riches. Samuel was known for his unwavering determination and resilience, braving the treacherous conditions of the mine with each passing day.

One fateful day, tragedy struck deep within the Copper Queen Mine. Samuel, driven by his dedication to his work, found himself trapped in a tunnel collapse. His fellow miners made desperate attempts to rescue him, but their efforts were in vain. Samuel's life was tragically cut short, his dreams and aspirations buried beneath tons of rubble.

It is said that Samuel's spirit never left the Oliver House, forever tethered to the place he once called home. Witnesses have reported encounters with the ghostly miner, describing a figure cloaked in tattered and soot-stained clothing. His face bears the weariness and pain of his untimely demise, forever etched in an expression of anguish.

Visitors to the Oliver House have recounted eerie experiences in the presence of Samuel's ghost. Some claim to have heard faint echoes of pickaxes striking rock, as if the miner's spectral form continues to toil away in the afterlife. Others have reported feeling an unexplained chill in the air, as if the ghostly miner has brought with him the cold depths of the mine.

There are those who believe that Samuel's spirit is restless, forever searching for closure or seeking solace from the mine that claimed his life. His apparition has become an integral part of the Oliver House's haunted reputation, drawing in those who yearn to witness the remnants of his tragic tale.

While the legend of the ghostly miner is passed down through generations, the truth behind Samuel's existence and the authenticity of his haunting remain subjects of speculation. Yet, his story intertwines with the history of Bisbee, serving as a haunting reminder of the sacrifices and perils endured by those who sought their fortunes in the depths of the Copper Queen Mine.

Today, the presence of the ghostly miner continues to capture the imagination of visitors to the Oliver House, beckoning them to explore the paranormal mysteries that reside within its walls. Whether true or born from the depths of folklore, the legend of the ghostly miner adds a touch of sorrow and intrigue to the rich tapestry of Bisbee's haunted past.

Children of the Oliver House

Within the mysterious confines of the Oliver House in Bisbee, an additional spectral presence is believed to haunt its halls—the spirits of ghostly children. This haunting legend adds a touch of innocence and curiosity to the paranormal reputation of the house.

Visitors and residents of the Oliver House have reported hearing the faint laughter and playful sounds of children echoing through the rooms and corridors. The disembodied giggles and pitter-patter of tiny footsteps evoke an atmosphere of both wonder and unease. Witnesses often describe the laughter as joyous and carefree, as if the ghostly children are reliving playful moments from their past.

These phantom children seem to have an ethereal presence, sometimes appearing as fleeting glimpses or felt as a gentle touch on the skin. Their presence can invoke a range of emotions, from a warm sense of nostalgia to a haunting sense of melancholy. Some accounts even suggest that the spirits of the children may attempt to interact with the living, tugging at clothing or playing mischievous pranks.

The origins and stories behind these ghostly children are veiled in uncertainty. While some speculate that they may be former residents of the house or children who lived in Bisbee during its mining heyday, concrete details about their identities remain elusive. The mysteries surrounding their presence only serve to deepen the intrigue and curiosity surrounding the Oliver House.

Visitors to the Oliver House who encounter the spirits of these ghostly children often experience a mix of fascination and a longing to understand their story. Some believe that these spirits may be lingering due to unfinished business, a longing to connect with the living, or simply a desire to revisit the joys of childhood.

As with any paranormal claims, skepticism persists, and it is important to approach these legends with an open mind. The experiences of encountering ghostly children at the Oliver House remain subjective and vary from person to person. However, the enduring tales and reported encounters with these spectral youngsters have woven themselves into the fabric of the house's haunted reputation, capturing the imaginations of those who visit and leaving an indelible mark on the lore of Bisbee's supernatural history.

The paranormal activity has undoubtedly contributed to the mystique and allure surrounding the Oliver House. Today, the building stands welcoming visitors who are eager to explore its architectural beauty and uncover the secrets it may hold. Whether one is drawn to its historical significance, architectural grandeur, or supernatural legends, the Oliver House offers a captivating glimpse into the past, making it an essential stop for those intrigued by the history and mystery of Bisbee.

The Screaming Banshee Pizza
200 Tombstone Canyon, Bisbee, Arizona

While tales of the paranormal in Bisbee are among the topics of this chapter, I could never write a chapter about Bisbee without mentioning the Screaming Banshee Pizza. This eatery, housed in a refurbished gas station and is the home of at least one ghost according to local legend, and is single-handedly responsible for my sear disappointment when I visit other pizza restaurants. Unfortunately, my wife is adamantly opposed to driving three and a half hours to for pizza, so I don't visit the Screaming Banshee as often as I would like. I have however convinced my wife on several occasions to go to Bisbee for the day, with the underlying motivation to stop in at the Screaming Banshee. This is, in my humble opinion as a guy who has spent a lot of time traveling around the state of Arizona over the last ten years, the best pizza in Arizona.

Figure 13: The Screaming Banshee. Photo by Timothy James Wilson

Every time I am in Bisbee, I go out of my way to visit this restaurant. There is even a story that my friends tell where I drove 50 miles out of the way to visit the Screaming Banshee and bring pizza to a hunting camp where I was meeting them for the weekend. Their disappointment in me being hours late through was relieved by the fact that I had brought a couple large Meat Lover's and a few orders of their Wood Fire Wings, along with a case of beer.

So, while you are in Bisbee, I strongly recommend going to the Screaming Banshee to fill up with food and then heading over to the Old Bisbee Ghost Tours for their haunted pub crawl to both wash down the deliciousness and walk off all those extra calories while having a few beers. I can assure you just about everything is within walking distance of your hotel.

The Bisbee Mining and Historical Museum
5 Copper Queen Plaza, Bisbee, Arizona

Figure 14: The Bisbee Mining and Historical Museum. Photo by Timothy James Wilson.

Hidden within the history of the city of Bisbee is a story so cynical that it might contribute to the hauntings experienced in this city today. This story is the story of the Bisbee Deportation of 1917, and searches on the internet will speak vaguely about a Bisbee Deportation Memorial; however, when you find the address and go there you will realize that the address has led you to the Bisbee Mining and Historical Museum.

To this day, the only recognition of the dark and malevolent event that I could find was in the Bisbee Mining and Historical Museum. The Museum has a very extensive exhibit in understanding this historic event.

The Bisbee Deportation of 1917

On the fateful day of July 12, 1917, that a strike erupted between the mining giants and the laboring souls that toiled beneath the unforgiving earth. The miners, their backs bent, and spirits crushed under the weight of exploitation, dared to rise against the wealthy mine operators. But little did they know that their uprising would awaken the dormant forces of evil that lurked within the hearts of those their oppressors.

As tensions escalated, the mining companies, with their thirst for wealth, conspired with the corrupt local sheriff and 2,000 merciless vigilantes. The dark alliance was formed, and their malevolence knew no bounds. This dark alliance was formed which exposed the extreme corruption in law-enforcement at the time.

The mining companies unleashed their wrath upon the striking miners, activists, and anyone deemed sympathetic to their cause. The miners, and those sympathetic to their cause where kidnapped, and loaded upon cattle cars. In total over a thousand people were rounded up, and deported on trains where they were dumped in the New Mexico desert. These deportees were abandoned to suffer the wrath of the desert throughout New Mexico.

Around the Plaza

One of the whispered legends tells of disembodied voices that drift through the stillness of the night, their words laden with anguish and despair. Visitors claim to have heard faint murmurs, as if the deported souls were eternally trapped within the walls of the plaza recounting their tales of suffering and injustice. Some believe that these spectral whispers serve as a chilling reminder of the horrors that unfolded during that ill-fated period.

Others speak of shadowy figures that flit across the peripheral vision, their presence fleeting yet undeniable. These apparitions are said to be remnants of the deported souls, forever trapped in a purgatorial limbo, unable to find peace after their untimely demise. Witnesses recount feeling a bone-chilling sensation as if they were being watched by unseen eyes, leaving them with a lingering sense of unease.

In the dead of night, when the moon casts its pale glow upon the building, some have reported witnessing ethereal manifestations. Ghostly figures, clad in the tattered clothing of the miners, are said to wander the grounds, their spectral forms shimmering with an otherworldly glow. These restless spirits are believed to be the lost souls of the deported, forever condemned to roam the earth in search of solace and redemption.

While these legends and myths cannot be substantiated by empirical evidence, they have woven themselves into the fabric of Bisbee's folklore. The tales persist, passed down from one generation to the next, contributing to the eerie reputation of the area. Whether they are figments of imagination or glimpses into a realm beyond our comprehension, they serve as a testament to the enduring impact of the past on the present and the power of collective memory to shape our perceptions of the world.

The Shadowy Miners

The legend of the Shadowy Miners adds an eerie dimension to the mystique surrounding the area. According to witnesses and accounts, these spectral figures manifest within the confines of the museum, appearing as ethereal beings that echo the laborers who were wrongfully deported.

Described as shadowy and insubstantial, the Shadowy Miners are said to materialize fleetingly, often observed in the peripheral vision or dimly lit corners. Witnesses claim to catch glimpses of them wearing tattered and worn clothing, resembling the attire of the miners who were forcibly expelled from Bisbee. Their presence seems to be transient, as if they are passing through solid objects or dissipating into the surrounding atmosphere.

These ghostly apparitions evoke an aura of mystery and sadness, their ethereal nature suggesting a connection to the tragic events of the Bisbee Deportation. The miners, who suffered unjustly and were subjected to harsh conditions, seemingly endure in spirit within the memorial. The legend of the Shadowy Miners reinforces the notion that the echoes of their suffering continue to resonate within the site, lingering as a poignant reminder of the past.

Encounters with the Shadowy Miners often leave witnesses with an unsettling feeling, as if they have glimpsed into a realm beyond our understanding. Their presence evokes a sense of the otherworldly, hinting at the profound impact of the Bisbee Deportation and the enduring legacy of those who suffered during that dark chapter of history.

It is worth noting that these accounts are based on personal experiences and local folklore, which may vary from person to person. Whether the Shadowy Miners are figments of imagination, manifestations of residual energy, or something beyond our comprehension, they contribute to the haunting aura that surrounds the Bisbee Deportation Memorial.

Apparitions of Mourning

The Apparitions of Mourning are part of the ghostly legends associated with the Copper Queen Plaza (this area). Witnesses claim to have encountered these full-bodied apparitions, which are believed to embody the grief and anguish of the miners who met tragic fates during the deportation.

According to the tales, these spectral figures manifest as individuals dressed in the attire of early 20th-century miners. Their countenances bear an expression of profound sadness, reflecting the immense suffering and injustice they endured. The Apparitions of Mourning are said to wander the grounds of the memorial, appearing lost and tormented, as if forever reliving the pain and hardships they experienced.

Witnesses describe encounters with these ghostly manifestations as deeply emotional and haunting. Some claim to have seen the apparitions standing in silent contemplation or moving with a sense of purpose, as if searching for solace or seeking to make their stories heard. Their presence exudes an atmosphere of sorrow and melancholy, evoking a deep sympathy and empathy for the plight of those affected by the Bisbee Deportation.

The Apparitions of Mourning contribute to the somber and introspective aura surrounding the memorial. They serve as poignant reminders of the human cost of the events that took place there, offering a glimpse into the profound impact of the past on the present. These ghostly figures, forever trapped between the realms of the living and the deceased, invite reflection on the injustices inflicted upon the miners and the ongoing struggle for social justice.

It is important to note that accounts of the Apparitions of Mourning are based on personal experiences and local folklore. While the emotional weight and impact of these encounters can be deeply felt by those who have witnessed them, their existence remains within the realm of supernatural and subjective interpretation. These apparitions symbolize the enduring legacy of the Bisbee Deportation and serve as a testament to the enduring power of memory and remembrance.

The Muheim Heritage House
207 Youngblood Hill, Bisbee, Arizona

The Muheim Heritage House is a captivating historic building nestled in the picturesque town of Bisbee. Built in 1898, this Victorian-style residence has witnessed numerous historical events and is steeped in rich lore and tales of the supernatural.

The building itself is a stunning example of late 19th-century architecture. It features a combination of Queen Anne and Classical Revival styles, with its distinctive red brick facade, ornate detailing, and a prominent wraparound porch. The Muheim Heritage House stands as a testament to the town's prosperous mining era and reflects the opulence and elegance of the time.

As for its historical significance, the Muheim Heritage House has played host to several notable events and people throughout the years. One prominent association is with the Muheim family, who were influential members of the Bisbee community. They occupied the house for several generations and contributed significantly to the town's development.

Moreover, the Muheim Heritage House has been rumored to have connections to famous individuals. It is said that notable figures such as Wyatt Earp and John Wayne were occasional visitors, adding an air of celebrity to the house's legacy. However, concrete evidence of their direct association remains elusive.

The Muheim Heritage House has also gained notoriety due to the paranormal occurrences reported within its walls. Over the years, visitors and residents alike have claimed to witness inexplicable phenomena. Reports of ghostly apparitions, mysterious footsteps, and unexplained sounds permeate the house's history. Some have even spoken of encountering ethereal figures dressed in clothing reminiscent of the Victorian era, further fueling the haunted reputation of the place.

Visitors have recounted chilling experiences, such as doors opening and closing on their own, objects moving inexplicably, and eerie whispers echoing through the rooms. The house's upper floors, in particular, have been cited as hotspots for supernatural activity. Many paranormal investigators and enthusiasts have sought to capture evidence of these phenomena, leading to the Muheim Heritage House becoming a subject of interest in the field.

The Curse of the Muheim Family

Long ago, nestled amidst the arid landscape of Bisbee, the Muheim Heritage House stood as a testament to the family's affluence and influence. But beneath its grandeur, a curse whispered through the halls, foretelling a destiny steeped in tragedy and misfortune.

Legend tells of a Muheim patriarch, a man who sought riches and power at any cost. In his pursuit, he crossed paths with a mysterious traveler who gifted him a coveted artifact—a twisted amulet with an otherworldly glow. Unbeknownst to the patriarch, this seemingly priceless treasure bore an ancient curse, an affliction that would befall generations to come.

The curse took root, infesting the Muheim family's lives with despair and anguish. Their wealth diminished, their prosperity crumbled, and their once harmonious household became a breeding ground for sorrow. Death visited the family relentlessly, claiming loved ones in the prime of their lives. The whispers of the curse became deafening, echoing through the corridors as a constant reminder of their ill-fated fate.

The curse manifested in various forms, each more devastating than the last. Some spoke of a spectral matriarch, a vengeful apparition with a mournful wail, whose presence heralded imminent doom for any Muheim descendant. Others whispered of the house itself turning against its inhabitants, walls oozing with dark secrets and rooms shifting and trapping those unfortunate enough to cross their threshold.

Madness, too, gripped the family's bloodline, a result of the curse's insidious influence. Descendants were plagued by visions and nightmares, tormented by shadows that danced at the edge of their vision. Sanity eroded as the curse gnawed at their souls, leaving behind mere shells of what once was.

The Muheim Heritage House became a place of desolation, shunned by the townsfolk who feared the curse's touch. The family's legacy, once admired and respected, became a cautionary tale, a chilling reminder of the consequences of unchecked ambition and the price paid for tampering with forces beyond mortal understanding.

To this day, the Curse of the Muheim Family lingers, a specter that haunts the Muheim Heritage House and its descendants. It serves as a reminder that wealth and power acquired through unscrupulous means are fleeting, and the pursuit of forbidden treasures can exact a heavy toll on those who dare to tread such treacherous paths.

The Secret Chamber

Deep within the enigmatic depths of the Muheim Heritage House, an elusive secret chamber lies concealed, its existence known only to a select few. Legends speak of this hidden enclave, a place of intrigue and mystery, where untold treasures or forbidden knowledge lay in wait.

Whispers of the secret chamber have echoed through the generations, enticing those who yearn for the unknown, for it is said that within its walls, secrets of the past are unveiled and truths long obscured are brought to light. Yet, those who have dared to seek its elusive entrance have found themselves ensnared in a web of enigma and uncertainty.

Legends describe the secret chamber as a realm apart from the mundane world—a sanctuary steeped in ancient lore and imbued with a palpable sense of power. Some believe it to be a repository of hidden artifacts, valuable beyond imagination, while others speak of sacred texts or arcane manuscripts that hold the keys to forgotten wisdom.

The chamber's location remains a closely guarded secret, concealed by intricate mechanisms and concealed passages. Many have ventured into the depths of the Muheim Heritage House, seeking the elusive entrance, only to be confounded by the house's deceptive architecture, its shifting corridors, and seemingly impassable walls. The chamber, like a mirage, evades discovery, teasing those who would unlock its secrets.

Rumors persist of those who claim to have glimpsed the chamber, speaking of ethereal light filtering through cracks, illuminating fragments of long-forgotten knowledge. They recount whispers that echo through the hidden passages, secrets whispered by unseen voices, teasing and tantalizing the curious souls who dare to venture too close.

But cautionary tales also abound. Whispers speak of those who uncovered the entrance, only to vanish without a trace, swallowed by the chamber's insatiable hunger for discovery. Their names etched into the annals of mystery, forever lost within the labyrinthine recesses of the Muheim Heritage House.

Whether the secret chamber is a manifestation of the collective imagination or a veritable sanctuary of enigmatic power, its allure continues to beckon the intrepid and the curious. The Muheim Heritage House, a guardian of secrets, stands as a testament to the unseen realms that lie beneath its storied facade, forever preserving the enigma of the secret chamber and the wonders it conceals within its mysterious depths.

The Unsettling Doll Collection

Within the dimly lit confines of the Muheim Heritage House lies a collection of dolls that exude an unsettling presence. These dolls, with their porcelain visages frozen in eerie expressions, whisper secrets of a darker realm, casting an aura of discomfort and unease upon those who dare to gaze upon them.

Each doll within the collection possesses an uncanny resemblance to its former owner, their glassy eyes seeming to follow visitors with an unsettling intensity. Their delicate features, once intended to convey innocence and joy, now bear an unsettling distortion—a twisted reflection of the innocence they once embodied.

Legends swirl around the origins of these dolls, attributing them to various macabre tales. Some whisper that they were created by a deranged artist, imbued with the essence of tortured souls to forever preserve their torment within the ceramic shells. Others believe they are vessels for lost spirits, yearning for release from their doll-like prisons.

As the shadows lengthen and daylight wanes, the dolls' presence becomes more pronounced. Visitors swear they have witnessed the dolls moving, their positions shifting imperceptibly when no one is looking. Whispers and hushed conversations have been overheard, originating from the very mouths of these lifeless figurines, their voices carrying a spectral chill that sends shivers down the spines of all who hear them.

Some claim that the dolls harbor a malevolent energy, capable of influencing the emotions and actions of those who draw near. The air around them grows heavy with a sense of foreboding, their silent gaze penetrating the soul and stoking the embers of dormant fears.

Visitors have reported a feeling of being watched, as if the dolls' painted eyes possess a maleficent sentience that can pierce through one's defenses. A sense of being manipulated, toyed with, and even cursed pervades the atmosphere when one delves too deeply into the unsettling doll collection.

Those who linger in the presence of these dolls may find their dreams haunted by nightmarish visions, their waking hours plagued by a perpetual sense of dread. Some claim the dolls hold a power to invoke madness, their very presence chipping away at the fragile boundaries of sanity.

The unsettling doll collection in the Muheim Heritage House stands as a haunting reminder that innocence can be corrupted, beauty can be twisted, and that which appears benign can hide a darkness that defies explanation. The dolls, forever trapped within their porcelain shells, serve as harbingers of an enigmatic realm where the boundaries between the living and the lifeless blur, where the innocence of childhood takes a sinister turn, and where the secrets of their existence remain locked within their haunting gaze.

The Haunted Clock

High upon a weathered wall within the Muheim Heritage House, a haunted clock stands as a testament to the passage of time and the ethereal forces that permeate its ancient gears. This clock, with its ornate craftsmanship and intricate mechanisms, possesses an eerie presence that transcends the boundaries of the physical realm.

Legends speak of the haunted clock, an object imbued with supernatural power, said to bridge the divide between the mortal world and the realm of spirits. Its hands move with an otherworldly grace, marking the hours with a spectral precision that echoes through the haunted corridors of the house.

As the midnight hour approaches, a palpable tension fills the air, and an otherworldly hush descends upon the Muheim Heritage House. It is at this time that the haunted clock awakens from its slumber, its pendulum swinging with an ethereal rhythm that beckons the spirits of the house to stir.

The chime of the clock is said to possess an otherworldly quality, resonating with a haunting melody that resonates deep within the soul. Its tolling seems to summon restless apparitions from the shadows, as if it were a signal for the spirits to emerge and roam the house, their ethereal presence weaving through the tapestries of time.

Witnesses have reported witnessing ghostly figures, translucent and ethereal, gliding in tandem with the ticking of the clock. These specters, remnants of past inhabitants or long-forgotten souls, drift through the rooms and hallways, caught between realms and forever trapped within the timeless embrace of the Muheim Heritage House.

The haunted clock is said to possess a mysterious influence over time itself. Some claim that its hands can spin backward, causing time to unravel and twist upon itself. Others speak of the clock's ability to halt time altogether, freezing the world in a suspended state, allowing glimpses into alternate dimensions or realms beyond mortal comprehension.

Yet, the haunted clock's presence is not without its dangers. To tamper with its mechanisms or disturb its delicate balance is to invite calamity and misfortune. Legend tells of those who dared to meddle with its inner workings, only to be cursed with a lifetime of perpetual torment or to vanish into the depths of time, forever lost to the annals of history.

The haunted clock remains a fixture within the Muheim Heritage House, a relic that transcends the boundaries of mere machinery and becomes a conduit for the supernatural. Its ghostly presence serves as a reminder that time is not a linear construct, but a tapestry woven with both the mortal and the ethereal, forever intertwined within the haunted halls of this storied dwelling.

The Wailing Specter

Deep within the Muheim Heritage House, when the moon is veiled by clouds and the hour is darkest, a mournful wail reverberates through the ancient walls. This haunting sound is attributed to the presence of the Wailing Specter, a ghostly apparition that is said to embody sorrow and despair.

Legend has it that the Wailing Specter is the tormented soul of a woman who met a tragic fate within the confines of the house. Her identity remains a mystery, lost in the mists of time, but her anguished cries echo through the generations, carrying with them an unyielding sorrow that tugs at the heartstrings of all who hear.

The wail of the specter is hauntingly distinct—a keening sound that pierces through the silence of the night, seeping into the very essence of the house. It evokes a profound sense of loss and desolation, as if the specter's grief transcends the boundaries of mortality and permeates the spiritual fabric of the dwelling.

Those who have encountered the Wailing Specter speak of an overwhelming sadness that accompanies her presence. The air becomes heavy with an invisible weight, and a chill envelops the space, leaving an indelible impression of sorrow upon the soul. Her cries are laden with an intensity that resonates deep within the bones, stirring emotions of empathy and melancholy.

Some speculate that the Wailing Specter is bound to the house, eternally trapped within its walls, unable to find solace or peace. The reasons for her unrest remain shrouded in mystery, but some believe it to be connected to a great tragedy or an unresolved injustice that occurred within the house's history.

Visitors recount moments of encountering the specter, describing her ethereal form as a misty figure clothed in tattered garments, her face obscured by a veil of sorrow. She floats silently through the corridors, her mournful cries echoing in her wake, leaving those who witness her presence filled with an indescribable sense of grief and melancholy.

While the origin and nature of the Wailing Specter remain enigmatic, her haunting presence within the Muheim Heritage House serves as a somber reminder of the depths of human suffering and the lingering echoes of sorrow that can reverberate through time. Her lamentations resonate through the halls, ensuring that the memory of her anguish will never fade, forever haunting the house and those who dare to venture into its embrace.

Step into the enigmatic world of the Muheim Heritage House, nestled in the heart of Bisbee, where history and mystery intertwine. Explore the grandeur of a bygone era but be prepared for the chilling secrets that lie within. Encounter the Lady in

White, a phantom in a white gown, whose ethereal presence will send shivers down your spine. Dare to enter the domain of the Muheim Children, the restless spirits of innocence turned eerie, and witness their spectral apparitions. Marvel at the unsettling doll collection, where porcelain figures exude an otherworldly aura. Traverse the haunted corridors and listen for the mournful cries of the Wailing Specter, a ghostly embodiment of sorrow. And discover the hidden depths of the house, where a secret chamber and a haunted clock await those who dare to unlock their mysteries. The Muheim Heritage House beckons, inviting the curious and the brave to unravel its history and encounter the supernatural, in a journey that will leave an indelible mark upon the soul.

Chapter Three: The Enigma of the Mountains

The Superstition Mountains

Figure 15: Picture

Among the rugged beauty of the Superstition Mountains, this weekend escape promises an unforgettable journey into Arizona's enigmatic past. Located in the eastern part of Maricopa County, are a rugged and iconic mountain range that has captivated the imagination of locals and adventurers for centuries. These striking peaks are characterized by their jagged terrain, distinctive red rock formations, and an air of mystery that goes back several centuries. These mountains are a prominent feature of the Sonoran Desert landscape and serve as a stunning backdrop to the cities and towns in the region, including Apache Junction, Superior, and Globe.

This mountain range covers an area of approximately 160,000 acres and is a popular destination for outdoor enthusiasts, hikers, rock climbers, and treasure hunters alike due to its diverse range of flora and fauna, including saguaro cacti, desert wildflowers, and various species of wildlife.

Figure 16: Spring wildflowers in the Superstition Mountains. Photo taken by Timothy James Wilson.

The Superstition Mountains are steeped in history and legend, contributing to their mystique and allure, including one of the most iconic treasure stories in the Southwest.

Before European settlers arrived in the area, various Indigenous peoples called the Superstition Mountains home. These people left behind petroglyphs and other archaeological evidence of their presence and many glimpses into their culture.

In the 16th century, Spanish explorers ventured into the region in search of gold and other valuable resources. The legendary Jesuit missionary, Father Eusebio Francisco Kino, is believed to have explored the Superstition Mountains in the early 1700s.

In the late 19th century, the Superstition Mountains served as a refuge for Apache warriors resisting both American and Mexican forces. The rugged terrain gave the Apache warriors an advantage over invading armies for several decades.

The Superstition Mountains continue to be a place of fascination, not only for their scenic beauty but also for the rich history and legends that surround them.

Many of the towns in the Superstition Mountains though are mining towns, that have suffered massive population busts over the past several decades. Most of this trip will center around State Route 60, which offers some breathtaking and amazing views, as well as plenty of quaint little towns that offer a variety of historic endeavors.

The Historic Hotel Magma
100 Main Street, Superior, Arizona
Reservations: (520) 689-2300

The Historic Hotel Magma is not a haunted hotel, so you can rest easy on this trip and know that I didn't send you to a hotel where you might be woken up by a ghost. However, the Magma is a beautifully restored hotel in Superior, right in the middle of the Superstition Mountain, which makes it the perfect place to venture from.

Constructed between 1910 and 1912 by Canadian John M. MacPherson, the Magma Hotel stands as a lasting testament in solid concrete. In 1923, an extension was added, crafted from local red brick, with John Davey, overseer of the local brick factory, overseeing the brickwork and contracting.

The Magma Hotel played a pivotal role in the town's history. It housed the inaugural issue of the Superior Sun weekly newspaper in 1916, serving as its publishing venue within its walls. In 1918, the hotel's restaurant, The Magma Cafe, was leased and managed by O. C. Hing. The early 1920s saw the installation of a phone booth by the Mountain States Telephone and Telegraph Company, allowing residents to engage in long-distance conversations.

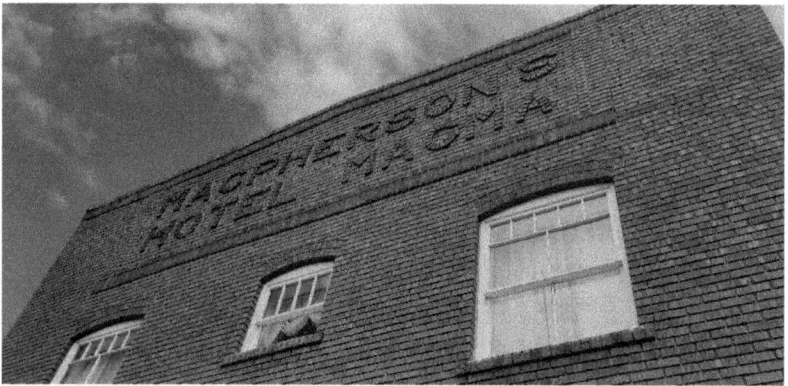

Figure 17: The Hotel Magma. Photo taken by Timothy James Wilson.

Throughout its rich history, the sprawling 13,000+ square foot Magma Hotel has served as both a boarding house and hotel. A screened-in seasonal sleeping porch for men was added during the 1920s, augmenting its facilities. Notably, the East Wing housed Seymour's Drug Store, later known as the Magma Pharmacy, which transitioned to Murphy's Pharmacy around 1950. In tandem, the O'Donnell & Hunt Insurance Agency opened its doors. Subsequently, the hotel became a hub for professionals, housing attorneys, realtors, and even a Greyhound bus depot.

In later years, the hotel underwent a transformative period. The ground floor was host to a hair salon and rentable rooms, while the once elegant lobby assumed a new role as a storage and distribution center for the Superior Food Bank. The East Wing accommodated La Esquina Restaurant.

Fast forward to 2010, the Magma Hotel entered a new chapter under the ownership of Los Cedros Superior, LLC, led by Miguel A. Sfeir. Miguel's introduction to Superior was facilitated by his close friend and flight instructor, Captain Curtis Pierce, who was actively involved in town development. Despite the hotel's dilapidated interior, Miguel was drawn to its historic significance. The restoration process was undertaken, meticulously preserving its original character. Over 300 photographs documented its deteriorated state, affirming the decision to embark on a restorative journey.

Upon acquisition, the Magma Hotel was in disarray. Its exterior was marred by peeling paint, while the surrounding area had succumbed to desert overgrowth. Inside, the aftermath of vandalism was evident, with broken fixtures, damaged infrastructure, and scattered debris. A silver lining amidst the wreckage was the resilient "Imperial Staircase," a remnant of its former grandeur that endured.

Today, the Magma Hotel is one of the most beautiful buildings in the historic downtown area of Superior.

Bella's Marketplace and Café
203 Main Street, Superior, Arizona
Information: (203) 297-1182

One of the best sandwich shops you will find in Arizona is across the street from the Hotel Magma, and I couldn't write this book without mentioning it, and my favorite sandwich The Godfather. Stop in the Café, while in Superior and have a great cup of coffee, or lemonade and a sandwich. I promise you won't be disappointed. Also, if you have a sweet tooth, you just can't go wrong with one of their lemon bars.

Figure 18: Historic Downtown Superior. Photo taken by Timothy James Wilson.

Goldfield Ghost Town
4650 North Mammoth Mine Road, Apache Junction, Arizona
Tickets: (480) 983-0333

Located in Apache Junction, Goldfield Ghost Town is a captivating historical site that offers visitors a glimpse into the Wild West era. Nestled at the foot of the Superstition Mountains, this ghost town showcases the rich history of the region and has become a popular destination for history enthusiasts and paranormal enthusiasts alike.

Goldfield Ghost Town was founded in 1893 when gold was discovered in the area. The town quickly grew, attracting miners, prospectors, and their families, turning it into a bustling community. At its peak, it boasted a population of approximately 4,000 residents, along with numerous businesses and services. However, as the gold vein eventually ran dry, the town's prosperity dwindled, leading to its eventual abandonment.

Today, Goldfield Ghost Town has been meticulously reconstructed to resemble its former glory. The architectural style of the buildings reflects the rustic charm and ruggedness of the Wild West. Visitors can explore the town's streets, lined with wooden storefronts, saloons, and other structures, giving them a genuine feel of stepping back in time. The attention to detail in the reconstruction ensures an authentic experience, allowing visitors to immerse themselves in the town's history.

Figure 19: Goldfield Ghost Town. Photo taken by Timothy James Wilson.

Several significant buildings stand out within the ghost town. The Goldfield Museum houses artifacts and exhibits that tell the story of the town's gold rush era, displaying items such as mining equipment, photographs, and personal memorabilia. The Mammoth Gold Mine offers guided tours, allowing visitors to descend into the depths of the mine and learn about the challenges and risks faced by the miners of that time. The Goldfield Superstition Narrow Gauge Railroad takes visitors on a nostalgic train ride through the town, providing an opportunity to appreciate the picturesque surroundings.

With its rich history and mysterious past, Goldfield Ghost Town has become the subject of numerous paranormal legends and haunted tales. Visitors and staff members have reported various unexplained phenomena, including ghostly apparitions, disembodied voices, and inexplicable sounds.

George

The most famous legend revolves around a ghostly miner named George, who is said to wander the premises, still searching for gold. Many visitors claim to have seen George or experienced his presence, adding an extra layer of intrigue to the town. George, the ghostly miner of Goldfield Ghost Town, is a central figure in the paranormal legends and stories surrounding the site. According to local lore, George was a miner who was deeply devoted to his pursuit of gold during the town's heyday. He tirelessly toiled in the mines, hoping to strike it rich.

Legend has it that George met a tragic fate while working in one of the mines at Goldfield. The circumstances surrounding his demise vary depending on the accounts, but it is believed that he either perished in a mining accident or met an untimely end while defending his claim against rival miners.

Since his passing, George's spirit is said to have remained attached to the ghost town, forever wandering its streets and mining areas. Numerous visitors and staff members claim to have encountered the apparition of George or experienced his presence in different ways.

Reports of George's ghost include sightings of a spectral miner dressed in tattered clothing and wearing a wide-brimmed hat. Witnesses often describe him as a haggard figure, appearing as though he is eternally searching for gold. Some visitors have reported seeing George in the Mammoth Gold Mine, where he is said to roam the dark tunnels and chambers.

In addition to visual sightings, many people claim to have felt an eerie presence or experienced unexplained phenomena attributed to George. Visitors have reported feeling sudden drops in temperature, hearing footsteps or voices when no one else is around, and witnessing objects moving or being knocked over by an unseen force.

The Mammoth Saloon

The Mammoth Saloon, a reconstructed establishment from Goldfield's past, is believed to be haunted by spirits from the town's heyday. Visitors and staff have reported hearing phantom footsteps, voices, and laughter within the saloon, even when it is empty. Some have witnessed objects moving on their own, glasses sliding off tables, or doors opening and closing inexplicably. The ambiance within the Mammoth Saloon often evokes a sense of nostalgia and a connection to the spirits of the past.

Visitors and staff have frequently reported hearing unexplained sounds within the Mammoth Saloon. These include footsteps, disembodied voices, whispers, laughter, and even the clinking of glasses. Witnesses have described the sounds as echoing through the saloon, often when no one else is present. The phantom sounds add an eerie and mysterious atmosphere to the location.

Some individuals claim to have witnessed ghostly apparitions or shadow figures while in the Mammoth Saloon. These spectral entities are often described as fleeting or transparent, appearing for brief moments before vanishing. Witnesses have reported seeing figures dressed in old-fashioned clothing, resembling cowboys, saloon girls, or patrons from the past.

Another intriguing aspect of the paranormal activity at the Mammoth Saloon is the apparent manipulation of objects by unseen forces. Some visitors have reported seeing glasses or other items on tables move or slide across the surface without any physical interaction. Doors and windows have been observed opening and closing on their own, adding to the sense of a supernatural presence within the building.

Many people have experienced sudden drops in temperature or encountered localized cold spots within the Mammoth Saloon. These cold spots are often associated with paranormal phenomena and are considered by some to be indications of spiritual energy or the presence of entities.

EMF Readings and Equipment Malfunctions: During paranormal investigations conducted in the Mammoth Saloon, electromagnetic field (EMF) readings have been known to spike unexpectedly. Some investigators believe that these spikes indicate the presence of paranormal energy or entities. Additionally, electronic equipment, such as cameras, audio recorders, or EMF meters, may malfunction or drain their batteries unusually quickly while inside the saloon.

The Bordello

The Bordello is known for its haunted reputation and numerous paranormal occurrences. As a former brothel, The Bordello holds a captivating and somewhat mysterious past, which has contributed to the reports of supernatural activity within its walls.

Many visitors and staff members have reported feeling a strong presence or being touched by unseen entities while inside The Bordello. Some have described feeling a gentle brush against their skin, as if someone or something is trying to make contact. Others have experienced cold drafts, sudden temperature changes, or a distinct sensation of being watched, even when alone in a room.

Witnesses have reported hearing disembodied voices and whispering within The Bordello. These whispers are often described as faint and indistinct, as if coming from distant corners of the building. Some visitors claim to have heard murmurs of conversation or laughter, as if echoes from the past still linger within the walls.

The Bordello has been the site of reported apparitions, with witnesses claiming to have seen ghostly figures resembling former inhabitants of the establishment. These spectral entities are often described as wearing period clothing, such as provocative attire associated with the brothel's heyday. Witnesses have described glimpses of shadowy figures or transparent forms, appearing briefly before fading away.

Similar to other haunted locations, The Bordello has its share of unexplained object movements. Visitors have reported witnessing items, such as furniture or personal belongings, shift or topple over seemingly by themselves. Doors and windows have been known to open or close on their own, sometimes with a noticeable force behind the movement.

The Bordello is believed to hold residual emotional energy from its past, which some visitors claim to sense. Reports include feeling a heavy atmosphere, sudden waves of sadness, or a general unease while exploring the building. It is as if the intense emotions and experiences of its former inhabitants have left an energetic imprint that can still be felt.

Paranormal investigators and enthusiasts have conducted extensive research and investigations within The Bordello, utilizing tools such as EVP (Electronic Voice Phenomena) recorders, EMF (Electromagnetic Field) meters, and thermal imaging cameras to capture potential evidence of the supernatural occurrences. These investigations have yielded audio recordings of unexplained voices and electronic fluctuations that suggest the presence of paranormal activity.

The combination of the building's history as a brothel, reports of apparitions, tactile sensations, mysterious object movements, and the lingering emotional imprints all contribute to

The Enigma of the Mountains
The Bordello's reputation as a haunted location within Goldfield Ghost Town. Visitors intrigued by the supernatural can explore The Bordello during ghost tours or participate in investigations, immersing themselves in the mystique of this intriguing and ethereal destination.

The Lady in Red at the Goldfield Hotel
While not located within the immediate confines of Goldfield Ghost Town, the nearby Goldfield Hotel is often associated with the ghostly legends of the area. The hotel was once a hub of activity during the gold rush era, attracting miners and travelers alike. It is rumored to be haunted by a variety of spirits, including former guests, employees, and even a phantom cowboy. Reports of apparitions, disembodied voices, and eerie sounds have made the Goldfield Hotel a popular destination for paranormal investigations.

The tragic love story of the Lady in Red at the Goldfield Hotel is one that has captured the imaginations of visitors and locals alike. According to the legend, the Lady in Red was a captivating and mysterious woman who graced the halls of the hotel during its vibrant era in the early 1900s.

The Lady in Red was said to possess a beauty that could enchant any man who laid eyes on her. Her allure and elegance were unmatched, drawing the attention of numerous suitors who visited the Goldfield Hotel. Among these admirers was a mining magnate, a man of wealth and power, who became captivated by the Lady in Red's charm.

The two fell deeply in love, but their romance faced insurmountable obstacles. It is whispered that the mining magnate was already bound in a loveless marriage or was engaged to a woman of high societal standing. Their love, forbidden by circumstances and societal expectations, was deemed impossible.

Despite the challenges, the Lady in Red and the mining magnate yearned to be together. They hatched a plan to elope, aiming to escape the confines of their respective lives and find happiness in each other's arms. They envisioned a life of freedom, away from the judgmental eyes of society.

However, fate had other plans. On the fateful night of their planned elopement, tragedy struck. The details of this ill-fated event are shrouded in mystery. Some accounts suggest that the mining magnate's family discovered their plan and intervened, forcing the Lady in Red to abandon her dreams of love. Others speak of a tragic accident that resulted in her untimely demise.

Heartbroken and shattered, the Lady in Red met a tragic end, leaving behind a legacy of unfulfilled love and sorrow. It is said that her spirit now haunts the Goldfield Hotel, forever trapped between the realm of the living and the dead. Her spectral presence, clad in a flowing red gown, wanders the hallways and lingers near the staircase, a constant reminder of the tragic love that was never meant to be.

The tragic love story of the Lady in Red adds an air of melancholy and romance to the Goldfield Hotel's haunted reputation. It has become an integral part of the hotel's lore, captivating those who visit in search of glimpses into the mysterious and sorrowful tale of love and loss.

The Drowned Man at the Goldfield Hotel

The story of the drowned man associated with the Goldfield Hotel adds another layer of mystery and tragedy to the hotel's haunted history. According to local legends and accounts, the drowned man is said to be a spirit that frequents the premises, leaving an indelible mark on the hotel's supernatural reputation.

The tale begins with a man whose identity remains unknown. He was believed to be an adventurous soul, drawn to the rugged beauty of the nearby Superstition Mountains. As an avid explorer, he often ventured into treacherous terrains in search of hidden treasures and unknown discoveries.

During one of his expeditions, fate took a cruel turn. While attempting to navigate the treacherous waters or cross a perilous river, the man met his untimely demise. Whether it was due to a sudden surge of the currents, an unforeseen accident, or simply an act of nature's unpredictability, he found himself at the mercy of the water's merciless embrace.

His body, unable to be recovered or lost in the depths of the water, was forever claimed by the river that had claimed his life. It is believed that the spirit of the drowned man returned to the Goldfield Hotel, forever haunted by the circumstances of his demise.

Witnesses have reported encounters with the apparition of a man who appears soaking wet, his clothing drenched, and his demeanor filled with anguish. The drowned man is often described as appearing distressed and disoriented, seemingly trapped between the realms of the living and the dead.

His spectral presence manifests himself in various ways. Some guests have claimed to see him walking through the corridors, leaving wet footprints in his wake. Others have reported encountering him near bodies of water or hearing the faint sounds of splashing, as if he is desperately trying to escape his watery fate.

The presence of the drowned man adds a somber element to the haunted reputation of the Goldfield Hotel. His unresolved tragedy and lingering spirit evoke feelings of sympathy and unease among those who experience his spectral presence.

While the identity and circumstances surrounding the drowned man remain shrouded in mystery, his story serves as a poignant reminder of the dangers and mysteries that lie within the natural landscapes surrounding Goldfield. The drowned man's spirit, forever tied to the hotel, continues to captivate visitors and paranormal enthusiasts, leaving an enduring imprint on the haunting legends of the Goldfield Hotel.

Whether one is drawn to its historical significance, architectural charm, or paranormal intrigue, Goldfield Ghost Town offers a captivating experience for visitors seeking a unique journey into the Wild West and the mysteries that surround it.

The Lost Dutchman State Park
6109 N Apache Trail, Apache Junction, Arizona
Park Information: (480) 982-4485

Figure 20: Lost Dutchman State Park. Photo taken by Timothy James Wilson.

The Lost Dutchman's Mine State park is one of the most remarkable places in Arizona. The views and the hikes are amazing. So much so, that I can understand why the Apache peoples regarded this area as a holy place just by looking at it. There is little evidence that the actual mine of the Dutchman, Jacab Waltz is here at the state park, or for that matter even exists, but this place is definitely worth a few hours of time.

The Enigma of the Mountains

The Lost Dutchman's Mine, located in the rugged Superstition Mountains, is a legendary and enigmatic place that has captivated treasure hunters, adventurers, and storytellers for generations. The mine's history is shrouded in mystery and tragedy, intertwined with tales of hauntings and supernatural occurrences. Let us delve into the detailed account of the haunting legends that surround the Lost Dutchman's Mine.

Jacob Waltz

The legend of the Lost Dutchman's Mine begins with the story of Jacob Waltz, a German immigrant who arrived in the United States in the mid-19th century. Born in Germany around 1810, Waltz immigrated to the United States in the mid-19th century, seeking a better life and the opportunity for prosperity during the California Gold Rush.

Waltz's life before his arrival in Arizona remains somewhat obscure. Some accounts suggest that he had mining experience in Europe, while others claim that he served as a soldier in the Mexican American War. Nevertheless, it was his journey to the Superstition Mountains that would cement his place in history.

According to the legend, Waltz first discovered the mine in the 1870s while working as a prospector in the Superstition Mountains. The exact circumstances of his discovery are a subject of speculation and myth. Some versions of the tale suggest that he stumbled upon the mine by accident, while others claim that he received a treasure map or directions from a passing traveler. There are even accounts that suggest Waltz might have learned about the mine from the Peralta family, who were said to have discovered it before him.

Regardless of how he came upon the mine, it is believed that Waltz was able to extract a considerable amount of gold from the rich vein he discovered. However, in keeping with the secretive nature of the Lost Dutchman's Mine, Waltz kept the location of the mine closely guarded. He supposedly trusted the secret to only a few individuals, including his close friend Jacob Weiser.

Over the years, Waltz and Weiser intermittently returned to the mine to extract more gold. However, as Waltz grew older and his health declined, he was unable to continue his expeditions to the Superstition Mountains. He passed away in 1891, taking the exact location of the mine with him to the grave.

It is rumored that Waltz killed several people in his attempt to keep the mine a secret. Some rumors even suggest that Waltz killed for the treasure map. Legend says that Waltz had become so recognizable that many people attempted to follow him to his mine, but Waltz was always one step ahead of them.

After Waltz's death, rumors of the legendary mine spread like wildfire, attracting numerous treasure hunters, prospectors, and adventurers to the Superstition Mountains. Many claimed to have found the mine, but their discoveries often ended in tragedy or disappointment.

It is said among many that if a person does discover the mine, they will also discover that to this day, the ghost of Jacob Waltz will shoot you dead with his .45 Colt revolver.

Jacob Waltz's legacy lives on through the tales of the Lost Dutchman's Mine. Whether he was a lucky prospector who stumbled upon unimaginable wealth or a skilled miner who meticulously discovered the gold vein, his name has become synonymous with both the treasure and the supernatural hauntings that are said to protect its location in the Superstition Mountains of Arizona.

The Enigma of the Mountains

The Peralta Massacre

Another famous story associated with the Lost Dutchman's Mine is the tale of the Peralta Massacre. The Peralta Massacre is a tragic event deeply entwined with the legend of the Lost Dutchman's Mine. According to the folklore, the Peralta family, a prominent Mexican mining clan, discovered the mine long before Jacob Waltz. The exact timeline and details of the Peralta Massacre are uncertain, as the event has become a part of local legend and historical accounts vary.

The story goes that in the early 1840s, members of the Peralta family, led by Don Miguel Peralta, ventured into the Superstition Mountains in search of gold. They are said to have found a rich gold vein, establishing a lucrative mining operation in the region. However, their success did not go unnoticed, and it is believed that their activities drew the attention of the Apache peoples who inhabited the area.

Even though the region was, at the time, part of Mexico, the Apache still would have seen the Peralta family as invaders, as the Apache had long been fighting to maintain their way of life despite Mexican and American interests encroaching of them.

In a fateful turn of events, the Peralta family and their miners were ambushed and brutally massacred by the Apache warriors. According to legend, not a single member of the Peralta party survived the attack. The Apache warriors, aiming to keep the location of the mine a secret, ensured that no witnesses would remain to reveal its whereabouts.

The exact location of the Peralta Massacre and the burial sites of the victims have never been definitively identified. Some accounts suggest that the massacre occurred near a natural formation known as Massacre Grounds, while others believe it took place at various locations throughout the Superstition

Mountains. The lack of concrete evidence has only added to the mystery and allure surrounding the Lost Dutchman's Mine and the Peralta Massacre.

In the years that followed, the tale of the Peralta Massacre and the lost gold mine intertwined with the legend of Jacob Waltz and his own discovery. Many believe that Waltz learned about the mine's location through interactions with survivors of the Peralta family or through recovered maps or documents left behind by the family. This connection further fueled the interest and fascination surrounding the Lost Dutchman's Mine.

While some historians question the authenticity of the Peralta Massacre and the involvement of the Peralta family in the Lost Dutchman's Mine, the legend has endured and become an integral part of the lore associated with the Superstition Mountains. It adds a tragic and dramatic element to the stories of gold, curses, and hauntings that continue to captivate those who seek the hidden riches within the rugged landscape.

The Petrasch-Thomas Disaster

The Petrasch-Thomas Disaster is a tragic event that is said to have taken place following the death of Jacob Waltz. As legend tells, on his death bed Waltz confessed to Julia Thomas, his neighbor, the location of the mine. Following his death, Julia enlisted the help of her brother Jacob and their friend Herman Petrasch to find the treasure.

The Petrasch-Thomas trio were determined treasure hunters who became consumed by their quest for the Lost Dutchman's Mine. Armed with little more than hope, and the tales told to Julia by Jacob Waltz, they ventured deep into the treacherous Superstition Mountains, seeking the legendary fortune rumored to be hidden within its rocky depths.

The Enigma of the Mountains

As they pressed forward into uncharted territories, the explorers faced a myriad of challenges: the harsh desert environment, the unforgiving landscape, and the ever-present specter of danger. They braved the scorching sun, navigated treacherous cliffs, and fought against the elements in their relentless pursuit of wealth.

However, it was during one fateful expedition that tragedy struck. As the Trio delved deeper into the heart of the Superstition Mountains, they unknowingly trespassed into sacred Apache lands. The Apaches, fiercely protective of their territory and suspicious of outsiders, saw the treasure hunters as intruders threatening their sacred heritage.

In a sudden and brutal confrontation, the Apache warriors ambushed the trio, unleashing a ferocious assault upon their camp. Outnumbered and caught off guard, the treasure hunters were overwhelmed by the swift and deadly attack. Although the three of them fought valiantly, but ultimately succumbed to the forces arrayed against them.

The Petrasch-Thomas Disaster sent shockwaves through the community of treasure hunters and adventurers who dared to seek the Lost Dutchman's Mine. The incident served as a grim reminder of the perils that awaited those who ventured too far into the Superstition Mountains, where danger and misfortune seemed to lurk around every bend.

The tale of the Petrasch-Thomas Disaster became intertwined with the folklore surrounding the Lost Dutchman's Mine, adding another layer of tragedy to the already haunted reputation of the Superstition Mountains. Though the specifics of this tragedy may differ from historical accounts, it reflects the dangers and risks associated with the pursuit of legendary treasures and the enduring allure of the unknown.

Persistence

Over the years, countless prospectors and treasure seekers ventured into the treacherous Superstition Mountains in search of the fabled mine. Many met with misfortune and tragedy, as the harsh desert conditions, treacherous terrain, and the mysterious curse associated with the mine seemed to thwart their efforts.

As the years passed, numerous individuals claimed to have found the Lost Dutchman's Mine, only to meet with misfortune or untimely death. Mysterious accidents, disappearances, and unexplained phenomena became synonymous with the pursuit of the mine's riches. Some believe that the spirits of those who perished in their search for the mine now roam the mountains, seeking revenge or guarding the secrets of the treasure.

Among the reported hauntings is the Ghost of the Lost Dutchman himself. Many hikers and treasure hunters have claimed to see a spectral figure resembling Jacob Waltz wandering the mountain trails, wearing a tattered hat and clutching a pickaxe. It is said that the ghostly figure warns adventurers to turn back, as if trying to protect them from the dangers that lie ahead.

There have also been accounts of disembodied voices, eerie laughter, and phantom footsteps echoing through the Superstition Mountains. Some visitors have reported seeing strange lights or orbs floating in the distance, while others claim to have witnessed ghostly apparitions near the supposed location of the mine.

Interestingly, the Apache people, who have long considered the Superstition Mountains sacred, have their own supernatural beliefs associated with the region. They believe that the mountains are home to a powerful spirit called the Thunder God, who guards the land and its treasures. Some locals and

The Enigma of the Mountains

researchers speculate that the hauntings and curses attributed to the Lost Dutchman's Mine might be influenced by the ancient Apache folklore, adding another layer of mystique to the legends surrounding the area.

Despite the tales of hauntings and curses, the allure of the Lost Dutchman's Mine persists, drawing adventurers and treasure hunters to the Superstition Mountains to this day. The search for the elusive mine continues, fueled by the hope of uncovering unimaginable riches and the thrill of solving a centuries-old mystery. But the legends, hauntings, and the supernatural aura surrounding the Lost Dutchman's Mine ensure that the treacherous Superstition Mountains will forever hold their secrets, captivating the imaginations of those who dare to seek its hidden wealth.

The Great Swindler

When the United States and Mexico signed the Gadsden Treaty, there certain protections, or clauses that the treaty contained, which included the US recognizing the validity of Spanish and Mexican land grants that existed prior to the Treaty. This clause was designed to protect the interests of Mexican citizens living in the area. The Missouri man, James Addison Reavis, also known as the Great Swindler, would be the man who would devise a plan to exploit this clause in the Treaty.

Reavis was a veteran of the Confederate army, who learned the cunning skill of forgery because he was homesick during the Civil War. His forgery of leave passes and orders were the beginning of what would become a lifetime of conning people. Reavis even forged his own discharge papers, so that he could get out of the war, and go back home. Upon returning to St. Louis, Reavis worked in Real Estate, and honed his forgery skills, conning people with dubious land deals. Reavis' forgeries were so convincing that a movie would be made about him in 1950.

In 1874, in Prescott, Reavis presented documentation that he was the rightful heir to Spanish land-grant that included nearly twelve million acres of land in Arizona and New Mexico, including the Superstition Mountains. Reavis would use these land rights to become the Baron of Arizona extorting thousands from prospectors, landowners, and ranchers for 15 years before it was discovered in 1889 that all of the documentation was forged. There was no Spanish Land Grant, and this was just one of the many St. Louis real estate swindles he had done, just on a much bigger scale. Reavis was arrested and found guilty of fraud. He was sentenced to two years in prison and fined $5,000.

Following his prison sentence, legend tells that the Baron returned to Phoenix, and peddled forged maps to the Lost Dutchman's Mine to newcomers to the area. He would walk the streets of downtown Phoenix, looking for suckers to con. Sometimes, in the midst of a warm night in the downtown region, you might encounter the old man, in his pristine antique suit, and his hair neatly combed. He will tell you tales of great riches of silver and gold in the Superstition Mountains and try to sell you a map to lead you straight to the mine. If you buy the map and follow it you might meet Jacob Waltz and his Colt revolver, but if you ignore the old man he will simply dissolve, right in front of you. While this is the end of the stories of James Addison Reavis, it is not the last that we will hear from him.

The Old Gila County Jail and Courthouse
177 East Oak Street, Globe, Arizona
Information: (928) 425-4449

The Old Gila County Jail and Courthouse is a historic site that holds a rich history and has gained a reputation for its haunted and paranormal occurrences. This unique structure serves as a tangible reminder of the county's past and has become a popular destination for history enthusiasts and ghost hunters alike.

The Old Gila County Courthouse is a massive red-brick building, constructed in the late 1800s. The architecture reflects the typical style of the era, with arched windows, a prominent entrance, and a clock tower rising from the center of the courthouse. The jail section is attached to the courthouse and is distinguishable by its thick stone walls and iron-barred windows. The interior consists of narrow corridors, small cells, and several rooms that were once used as courtrooms and offices.

Figure 21: The Gila County Courthouse (left) and Jail (right). Photo taken by Timothy James Wilson.

The site's history dates back to 1005 when the courthouse was established to serve the growing population of Gila County. It played a significant role in the region, serving as a place for trials, hearings, and other legal proceedings. The jail section of the building housed numerous prisoners awaiting trial or serving their sentences.

Figure 22: The Old Gila County Jail (right) and Courhouse (left). Photo taken by Timothy James Wilson.

One of the more unique features of the Old Gila County Courthouse and Jail is the bridge connecting the courthouse to the jail. This allowed prisoners to be transported from there cell to the courtroom without risking the prison escape, or the convoy being attacked by fellow gang members.

Haunted and Paranormal Occurrences

The Old Gila County Jail and Courthouse is renowned for its haunted and paranormal occurrences, with numerous reports and stories from visitors, staff, and paranormal investigators. Within the walls of this historic building, eerie phenomena have been experienced, leaving an indelible mark on those who dare to explore its haunted corridors.

One of the most common occurrences reported by visitors is the sound of disembodied voices. People have claimed to hear whispers and hushed conversations echoing through the empty hallways, as if the spirits of the past are still engaged in their ethereal discussions. Some have even reported hearing

The Enigma of the Mountains

distinct names being called out, evoking a sense of otherworldly presence.

Cold spots, which are localized areas of intense coldness, are frequently encountered within the building. Visitors have described sudden drops in temperature, even in rooms that are otherwise warm. These chilling pockets of air seem to defy natural explanations, leaving individuals with a distinct feeling of unease as they move through the haunted structure.

Unexplained footsteps and the sensation of being watched are commonly reported in the Old Gila County Jail and Courthouse. Visitors have described the distinct sound of footsteps echoing through the empty corridors, as if someone is pacing or wandering aimlessly. Some have also reported the unnerving feeling of being observed, as if invisible eyes are fixed upon them, causing a heightened sense of anxiety.

One area of the building that is particularly notorious for paranormal activity is the old jail section. Visitors have reported hearing the rattling of chains and the clanging of cell doors, despite there being no physical source for these sounds. Some have even claimed to see shadowy figures moving within the cells, their forms flickering and dissipating as they vanish into the darkness.

In addition to these auditory and visual encounters, visitors have experienced tactile paranormal phenomena. Sensations of being touched or brushed against by unseen entities have been reported, often accompanied by a sudden feeling of dread or a rush of cold air. These physical interactions, though subtle, leave a lasting impression on those who experience them.

While exploring the Old Gila County Jail and Courthouse, some individuals have encountered full-bodied apparitions. These ghostly figures are said to manifest briefly before fading away, offering glimpses into the past. Among the reported apparitions is the ghost of James Hale, an infamous outlaw who was held in the jail section. Witnesses have described seeing a spectral figure resembling Hale, wearing tattered clothing and a haunted expression, wandering through the cells or peering out from behind the iron bars.

The paranormal occurrences at the Old Gila County Jail and Courthouse are believed to be connected to the turbulent history of the site. The anguish, suffering, and emotional intensity that permeated the building during its time as a jail and courthouse may have left residual energy, creating a spiritual imprint that continues to manifest to this day.

As visitors brave the shadows and explore the haunted corridors, the Old Gila County Jail and Courthouse reveals itself as a place where the boundaries between the living and the dead blur. It stands as a testament to the enduring power of history and the lingering spirits that refuse to fade away, ensuring that its haunted reputation remains intact for those who dare to venture into its paranormal realm.

The Pleasant Valley War

The Old Gila County Jail and Courthouse witnessed several notable events during its existence. One such event was the infamous "Pleasant Valley War" that occurred in the late 19th century.

The Pleasant Valley War, also known as the Tonto Basin Feud, was a violent and protracted conflict that took place in the late 19th century in the Tonto Basin. It was a bloody and bitter feud between two prominent ranching families, the Grahams and the Tewksburys, and their respective allies. The war spanned nearly a decade and resulted in numerous deaths, property destruction, and legal battles.

The Enigma of the Mountains

The origins of the conflict can be traced back to the late 1880s when tensions between the Grahams and the Tewksburys began to escalate. The Grahams, led by brothers Tom and John Graham, were cattle ranchers who had established a successful operation in the Tonto Basin. On the other hand, the Tewksburys, led by the Tewksbury brothers, Bill and John, were sheep herders who had recently settled in the same area.

The feud erupted over disputes related to grazing rights, water resources, and competition for control of the lucrative cattle industry in the region. Both families resorted to acts of violence and intimidation, leading to a cycle of revenge and retaliation that spiraled out of control.

Killings became a frequent occurrence during the war, with members of both families and their supporters falling victim to ambushes and targeted attacks. The remote and rugged nature of the Tonto Basin provided an ideal backdrop for these violent clashes, as it allowed the warring factions to wage their battles away from prying eyes.

The conflict drew the attention of local law enforcement and the Arizona territorial government, who struggled to maintain peace in the area. The Graham and Tewksbury families became entangled in a series of legal battles, resulting in numerous arrests, trials, and acquittals. The trials themselves were often marred by witness intimidation and the difficulty of gathering evidence in such a hostile environment.

One of the most notable events of the war was the infamous "Pleasant Valley Massacre" that occurred in 1887. A group of Tewksbury supporters ambushed a cabin where several members of the Graham family were taking shelter. In the ensuing gunfight, several Grahams were killed, including Tom Graham himself. This violent event marked a turning point in the feud, further escalating tensions and solidifying the resolve of both sides.

The Pleasant Valley War finally came to an end in the early 1890s when the Arizona Rangers, a territorial law enforcement group, intervened and managed to bring some semblance of peace to the region. By that time, many lives had been lost, properties destroyed, and families torn apart. The war left a lasting impact on the Tonto Basin community, with scars that continued to linger for generations.

Today, the Pleasant Valley War is remembered as a dark chapter in Arizona's history, representing the lawlessness and violence that characterized the American West during that era. The legacy of the conflict serves as a reminder of the challenges faced by early settlers and the intense struggles for control over resources in the untamed frontier.

This bloody feud between rival cattle ranching families resulted in numerous deaths and trials that were held within the courthouse.

Prohibition

During the era of Prohibition in the United States (1920-1933), the Old Gila County Jail and Courthouse in Gila County, played a role in enforcing and addressing the challenges posed by the nationwide ban on the production, sale, and distribution of alcoholic beverages.

The prohibition of alcohol gave rise to various illegal activities, including bootlegging, speakeasies (underground bars), and organized crime. Gila County, like many other areas across the country, had its share of clandestine alcohol production and distribution.

The Old Gila County Jail and Courthouse became a central location for addressing cases related to Prohibition violations. The courthouse section of the building served as the venue for trials and hearings concerning illegal alcohol-related offenses. Judges presided over these cases, and the court played a crucial role in prosecuting individuals involved in bootlegging operations.

The enforcement of Prohibition in Gila County faced numerous challenges. The vast and rugged landscape provided ample opportunities for illegal alcohol production and smuggling. Remote areas, hidden caves, and secret routes were used by bootleggers to evade authorities. The Old Gila County Jail and Courthouse became a symbol of the ongoing struggle between law enforcement and those involved in the illicit alcohol trade.

Despite efforts to crack down on illegal alcohol activities, Prohibition faced widespread criticism and encountered resistance across the country. The ban led to an increase in organized crime, corruption, and the development of a black market for alcohol. Speakeasies and underground bars thrived, catering to those who sought to indulge in alcoholic beverages despite the prohibition laws.

The failure of Prohibition to curb alcohol consumption eventually led to its repeal in 1933 with the ratification of the 21st Amendment. The Old Gila County Jail and Courthouse witnessed the changing tides of public opinion and the eventual end of the Prohibition era.

Given the violent and intense history associated with the Pleasant Valley War and the criminal activities during Prohibition, some believe that the residual energy of turmoil and suffering still lingers within the site. This residual energy is thought to contribute to the overall haunting and paranormal activity experienced by visitors.

The Ghostly Judge

The legends surrounding the ghostly judge at the Old Gila County Jail and Courthouse add an intriguing element to the site's supernatural lore. According to these legends, the spirit of a former judge is said to linger within the courthouse section of the building, perpetually connected to the halls of justice where he once presided.

Witnesses have reported encountering a figure dressed in judicial robes, often described as appearing distinguished and authoritative. The ghostly judge is said to be seen walking the corridors, silently observing court proceedings, or even sitting on the judge's bench as if still overseeing trials from beyond the grave. Some accounts suggest that he may also exhibit gestures or expressions of disapproval or solemn contemplation, as if silently passing judgment on the living.

The presence of the ghostly judge is often accompanied by a sense of gravitas and a distinct feeling of being in the presence of authority. Witnesses claim to have felt a tangible atmosphere of reverence and formality when encountering this apparition, as if the spirit maintains a strong connection to the courthouse's history and purpose.

The origins and identity of the ghostly judge are shrouded in mystery. It is unclear who the judge was in life or the specific cases he presided over. Without concrete historical records, it's challenging to verify the accuracy of these legends or determine if there was indeed a judge who left a lasting spiritual imprint on the Old Gila County Jail and Courthouse.

However, the ghostly judge legends contribute to the overall supernatural ambiance of the site. They evoke a sense of justice, solemnity, and lingering responsibility that is often associated with the legal system.

The Crying Woman

The legend of the crying woman adds a poignant and sorrowful element to the supernatural tales associated with the Old Gila County Jail and Courthouse. According to local accounts and witness testimonies, visitors and staff have reported hearing the sounds of a woman sobbing or crying within the vicinity of the site.

The source and identity of the crying woman remain a mystery. There are no specific historical records or documented incidents that definitively explain the origin of this ghostly manifestation. However, speculations and local legends suggest that her presence may be linked to the hardships and tragedies experienced within the jail and courthouse throughout its history.

One theory is that the crying woman could be connected to the female prisoners who were held within the jail. It is possible that she represents the anguish and despair endured by women who found themselves incarcerated, separated from their families and facing uncertain futures. The sorrowful cries may echo the pain and suffering they endured during their confinement.

Another possibility is that the crying woman is associated with the emotional toll of the turbulent times when the jail was operational. The Pleasant Valley War and Prohibition era were marked by violence, loss, and intense emotions. The residual energy of those tumultuous times may have imprinted itself on the site, manifesting as the mournful cries of a tormented spirit.

The crying woman's presence is often described as evoking a deep sense of sadness and empathy in those who hear her cries. Witnesses have reported feeling a profound sorrow and a desire to offer comfort to the unseen entity. Some individuals have even attempted to investigate the source of the cries, only to find no visible or tangible explanation for the haunting phenomenon.

As with many supernatural legends, the crying woman's story relies on personal experiences and local folklore. While her true identity and the reasons behind her ghostly presence remain unknown, her presence adds to the mystique and emotional depth of the Old Gila County Jail and Courthouse's haunted reputation.

In recent years, efforts have been made to transform the Old Gila County Jail and Courthouse into a museum. The site now offers visitors the opportunity to explore its historic exhibits, learn about the region's history, and gain insights into the daily lives of those who lived and worked in Gila County.

Today, the Old Gila County Jail and Courthouse stands as a historical landmark, offering visitors a glimpse into the region's past. Whether exploring its intriguing architecture, delving into its haunted history, or appreciating the notable events and figures associated with it, the site continues to captivate the imaginations of those seeking a unique blend of history and the supernatural.

Besh-Ba-Gowah Park and Museum
1276 South Jesse Hayes Road, Globe, Arizona
Information: (928) 425-0320

In the heart of Globe, Besh-Ba-Gowah Archaeological Park and Museum stands as a living testament to the vibrant history and cultural legacy of the Salado people who once inhabited the region. The site's name, derived from the Apache language, translates to "place of metal" due to the abundant copper deposits nearby, which played a crucial role in the Salado culture's development. In your exploration of Arizona's dark history,

The Enigma of the Mountains

Besh-Ba-Gowah offers a unique opportunity to delve into the mysteries of the past.

Figure 23 The Besh-Ba-Gowah Achelogical Sight. Photo taken by Timothy James Wilson.

Besh-Ba-Gowah dates back to around 1225 to 1400 AD, a period marked by the flourishing Salado culture. The ancient pueblo settlement comprises ruins of dwellings, a plaza, and an intricate network of rooms and corridors that once housed families, craftsmen, and spiritual activities. As you wander through these ruins, you'll be transported to a time when the site was a bustling hub of social interaction, trade, and daily life.

The park not only showcases the physical remnants of the past but also provides a window into the cultural practices, traditions, and ingenuity of the Salado people. Guided tours and interpretive displays unravel the stories behind the pottery, tools, and artifacts that have been unearthed. This immersive experience offers insights into the lives of these ancient inhabitants, their agricultural practices, and their connection to the land.

Besh-Ba-Gowah's history also carries with it a tinge of melancholy. The site was eventually abandoned, leaving behind the ruins that now serve as a poignant reminder of the passage of time. Standing amidst these ancient walls, you can contemplate the narratives that unfolded within them and the stories that have been lost to history.

Mystery of Abandonment

The abandonment of Besh-Ba-Gowah Archaeological Park remains a captivating enigma that continues to intrigue archaeologists and historians alike. While the exact reasons for the departure of the Salado people from this once-thriving settlement may never be fully unraveled, several theories shed light on the factors that might have contributed to the site's abandonment.

One prevailing theory suggests that environmental challenges played a significant role. The region's arid climate and reliance on agriculture may have made the Salado people vulnerable to droughts and changing weather patterns. As water sources became scarce and crops faced failure, the inhabitants may have faced difficulties sustaining their way of life.

Besh-Ba-Gowah's proximity to copper deposits played a vital role in the Salado culture's development. However, over time, the exhaustion of copper reserves could have impacted trade networks and economic stability. Depletion of essential resources could have contributed to the decline of the settlement's economic foundation.

Cultural shifts and societal changes might have also influenced the abandonment of Besh-Ba-Gowah. The Salado culture might have undergone transformations, leading to shifts in community dynamics and traditional practices. As new social and economic dynamics emerged, some inhabitants might have chosen to relocate, leaving the settlement behind.

Interaction and contact with neighboring groups could have played a role in the site's abandonment. Changes in trade networks, alliances, or conflicts with other indigenous groups might have disrupted the flow of resources and the stability of the settlement.

Despite these theories, the true reasons for the abandonment of Besh-Ba-Gowah remain shrouded in mystery. Archaeologists continue to piece together the puzzle through careful excavation, artifact analysis, and the study of the surrounding environment. By examining the clues left behind by the Salado people, modern researchers aim to gain insights into the complex interplay of factors that led to the site's eventual abandonment.

Historic Downtown Globe
Broad Street, Globe, Arizona

Amidst the picturesque landscapes of Arizona, Historic Downtown Globe stands as a testament to the town's rich history, vibrant culture, and the echoes of the past that continue to resonate through its streets. As you wander through its charming alleys and historic buildings, you'll find yourself immersed in a tapestry of stories that have shaped Globe's evolution over the decades.

Figure 24: Downtown Globe. Photo taken by Timothy James Wilson.

The heart of Globe's history beats in its architecture. Victorian facades stand shoulder-to-shoulder with Territorial-style buildings, painting a vivid portrait of the eras that have left their mark. Stroll down Broad Street, where ornate facades tell tales of prosperous merchants and determined settlers. Be sure to visit the old Gila County Courthouse, a striking example of the Territorial style, which has witnessed the ebb and flow of justice for generations.

Behind the façades of these historic buildings lie untold stories, some darker than others. As the sun dips below the horizon, casting long shadows over the cobblestone streets, it's not difficult to imagine the miners and pioneers who once called this place home. Visit the Old Dominion Historic Mine Park, a chilling reminder of the town's mining roots, where tales of hard labor and mysterious accidents linger in the air. The Old Dominion Historic Mine Park is rumored to be haunted by a ghostly presence, but I could not find any information to confirm that.

Globe's charm extends beyond its architecture; it pulses through the veins of its vibrant community. Explore art galleries that showcase the talent of local artists, offering a contemporary contrast to the historical backdrop. Stop by the Gila County Historical Museum, where artifacts and exhibits reveal the region's rich heritage, from mining to Indigenous culture.

Come Halloween, Historic Downtown Globe takes on an even more enchanting atmosphere. The town's history comes alive during the annual walking ghost tours. With lanterns casting an eerie glow, visitors are led through the streets by guides who share tales of restless spirits, haunted buildings, and the mysteries that have endured through the ages. These tours offer a unique blend of history and the supernatural, giving participants a chance to walk alongside the past and experience the town's haunted legends firsthand.

In Historic Downtown Globe, every step is a journey through time. The district's historic charm, cultural vibrancy, and tales of the past weave together to create an experience that captivates the imagination and leaves an indelible mark on those who venture through its streets. Whether you're drawn to its architecture, curious about its dark history, or simply seeking an encounter with the otherworldly, Historic Downtown Globe promises an unforgettable exploration of Arizona's heritage.

Chapter Four: Central Paranormal Phenomena

Casa Grande, Picacho, Coolidge, Florence

Figure 25: the small town of Sacaton, 14 miles north of Casa Grande. Photo taken by Timothy James Wilson.

Nestled between the two biggest cities in the state, Casa Grande emerges as a captivating chapter in the history of the American Southwest. This vibrant city, along with its neighboring towns of Florence, Coolidge, Eloy, and the Iconic Picacho Peak, weaves a unique blend of geography, industry, and rich cultural tapestry, beckons explorers to delve into its past and present.

Casa Grande finds itself in a landscape that's as awe-inspiring as it is challenging—the Sonoran Desert. Towering saguaro cacti punctuate the horizon, casting shadows that dance with the rhythm of the desert wind. The city's proximity to the majestic Casa Grande Mountain adds to the allure, as it stands as a silent sentinel guarding the stories etched into the land.

Beyond the arid beauty lies a history woven with threads of Indigenous heritage. The city's very name, "Casa Grande," pays homage to the Ancient Sonoran Peoples who once inhabited the area. Their legacy is embodied by the Casa Grande Ruins National Monument—a testament to the ingenuity of these ancient engineers who crafted a bustling community amid the desert's challenges.

Casa Grande's history isn't confined to the distant past. It's a place where cultures converged, and history unfolded. Spanish explorers left their mark, and later settlers and pioneers established a sense of community. As the city grew, it became a crossroads where the past intertwined with the present, creating a unique blend of traditions and stories that continue to shape its identity.

Modern Casa Grande is marked by diverse industries that complement its historical significance. Agriculture thrives in the fertile soil, while manufacturing and commerce have found a home within its borders. The city's growth has been guided by the promise of progress while preserving the threads of its heritage.

The desert sun and wind shape the rhythms of life in Casa Grande. From scorching summers to mild winters, the climate is a reflection of the challenges faced by those who have called this land home. Yet, it's also a testament to the resilience of a community that thrives amidst the elements.

As we embark on this journey through the pages of history, let us immerse ourselves in the rich tapestry of Casa Grande—a city where ancient footprints blend seamlessly with modern aspirations. Let us uncover the stories that echo through time, carried by the wind that sweeps across the Sonoran Desert, and let us embrace the captivating spirit that has woven this city's past into the fabric of the American Southwest.

The Blue Mist Motel
40 South Pinal Parkway Avenue, Florence, Arizona
Reservations: (928) 683-2273

Figure 26: The Blue Mist Motel in Florence. Photo taken by Timothy James Wilson.

In the charming town of Florence, the Blue Mist Motel stands as a testament to both history and intrigue. This quaint and unassuming motel carries with it a legacy that spans decades, while local legends whisper of an enigmatic aura that has sparked tales of the paranormal.

Established years ago, the Blue Mist Motel has silently witnessed the ebb and flow of time in Florence. Its walls have borne witness to countless stories, offering respite to travelers, adventurers, and seekers of the unknown. While exact dates and origins are as mysterious as the motels' legends, the motel's legacy is undeniable, leaving traces of its presence etched into the town's narrative.

What lends the Blue Mist Motel an air of mystique is the local legends that swirl around it—whispers of hauntings and eerie encounters. These stories, shared among residents and visitors alike, tell of inexplicable phenomena that have left an indelible mark on the motel's reputation. It's said that in the stillness of the night, echoes of the past may come alive, bridging the gap between the living and the ethereal.

While tales of hauntings may capture the imagination, the Blue Mist Motel remains a place where travelers find a welcoming haven. With its classic charm and unpretentious ambiance, it offers a slice of nostalgia for those seeking a connection to the past. Whether you're drawn by the intrigue of local legends or simply seek a comfortable stay in a historic setting, the Blue Mist Motel offers an experience that goes beyond the ordinary.

As you step through its doors, you become part of a continuum—a lineage of travelers who have ventured into the heart of Florence and embraced the enigma that is the Blue Mist Motel. Here, history intertwines with mystery, inviting you to delve into the unknown, to explore the stories that have woven their way into the fabric of this timeless place.

Enigmatic Whispers of the Blue Mist Motel

Situated just a stone's throw away from the imposing walls of the Florence prison, the Blue Mist Motel carries a weighty legacy that intertwines with local legends and chilling events.

In the annals of 1984, the stage was set for a grim tragedy. A man named Robert Moormann, grappling with mental handicaps, found himself released on furlough from the Correctional Facility. The walls of the prison could not contain the turmoil that would unfold as he reunited with his abusive mother. Seeking refuge from the world outside, they checked into the Blue Mist Motel—a decision that would seal their fate in horror.

Within those motel walls, a harrowing tale played out—a tale of unfathomable violence. In the grip of a tortured mind, Robert Moormann committed an unspeakable act. His mother, bound by blood but not by compassion, became a victim of his pent-up rage. The motel room, once a sanctuary of anonymity, witnessed a twisted tragedy as he beat and stabbed his mother to her untimely demise.

What followed was a gruesome aftermath. Robert Moormann dismembered his mother's body, casting her remains into dumpsters scattered across the town that had unknowingly played host to this horror. Justice, however, would find its way. Sentenced to death, he met his fate on February 29, 2012, executed for the unspeakable crime that had stained the walls of the Blue Mist Motel.

The tale persists, lingering like an unsettling shadow in the night. Locals and visitors speak of hearing a woman's cries echoing through the vacant corridors of the motel, even when solitude reigns. These mournful wails, carried by an unseen wind, intertwine with an overwhelming sense of foreboding—an unshakable urge to flee from the chilling presence that lingers.

The Blue Mist Motel, once an unremarkable stopover, now stands as a testament to the haunting intersections of history, tragedy, and the unknown. It's a place where the past refuses to remain silent, its echoes haunting those who dare to listen, and reminding us that within every facade lies a tale waiting to be uncovered. On dark nights you can sometimes still hear the screams of Robert Moormann, and some have even claimed to encounter her ghostly spirit.

The Arizona State Prison Complex in Florence
1305 East Butte Avenue, Florence, Arizona

Imagine being incarcerated in a haunted prison. For thousands of inmates at Arizona State Prison Complex in Florence this is the reality that they live in every day. This prison complex is a sprawling correctional facility that weaves together a tapestry of incarceration, history, and, according to whispers, the echoes of the past that refuse to fade. This complex, often shrouded in legends of the paranormal, stands as a testament to a bygone era and the enduring spirits that may still roam its corridors.

Figure 27: *Arizona State Prison Complex, Florence. Photo taken by Timothy James Wilson.*

The Arizona State Prison Complex in Florence is a cluster of correctional facilities that house both male and female inmates, creating a complex world within its barbed wire and towering walls. With various units and housing options, it accommodates a substantial population of individuals who, for a multitude of reasons, find themselves confined within its borders.

The complex's history dates back to the late 1800s, when the territorial prison was established in the area. Over the decades, it has evolved into a network of facilities, each with its own stories of triumph and tragedy. Notably, the complex has witnessed executions, high-profile cases, and pivotal moments in Arizona's criminal justice history.

Yet, amidst the concrete and iron, there are tales that transcend the tangible. Stories of eerie encounters, unexplained sounds, and shadowy apparitions often cast a chilling pall over the complex. While these stories are whispered among inmates, staff, and those who venture near, they remain as enigmatic as the very walls that confine them.

With its rich history and the complex interplay of lives within its confines, the Arizona State Prison Complex in Florence is a microcosm of the human experience. Beyond the tales of reformation and redemption, there exists a narrative that extends beyond the bounds of the known—an intangible tale that hints at the restless souls that may still walk the halls, prisoners not of the law, but of their own unfinished stories.

As we explore the layers of history and mystery, let us tread carefully through the stories that have been woven into the fabric of this complex. It is a place where the echoes of the past merge with the reality of the present, inviting us to contemplate the unseen forces that linger in the shadows and the haunting resonance of lives intersecting in the heart of the Arizona State Prison Complex in Florence.

Cell Block 14

Within the imposing walls of the Arizona State Prison Complex in Florence, a particular area has emerged as a nexus of paranormal tales—Cell Block 14. This section, shrouded in mystery and whispered legends, is said to harbor unsettling energies and eerie encounters that defy the realm of the living.

Cell Block 14, a place that once echoed with the footsteps of inmates and the clang of iron doors, now resonates with a different kind of presence—one that seems to belong to the realm of the otherworldly. Guards and inmates alike have reported inexplicable phenomena that have left an indelible mark on their memories.

One of the most common reports from Cell Block 14 is the appearance of shadowy figures that seem to move of their own accord. These spectral silhouettes have been spotted by both guards and inmates, often manifesting in the periphery of vision before disappearing into thin air. Whether they linger as silent observers or remnants of former inmates, these shadows have instilled a sense of unease.

Many who have spent time in Cell Block 14 claim to have heard faint whispers that defy explanation. These disembodied voices seem to emanate from nowhere in particular, their words often unintelligible or too distant to fully comprehend. Some have described hearing their names being whispered in hushed tones, even when the block is devoid of other human presence.

A phenomenon often reported by those who venture into Cell Block 14 is the sudden drop in temperature accompanied by an overwhelming sense of dread. This chilling effect seems to settle in the air like a heavy mist, lending an atmosphere of melancholy to the already somber surroundings.

While shadows and whispers are unsettling enough, some individuals have reported witnessing full-bodied apparitions of former inmates or guards. These phantom figures manifest briefly, often disappearing as suddenly as they appeared. Yet, their presence lingers, leaving witnesses questioning whether they've glimpsed into a parallel plane of existence.

As the stories of Cell Block 14's paranormal activity spread, a frightening environment of the supernatural has enveloped the area. Whether these phenomena are the result of residual energies, the manifestation of long-forgotten stories, or the restless spirits of those who once dwelled within the cells, the legends endure, serving as a reminder that the past and present can intertwine in ways that transcend our understanding.

As we reflect on the tales whispered within Cell Block 14's confines, let us acknowledge that these stories serve as a testament to the complexity of the human experience—even in the realm beyond. Whether skeptics dismiss them as mere figments of the imagination or believers embrace them as evidence of an unseen realm, Cell Block 14 remains a focal point of intrigue within the enigmatic history of the Arizona State Prison Complex in Florence.

Violent Clash of Turmoil

In the long history of the Arizona State Prison Complex in Florence's history, the year 1981 stands out as a somber chapter marked by an eruption of violence that would forever leave its mark on the facility's legacy. This tumultuous event, commonly referred to as the 1981 Prison Riot, would reveal the underlying tensions, dire conditions, and strained dynamics that had been building within the prison's walls.

The stage was set for the riot on June 30, 1981, when a confrontation between prison staff and inmates sparked an explosion of pent-up frustration and anger. The prisoners, already grappling with issues such as overcrowding, inadequate living conditions, and perceived mistreatment, seized this moment as an outlet for their collective discontent.

What began as a skirmish between a small group of inmates and guards quickly escalated into a full-scale riot. The complex, usually governed by a tense but manageable atmosphere, was suddenly consumed by chaos. Inmates seized control of portions of the prison, setting fires and wreaking havoc that spread like wildfire through the cell blocks.

As the riot raged on, the situation grew increasingly dire. Tragically, two inmates lost their lives during the violence, and numerous others suffered injuries. The riot resulted in extensive damage to the prison infrastructure, leaving its mark on the physical landscape as well as the emotional fabric of those involved.

It took the combined efforts of law enforcement, corrections officials, and specialized units to quell the uprising and restore order within the prison complex. The riot revealed the urgent need for reforms within the Arizona penal system, shedding light on issues such as overcrowding, inadequate rehabilitation programs, and deteriorating conditions.

The 1981 Prison Riot left an indelible mark on the Arizona State Prison Complex in Florence and prompted a reckoning within the state's corrections system. It served as a catalyst for policy changes, improvements in inmate treatment, and increased attention to the rehabilitation and management of prisoners. The riot's legacy continues to influence discussions surrounding prison reform, inmate rights, and the delicate balance between maintaining order and ensuring humane treatment.

As we look back on the events of that fateful year, the 1981 Prison Riot serves as a reminder that the walls of a prison hold not only inmates but also the complexities of human emotions, systemic challenges, and the potential for upheaval. It stands as a testament to the enduring need for a fair and just penal system—one that seeks to rehabilitate, protect, and ultimately prevent the outbreak of violence that once shook the foundations of the Arizona State Prison Complex in Florence.

Sensational Murderess

One of the most famous residents of the Arizona State Prison Complex in Florence in recent history is Jody Arias, a name that became synonymous with a sensational trial that captured the attention of the media and the public alike. In 2008, Arias was arrested and charged with the brutal murder of her ex-boyfriend, Travis Alexander. The trial that followed would become a media spectacle due to the shocking details of the crime, the intense courtroom drama, and the high-profile nature of the case.

The trial painted a grim picture of the events leading up to Alexander's death. Prosecutors alleged that Arias had meticulously planned the murder and executed it with a level of brutality that sent shockwaves through the nation. The crime was committed in a deeply personal manner, involving both a stabbing and a gunshot wound. Arias initially denied any involvement but eventually changed her story multiple times, claiming self-defense, and then finally admitting to killing Alexander.

What catapulted the trial to national attention was the salacious nature of the evidence presented. The court was presented with explicit photographs, text messages, and recordings that offered a window into the complex and tumultuous relationship between Arias and Alexander. The trial's live broadcast allowed viewers to witness the emotional rollercoaster of the proceedings, and it also sparked debates about media sensationalism, ethics, and the impact of such coverage on the justice system.

The trial culminated in a guilty verdict in 2013, with Arias being found guilty of first-degree murder. The sentencing phase further fueled controversy as the jury failed to reach a unanimous decision on whether she should receive the death penalty or life in prison. This led to the final sentencing of life imprisonment without the possibility of parole.

The Jody Arias trial remains a prominent example of the media's fascination with criminal cases and the intersection of justice and public attention. The compelling and often disturbing details of the crime, combined with the extensive media coverage and courtroom drama, turned the trial into a cultural phenomenon, making Arias a name that is indelibly etched into the annals of the Arizona State Prison Complex in Florence's history.

Old Pinal County Courthouse
24 West Ruggles Street, Florence, Arizona
Park Information: (877) 697-2757

Figure 28: The Old Pinal County Courthouse. Photo by Timothy James Wilson.

The Old Pinal County Courthouse in Florence is a historic building that holds great significance in the region. The courthouse is located on the McFarland State Historic Park, which offers tours and information about the courthouse. The courthouse is a prominent example of territorial architecture and stands as a reminder of Arizona's rich history.

The Old Pinal County Courthouse is an impressive two-story structure made primarily of brick and stone. Constructed in 1878, it showcases a combination of Victorian architectural elements and territorial style. The courthouse features a symmetrical design with a central entrance, large arched windows, and a clock tower rising majestically above the structure. The red-brick exterior gives the building a stately appearance, while the interior boasts ornate detailing and period furnishings that transport visitors back in time.

The courthouse played a crucial role in the development of Pinal County and witnessed several historically significant events. It served as the county's main seat of justice, hosting numerous trials, hearings, and legal proceedings that shaped the region. The courthouse was also a gathering place for local residents, where community meetings and social events took place.

The legend of the Hanging Judge

The legend of the Hanging Judge is the story of a former judge known for his severe sentencing during the territorial period. This judge earned his nickname due to his reputation for handing down harsh judgments, particularly in cases involving serious crimes. While the details of the legend may vary, the overarching narrative centers around the judge's lingering spirit haunting the courthouse.

According to the legend, the Hanging Judge was known for his unwavering commitment to law and order, but his relentless pursuit of justice sometimes led to controversial decisions. It is said that he had a particular affinity for the death penalty, frequently sentencing criminals to be hanged for their crimes. This earned him a reputation as a stern and uncompromising figure in the community.

The legend suggests that the judge's spirit remains trapped within the Old Pinal County Courthouse, where he once presided over numerous trials. Witnesses have reported eerie occurrences associated with his ghostly presence. Some claim to have heard the sound of a gavel striking, as if he continues to oversee spectral trials from beyond the grave. Others have described encountering a somber and authoritative figure, dressed in judicial attire, within the courthouse or near the judge's chambers.

The Hanging Judge's ghost is often portrayed as a restless spirit, possibly driven by a sense of duty to ensure justice is served. While some versions of the legend depict him as a malevolent entity seeking retribution, others present a more sympathetic portrayal, suggesting that he seeks redemption or resolution for the souls affected by his harsh sentences.

The Vengeful Prisoner

The legend of the Vengeful Prisoner revolves around the spirit of a former inmate who met an unjust fate within the walls of the courthouse. This haunting tale depicts the vengeful ghost of a prisoner seeking retribution for a wrongful conviction and execution.

According to the legend, the prisoner was wrongly accused of a crime he did not commit. Despite maintaining his innocence, he was convicted and sentenced to death, with his execution taking place within the confines of the courthouse. The injustice and suffering he endured during his time in captivity and the wrongful loss of his life fuel the vengeful spirit that is said to linger within the building.

Witnesses of paranormal activity at the courthouse have reported experiencing an intense and oppressive atmosphere, particularly in areas associated with the prison cells or the execution site. Some claim to have felt an overwhelming sense of anger and unease when in proximity to the vengeful prisoner's presence.

The legend suggests that the vengeful spirit seeks to rectify the injustice he suffered by haunting the Old Pinal County Courthouse. His restless ghost may manifest through unexplained phenomena such as unexplained cold spots, disembodied voices expressing anguish or anger, or objects moving seemingly of their own accord.

The Vengeful Prisoner legend adds a chilling aspect to the haunted reputation of the courthouse, evoking sympathy for the spirit trapped within its walls.

The Legend of the Haunted Clock Tower

Adding a mysterious and eerie element to the paranormal tales surrounding the historic building is the legend of the haunted clock tower. According to local legend, the clock tower is believed to be a focal point of spectral activity and serves as a gathering place for the spirits of former prisoners or victims of the courthouse's turbulent past.

In this haunting legend, the clock tower is associated with the souls of individuals who met tragic or untimely ends within the courthouse's walls. The stories often revolve around prisoners who were incarcerated, executed, or even wrongfully accused, and whose spirits linger within the tower, trapped in a restless state.

Witnesses have reported a variety of eerie phenomena associated with the clock tower haunting. It is said that phantom footsteps can be heard ascending the tower's staircase when no one is present. The chimes of the clock sometimes sound spontaneously, without any apparent external cause, leading some to believe that spirits manipulate time itself. Others claim to have glimpsed ghostly figures peering out from the tower's windows or lurking within its shadowy corners.

The legend may also incorporate the notion that the clock tower acts as a portal or focal point for spiritual energy. It is believed that the souls of the departed are drawn to the tower, perhaps seeking solace, or attempting to communicate their presence to the living. The haunting of the clock tower is often portrayed as a reminder of the courthouse's tumultuous history, where past events and emotions continue to resonate within its structures.

The Domes
8109 South Thorton Road, Casa Grande, Arizona

The Domes at Casa Grande were a captivating testament to architectural innovation and the enduring mysteries of the paranormal. These unique structures have a rich history and have become renowned for the tales of ghostly encounters and unexplained phenomena that surround them. Join us on an immersive journey as we delve into the origins, purpose, construction, abandonment, and the haunting incidents that have made the Domes at Casa Grande an enigmatic landmark.

The story of the Domes at Casa Grande begins in the late 1980s when a man named Floyd "Skip" Measelle was inspired by the visionary architect Buckminster Fuller and his geodesic dome designs. Measelle envisioned creating an eco-friendly and sustainable community within a cluster of interconnected domes. His vision was to reduce energy consumption, promote self-sufficiency, and foster a sense of unity among its residents.

Construction on the Domes project commenced in 1982, with Measelle at the helm, leading a group of volunteers who shared his vision. The construction process was a labor of love, as they utilized reclaimed materials to bring the domes to life. Salvaged car hoods, discarded refrigerators, and other reclaimed materials were repurposed to form the triangular panels that comprised the domes. The interconnected structures began to take shape, creating a sprawling complex spanning approximately 3.8 acres.

Each dome was meticulously constructed using a geodesic framework, consisting of a network of interconnected triangles. This unique design not only provided structural stability but also resulted in visually striking and aesthetically pleasing structures. The domes stood as a testament to the innovative architectural principles championed by Buckminster Fuller.

As the construction progressed, the Domes at Casa Grande garnered attention and admiration from the local community and beyond. The ambitious project captured the imagination of many who saw it as a glimpse into a sustainable future, a harmonious fusion of nature and human habitation.

However, despite the initial excitement and momentum, the Domes faced significant financial challenges. Funding became scarce, and the project struggled to maintain its momentum. As a result, construction on the domes was eventually halted, and the site was left in a state of unfinished beauty.

The Domes at Casa Grande stood as an unfinished vision, an architectural masterpiece frozen in time. While the original purpose of the domes was never fully realized, they became a symbol of the spirit of innovation and experimentation that characterized the era.

Over time, the abandoned Domes acquired a reputation for being haunted, attracting reports of paranormal activity and unexplained phenomena. The stories of ghostly encounters and strange occurrences only added to the allure and intrigue surrounding the domes.

Local residents and visitors began to share accounts of their experiences within the deserted structures. Some claimed to have heard unexplained footsteps echoing through the empty chambers, as if an invisible presence roamed the halls. Whispers of phantom voices were reported, seemingly emanating from unseen sources. Witnesses described witnessing shadowy figures moving mysteriously between the interconnected domes, disappearing into thin air.

Central Paranormal Phenomena

The paranormal incidents at the Domes at Casa Grande were not limited to apparitions and strange sounds. Some visitors experienced sudden drops in temperature, even on warm days, accompanied by a chilling breeze that seemed to have no logical explanation. Others reported unusual gusts of wind within the domes, despite the absence of any open windows or doors. Visitors often described an overwhelming feeling of unease, as if being watched or surrounded by an invisible presence.

The accounts of alleged encounters with the supernatural gained traction, capturing the attention of paranormal enthusiasts and investigators. Ghost tours, paranormal investigations, and storytelling sessions became popular activities for those seeking to explore the mysteries of the Domes at Casa Grande and potentially experience their own brush with the unknown.

Despite the skepticism, the allure of the haunted Domes continues to captivate both locals and those with a fascination for the supernatural. The legends and stories surrounding the Domes at Casa Grande have become an integral part of their identity, adding to their mystique and drawing visitors from far and wide.

There were efforts to revitalize and preserve the Domes. Community-driven initiatives and preservation organizations have recognized the architectural and historical significance of the structures. The hope is to transform the site into a vibrant cultural and artistic hub, celebrating not only the haunted reputation of the domes but also their unique architectural heritage.

These efforts aim to honor the original vision of Floyd "Skip" Measelle and the volunteers who dedicated their time and energy to constructing the Domes. They seek to create a space where art, creativity, and community engagement can flourish, breathing new life into these abandoned structures while preserving their unique legacy.

Unfortunately, in 2016 the largest of the Domes collapsed, and thus the entire sight was condemned. Following the Condemnation of the sight, the sight became a magnet for criminal activity. In January of 2023 the Domes were demolished following a five-year legal battle between the property owners and county officials.

The Casa Grande Ruins National Monument
1100 West Ruins Drive, Coolidge, Arizona
Information: (520) 723-3172

Prior to the construction of Phoenix, and to Arizona becoming a state, or even a single European settler stepping foot on the Sonoran Desert, there was another group that called this area home: the Ancestral Sonoran Desert Peoples. These people are a mysterious group, whose arrival in modern day Arizona is as confusing as their disappearance. Some might call them the Hohokam Peoples, however, in my research for this book I found this name can be offensive to some native peoples of the Southwest.

In some records, it is said that the Ancient Sonoran Peoples disappeared off the landscape sometime in the 15th century; however, I believe it is most likely that these people never really disappeared, but instead fractioned off into the O'odham, the Hopi, and the Zuni peoples. They might have occupied Arizona as early as 5000 BC according to some archaeological evidence. Over the span of several millennia, this society evolved from a simple hunter and gather group to sophisticated peoples who farmed land using large irrigation systems. They engineered some of the most elaborate canal systems in North America, despite not having shovels, oxen, or horses.

It is also important to note here that the alleged disappearance of the Ancestral Sonoran Desert Peoples happens at the same time as European settler's arrival to the American continent. In Jared Diamond's book *Guns, Germs, and Steel*, Diamond makes the case that many Indigenous civilizations suffered greatly in the 15th and 16th centuries due to the arrival of Europeans to the continent, because in many cases the germs that these European settlers brought traveled much faster across the Americas that the settlers themselves. These germs, such as Smallpox, transmitted as great plagues to indigenous people who had not developed immunity to these diseases. Is it possible the "disappearance" of the Ancestral Sonoran Desert Peoples was just the fracturing of their civilization into several smaller civilizations because of these plagues?

Figure 29: The Great House at the Casa Grande Ruins National Monument. Photo by Timothy James Wilson.

One of the Ancestral Sonoran Desert Peoples greatest surviving structures is the "Great House" or "Casa Grande" in Spanish, which is the origin of the name of the city Casa Grande, that lies just under 50 miles south of Phoenix. The Great House is a four-story compound built of adobe, built about 1000 years ago, that sits in the Casa Grande Ruins National Monument. It was comprised of at least seven separate residential areas and was home to about 2000 people. They left behind plenty of beautiful pieces of art, woven baskets, and architecture.

The Ancestral Sonoran Desert Peoples people will come up time and time again in this book, so I thought it appropriate to start with the crown jewel of their achievement that has survived the six centuries since their civilization dissolved. While mostly thought of as peaceful people who understood the principles of irrigation and astronomy, they are also thought to have never left certain places, including the Great House.

The Ancestral Sonoran Desert Peoples had an intricate understanding of astronomy and built the Great House to have calendar holes to mark certain dates that were significant to them, such as the solstices, and the equinoxes. Calendar holes were used by several other historic civilizations to mark dates on a calendar and are the practice of having holes in multiple walls that will align from an outer wall to an inner wall at a certain time during the year. The Ancestral Sonoran Desert Peoples built these calendar holes to signify the spring and fall solstice, as well as the summer and winter equinoxes. These dates are significant as they were used to indicate to these people the upcoming seasonal shifts and helped them prepare for the upcoming season. For any ancient people that relied on agriculture, knowing when to plant and harvest was the difference between life and death, especially in a region like Arizona with such hot summers. They also build calendar holes to signify March 7, and October 7; the significance of these dates is unknown.

In the second half of the 15th century the Ancestral Sonoran Desert People began migrating out of the Casa Grande area, abandoning this great marvel they built. Some believe this was due to continued stress on the water sources; however, the Tohono O'odham people have an oral tradition that people left the area when the once peaceful settlement found themselves at war. Historians also point to the fact that in the 15th century there were several floods that happened in the area that could have caused devastation.

In 1694, Father Eusebio Francisco Kino of Spain arrived, and would be one of the first Europeans to write about the Casa Grande, likening it to a European palace. In the 1800s it would become a popular rest stop for stagecoaches traveling through the Arizona desert. Often people would gather souvenirs from the area and carve their names into the walls of the Casa Grande. In 1892 was set aside as the first Archaeological reserve in the US, and in 1918 it became a National Monument.

The Ancestral Sonoran Desert Peoples spirits are said to have never left the Great House though, and while the significance of March 7 and October 7 are unknown to modern day, the spirits remain on the premises, and remember the significance of these dates. Legend says that anyone who approaches the Great House during this these nights would be found dead the next morning, their mouths filled with sand.

Today, the Ruins stand under a giant roof that was constructed to preserve the ruins themselves.

Picacho Peak State Park
15520 Picacho Peak Road, Picacho, Arizona
Park Information: (520) 723-3172

Rising majestically from the arid landscape of southern Arizona, Picacho Peak stands as a striking geological formation with a history that spans both natural wonder and human endeavor.

This iconic peak, located between Phoenix and Tucson, offers visitors a unique blend of rugged beauty, historical significance, and outdoor exploration.

Figure 30: Picacho Peak. Photo taken by Timothy James Wilson.

Picacho Peak's distinct shape and towering presence are the result of ancient volcanic activity and erosion. Composed of volcanic rock and sedimentary layers, the peak's dramatic silhouette is visible from miles away. Its unique features make it a prominent landmark in an otherwise flat terrain, attracting the attention of travelers and adventurers for generations.

Beyond its geological allure, Picacho Peak has played a role in American history. During the Civil War, it served as a pivotal site for the Battle of Picacho Pass, a skirmish between Confederate and Union forces. This clash marked the westernmost engagement of the Civil War and is remembered as a key event in Arizona's history.

For nature enthusiasts and hikers, Picacho Peak State Park offers a range of recreational opportunities. Hiking trails wind through the park, providing various levels of challenge and breathtaking views. The most iconic trail, known as the Hunter Trail, leads to the summit, rewarding intrepid hikers with panoramic vistas of the surrounding desert landscape.

Central Paranormal Phenomena

One of the most captivating times to visit Picacho Peak is during the spring, when the desert bursts into a colorful display of wildflowers. The vibrant blooms transform the arid landscape into a living tapestry of color, attracting visitors and photographers eager to capture the fleeting beauty of this natural phenomenon.

Picacho Peak offers more than just stunning vistas; it's an invitation to adventure. Rock climbing enthusiasts are drawn to its challenging routes, while birdwatchers can spot a variety of desert-dwelling species. The park's visitor center provides information about the peak's natural and cultural history, enhancing the experience for curious minds.

Whether you seek a physical challenge, a glimpse into history, or a serene encounter with the natural world, Picacho Peak promises an unforgettable journey. Its geological grandeur, historical significance, and abundant recreational opportunities come together to create a destination that showcases the multifaceted beauty of the American Southwest.

The Legend of the Ghost Rider of Picacho Peak

The legend of the Ghost Rider of Picacho Peak is a tale of mystery and intrigue. While there are variations of the story, here's a general version of the legend.

Long ago, during the time of the Civil War, a group of Confederate Soldiers was sent to explore the desert region around Picacho Peak. These soldiers were on a mission to find and secure treasure rumored to be hidden somewhere in the area.

One night, as the soldiers camped near the base of the peak, they were attacked by a group of Indigenous warriors. A fierce battle ensued, and the soldiers were overwhelmed. In the chaos of the conflict, the treasure they sought was lost, buried, or hidden away to prevent its capture.

Legend has it that one of the soldiers, a brave and determined leader, vowed never to abandon his quest for the treasure. He made a pact with dark forces or the spirit of the desert, sealing his fate as the Ghost Rider of Picacho. As punishment for his unwavering greed and ambition, he was cursed to forever ride the desert at night, searching for the lost treasure that had eluded him in life.

To this day, it is said that the Ghost Rider can be seen riding through the desert around Picacho Peak, often accompanied by the eerie sound of phantom hooves and gusts of wind. Some versions of the legend claim that the treasure remains hidden, waiting for a brave and virtuous soul to discover it and free the Ghost Rider from his eternal quest.

Central Paranormal Phenomena

Chapter Five: Restless Spirits of the Old West

Tombstone

Figure 31: Allen Street. Photo by Timothy James Wilson

Welcome to the heart of the Wild West, where dusty streets whisper tales of outlaws and lawmen, and the echoes of gunshots still resonate through time. In the pages that follow, we invite you to journey into the shadowed corners of Tombstone—an iconic destination for dark tourists seeking to unravel the enigmatic tapestry of the past. As you step onto these hallowed grounds, prepare to immerse yourself in a realm where history, mystery, and the paranormal intertwine.

Tombstone's legacy is a testament to an era characterized by lawlessness, feuds, and the pursuit of riches. This chapter serves as a guide to the key sites that epitomize the darker facets of the Old West, where legends of shootouts, ghostly apparitions, and untamed spirits come to life. From the moment you set foot in this storied town, you will find yourself drawn into narratives that span from the legendary Gunfight at the O.K. Corral to the ethereal whispers of the Crystal Palace Saloon.

Allow your imagination to roam as you explore the historic streets and alleys that have borne witness to the deeds of famed outlaws, the valiant efforts of lawmen, and the tales of everyday citizens caught in the crossfire. Stand where legends clashed, and let the stories of the Clanton Gang, Wyatt Earp, and Doc Holliday paint vivid images of a time when justice was often defined by the barrel of a gun.

As the sun sets and the moon casts its pale glow, venture into the realm of the paranormal at Boot Hill Cemetery—a resting place that hints at restless spirits and lingering shadows. Experience the eerie allure of The Birdcage Theatre, where the echoes of long-forgotten performances may still be heard and discover the haunted corners of the Tombstone Grand Hotel, where the past and the present intertwine in mysterious ways, and where you should be staying for this trip.

From the lavish interiors of the Crystal Palace Saloon to the preserved elegance of Historic Allen Street, each site beckons you to peel back the layers of history, uncover the truth behind the legends, and engage with the intriguing facets of dark tourism. As you explore Tombstone Courthouse State Historical Park, step into the shoes of those who once stood trial and immerse yourself in the trials and tribulations that defined this tumultuous era.

Prepare to embark on a journey that bridges the gap between the mundane and the mysterious, the historical and the supernatural. Tombstone awaits, ready to reveal its secrets and stories to those who dare to embrace the allure of the darker side of history.

The Tombstone Grand Hotel
580 West Randolph Way, Tombstone, Arizona
Reservations: (520) 457-9507

The Tombstone Grand Hotel, located within a 5-to-15-minute walk of most of the sights that we will see on this road trip, so it's unique blend of historical ambiance and modern comfort will resonate as a great place to stay for this weekend's immersive experience. While not explicitly a dark tourist site, the hotel's Victorian-style architecture and attention to detail evoke the town's Wild West era, providing a captivating backdrop for those intrigued by historical events and the paranormal.

Within the hotel, guests will find a range of accommodation, each designed to transport them to the past while offering modern amenities. For dark tourists, the appeal lies in the historical ambiance and the sense of connection to Tombstone's rich history. The opportunity to explore the town's attractions during the day and return to a hotel that complements the overall theme of the trip could enhance the overall experience.

The O.K. Corral
326 East Allen Street, Tombstone, Arizona

Standing as an enduring symbol of both the tumultuous Wild West era and one of the most the storied gunfights in the history of the Old West, is the O.K. Corral. Nestled behind the façade of Tombstone's buildings on Fremont Street, this small vacant lot became the stage for a brief yet dramatic confrontation that left an indelible mark on history.

Figure 32: The O.K. Corral. Photo taken by Timothy James Wilson.

The setting was tense, with the backdrop of a town rife with lawlessness and simmering feuds. On that fateful day, October 26, 1881, the Earp brothers—Wyatt, Virgil, and Morgan—joined forces with the sharp-witted and sharp-shooting Doc Holliday, a close friend, to confront a group of lawless outlaws known as the "Cowboys." Led by Ike Clanton, Billy Claiborne, and the McLaury brothers—Tom and Frank—the Cowboys symbolized a dark underbelly of the Old West, engaging in rustling and other illicit activities.

The confrontation erupted in a sudden exchange of gunfire at close quarters, lasting mere minutes but echoing through history. The piercing reports of revolvers reverberated off the nearby buildings, smoke hung in the air, and when the dust settled, three members of the Cowboys lay dead—the McLaury brothers and Billy Clanton. Virgil and Morgan Earp sustained injuries, and Doc Holliday was slightly grazed.

The gunfight sent shockwaves beyond the town, capturing national attention through newspapers and stoking debates about frontier justice. The incident marked a crucial turning point in Tombstone's law enforcement dynamics and exacerbated tensions between the Earps and the Cowboys, leaving an indelible imprint on the town's historical narrative.

Beyond its historical weight, the O.K. Corral area has also become enshrouded in whispered tales of the paranormal. Visitors and residents have recounted eerie experiences, speaking of phantom gunshots echoing through the alleys, spectral footsteps that resonate when all is quiet, and ethereal figures that materialize in the corners of vision. These haunted perceptions lend an added layer of mystique to the O.K. Corral, suggesting that the restless spirits of those who once stood there continue to cast a spectral presence over the historic site.

Ultimately, the O.K. Corral's significance is intertwined with its dual nature: a place where history's defining moments unfolded and a realm where shadows of the past seem to dance on the periphery of perception. It encapsulates the essence of the Wild West, where history and mystery intertwine in a tapestry that continues to captivate and intrigue.

Boot Hill Cemetery
408 AZ-80, Tombstone, Arizona

Boot Hill Cemetery is a historic graveyard located in Tombstone. It's renowned for its association with the Old West and the town's vibrant mining and cowboy past. Boot Hill Cemetery earned its name from the popular saying that "those buried here had died with their boots on," which was often used to describe individuals who met violent deaths in the Old West. The cemetery served as the final resting place for many of

Tombstone's early residents, including miners, cowboys, lawmen, and outlaws.

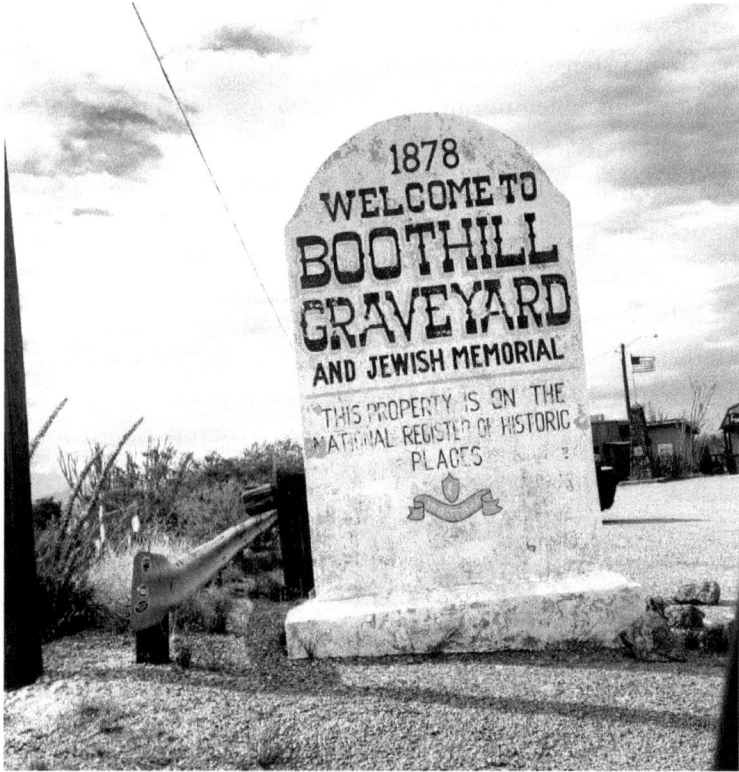

Figure 33: Boothill Graveyard. Photo by Shirley Marie Wilson.

Boot Hill Cemetery is significant due to its role in reflecting the diverse and often harsh realities of life during the Wild West era. Many of those interred at Boot Hill met their ends through accidents, disease, gunfights, and other violent circumstances. The graves offer a curious glimpse into the challenges and dangers faced by the people who contributed to Tombstone's history. Additionally, the simple wooden markers and rough stone gravestones create a stark yet evocative landscape. Some graves have inscriptions that offer insights into the lives and circumstances of the deceased.

Timothy James Wilson

Among the graves at Boot Hill Cemetery, there are a few notable figures whose stories have captured historical attention: such as Billy Clanton, Frank McLaury, and Tom McLaury, the three men were involved in the Gunfight at the O.K. Corral in 1881, all members of the Clanton Gang. Additionally, Marshal Fred White who was a Tombstone city marshal who accidentally shot himself in the groin while attempting to disarm an outlaw. He is one of the earlier burials in Boot Hill Cemetery.

The Clanton Gang

In the vast expanse of the American Old West during the late 19th century, amidst the dust and lawlessness, the Clanton gang emerged as a notorious and enigmatic faction. Led by the brash and tempestuous Ike Clanton, this group of outlaws and rustlers left an indelible mark on the history of the frontier. At the heart of this criminal fraternity was Ike Clanton, a figure known for his quick temper and involvement in a web of nefarious activities. From cattle rustling to horse thievery, Clanton and his gang were no strangers to illicit deeds.

Walking in the shadow of their leader were Billy Clanton, Ike's younger brother, and Phineas "Phin" Clanton, another sibling who was entangled in the web of lawlessness. The trio, connected by blood and shared ventures, engaged in a lifestyle that defied the confines of the law. Additionally, the gang boasted the presence of Finis "Frank" McLaury, a man whose ties to Ike Clanton sealed his fate within this band of outlaws. Frank McLaury shared in their criminal endeavors, weaving his own tale of lawlessness in the annals of the frontier.

Within the intricate tapestry of the Old West's lawlessness, the Clanton gang carved a niche for themselves by partaking in various criminal exploits. Their activities ranged from brazen thefts to acts of intimidation that reverberated through the towns and settlements of the region. Their encounters with rival factions and brushes with law enforcement served to intensify the air of tension and chaos that characterized the era.

However, it was the notorious Gunfight at the O.K. Corral that etched the Clanton gang's name into the pages of history with indelible ink. The simmering conflicts between the Earp family and their associates reached a boiling point on that fateful day in 1881. As tensions flared, the O.K. Corral became the crucible of fate, witnessing a confrontation that would forever define the legacy of the Clanton gang. The outcome of that day was a devastating one for the gang, as the lives of Billy Clanton, Tom McLaury, and Frank McLaury were claimed by the echoes of gunfire.

The legacy of the Clanton gang endures not only through their criminal exploits but through their role in shaping the narrative of the Old West's lawless and tumultuous years. In the midst of the frontier's chaos, they stand as a stark reminder of the complexities and contradictions that defined a time when justice often took a back seat to survival and retribution.

Paranormal Activity at Boot Hill Cemetery

Boot Hill Cemetery—an unassuming graveyard whose reputation extends beyond the earthly realm. Fabled to be haunted, Boot Hill has woven itself into the tapestry of the Old West, where tales of the paranormal intertwine with the echoes of history. Just like the spectral remnants that are said to wander its grounds, the cemetery has collected a trove of stories—ghostly encounters, unexplained phenomena, and eerie experiences—that speak of a world unseen.

Among these spectral narratives, the most haunting are the apparitions that have materialized amid the silent tombstones. Visitors have reported glimpses of shadowy figures, ethereal specters that wear the attire of a bygone era, with whispers of cowboys and settlers adorning their enigmatic presence. These ghostly forms seem to emerge from the pages of history, transient visitors from another time who continue to roam the resting place they once inhabited.

Yet, it's not just the visual that carries a hint of the otherworldly at Boot Hill. Echoes of the past are said to reverberate through the air, manifesting as unexplained sounds that disturb the stillness. Footsteps, whispers, and even the faint murmur of distant conversations have been heard, though the source remains elusive. Within this realm of the inexplicable, even the ambient temperature is not immune—a phenomenon known as cold spots chills the air, perhaps hinting at a lingering presence that seeks to make itself known.

In the age of technology, the ethereal meets the tangible as orbs and anomalies manifest in photographs captured at the cemetery. These curious light formations, often referred to as orbs, dance across the frames, evoking questions about their origin and meaning. Some believe them to be manifestations of spirits captured in a fleeting moment—a visual echo of the tales whispered through generations.

However, it's the palpable feeling of unease that often leaves the deepest imprint on those who tread these hallowed grounds. Visitors recount sensations of being watched, of an unseen gaze that lingers and a presence that defies the visible realm. An indescribable atmosphere surrounds them—a combination of reverence for the history that lies beneath and a curiosity that bridges the gap between the living and the spectral.

As the sun sets on Tombstone and the veil between the worlds thins, Boot Hill Cemetery emerges as a realm of mystery and intrigue. These reports of the paranormal, carried forth through word of mouth and shared experiences, etch an additional layer onto the already rich canvas of its historical significance. Yet, in the realm of the supernatural, subjectivity reigns supreme. What one encounters in this enigmatic space might elude another entirely—a reminder that, in the pursuit of the otherworldly, the heart of the beholder becomes the compass to navigate the realms that remain beyond explanation.

The Restless Outlaws

The legends of Boot Hill Cemetery are as diverse as the characters who rest beneath its rugged landscape. Among these tales, none resonates more eerily than the stories of restless spirits, particularly those of the outlaws who found their final repose within its hallowed grounds.

As the sun sets on the Old West, a sense of quiet unease descends upon Boot Hill, a graveyard bearing witness to lives cut short by violence, tragedy, and a lawless existence, a perfect place for a dark tourist to spend the evening. The restless spirits of outlaws are said to wander its rows, their ephemeral forms stirring with a spectral restlessness that mirrors the tumultuous lives they once led.

These apparitions, as the stories go, are remnants of individuals who met their fate through violent means—gunfights, skirmishes, and altercations that defined the unforgiving landscape of the frontier. Their lives, marked by criminal pursuits and defiance of the law, have left an indelible imprint on the soil of Boot Hill, and it's said that their essence lingers still.

One of the most haunting aspects of these legends is the notion that these spirits seek solace or perhaps redemption. Their presence is not always ominous; some tales suggest that they wander the grounds in search of something left unresolved in life. Perhaps it's a desire to set the record straight, to find closure in a world that was anything but certain, especially when history has a tendency to omit the loser's story. These restless spirits, once formidable in life, now navigate the afterlife with a purpose that defies time.

Visitors recount encounters with these ghostly figures, describing fleeting glimpses of shadowy forms in the corners of their eyes. The atmosphere is said to change, thickening with an energy that defies explanation. Apparitions in period clothing—cowboy hats and rugged attire—manifest as whispers from another era, reminding those who dare to venture into Boot Hill of the legacy of the Old West.

While the legends may be steeped in mystery and the ethereal, they bear testament to the duality of life in the frontier. In life, these outlaws were both the architects of their own destinies and the products of a turbulent era. In death, they become spectral echoes that serve as a reminder of the trials and tribulations of the past. As the winds sweep through Boot Hill, they carry with them the whispers of those who met their end too soon, leaving their stories etched upon the tombstones and lingering in the hearts of those who dare to listen.

Is it possible that an evening in Boot Hill Cemetery could end with you face to face with Billy Clanton, Frank McLaury, or Tom McLaury, who might have a different account of the factors that led up to the Shootout at the OK Corral?

The Lady in White

The Lady in White is said to be a ghostly figure that roams Boot Hill, her presence adding an additional layer of mystery and intrigue to the site's already haunted reputation. Accounts of the Lady in White often describe her as a sorrowful or melancholic figure, appearing during twilight hours or under the cover of darkness. She is typically depicted wearing a white gown or attire that harkens back to an earlier time, evoking an aura of timelessness.

The origin stories of the Lady in White can be quite varied. In some versions, she is believed to be the spirit of a woman who died tragically or under mysterious circumstances. She might be associated with a tragic love story, a betrayal, or a heart-wrenching loss that ties her to a specific place, such as a cemetery. In other interpretations, the Lady in White might represent a guardian spirit or a spectral presence that watches over the resting souls in the cemetery.

Encounters with the Lady in White are often accompanied by eerie experiences. Visitors and witnesses claim to have seen her gliding among the tombstones, her presence marked by an otherworldly radiance. Some accounts speak of a feeling of cold or a sudden drop in temperature when she is near, adding to the sense of the supernatural.

The Birdcage Theatre
535 East Allen Street, Tombstone, Arizona

The Birdcage Theater is a captivating landmark that holds a rich history and a reputation for paranormal occurrences. Built in 1881, this iconic theater is a testament to the wild and rugged spirit of the Old West. Its unique name stems from the 14 birdcage-like boxes that adorned the theater's upper level, where ladies of the night would entertain patrons.

The Birdcage Theater itself is a two-story structure constructed primarily out of wood and brick. Its façade showcases an inviting Wild West aesthetic, with a weathered exterior that speaks to the passage of time. As you step inside, you're transported back to the vibrant atmosphere of the late

19th century, surrounded by original artifacts and remnants of the theater's storied past.

Figure 34: The Birdcage Theatre. Photo by Timothy James Wilson.

This theater witnessed a myriad of historically significant events during its operation. As a hotspot for entertainment and revelry in the lawless town of Tombstone, it hosted a variety of performances, ranging from vaudeville acts to melodramas and opera. It was an integral part of the booming mining town's social scene, providing a sanctuary from the tumultuous streets.

The Birdcage Theater also has close associations with numerous famous and historically significant individuals. Notably, legendary figures such as Wyatt Earp, Doc Holliday, and Bat

Masterson were known to frequent the establishment. These iconic figures of the Old West visited the Birdcage Theater to unwind, gamble, and perhaps seek solace from their adventurous lives.

However, the Birdcage Theater is not just renowned for its historical significance—it has gained a reputation for being haunted. Over the years, countless reports of paranormal activity have emerged from the theater. Visitors and staff have claimed to witness ghostly apparitions, eerie sounds, and inexplicable movements. Some attribute these occurrences to the turbulent past of Tombstone, where violence and tragedy were commonplace. The Birdcage Theater's numerous deaths, resulting from gambling disputes and gunfights, are believed to contribute to its haunted reputation.

The Lady in White

The legend of the Lady in White at the Birdcage Theater is one of the most enduring and captivating ghost stories associated with the historic landmark. According to local folklore and numerous witness accounts, the apparition of a lady dressed in a flowing white Victorian-era gown has been seen wandering the halls and corridors of the theater.

The identity of the Lady in White remains a mystery, but various theories and speculations have emerged over the years. Some believe that she may have been a former actress who graced the Birdcage Theater's stage during its heyday. Others suggest that she was a lady of the night, one of the women who entertained patrons in the birdcage-like boxes that lined the theater's upper level.

Legend has it that the Lady in White met a tragic fate within the walls of the Birdcage Theater. The circumstances surrounding her death are unclear, but it is said that her spirit still lingers, forever bound to the place where she met her untimely end. Witnesses describe her as a sorrowful figure, often appearing melancholic or lost as she roams the theater's halls.

Encounters with the Lady in White are often accompanied by a faint scent of lavender, adding an eerie sensory element to the ghostly apparition. Some claim to have seen her floating through the air, while others catch glimpses of her reflection in mirrors or windows, only to have her vanish upon closer inspection.

The Lady in White has become a staple of the Birdcage Theater's haunted reputation, attracting ghost hunters, paranormal enthusiasts, and curious visitors hoping to catch a glimpse of her ethereal presence. Her story has been passed down through generations, adding to the theater's allure and mystique.

The Gambler

The legend of the Gambler at the Birdcage Theater adds another layer of intrigue to the paranormal tales associated with the historic venue. According to accounts and eyewitness testimonies, a ghostly figure resembling a cowboy can often be seen in the gambling area of the theater.

The Gambler is described as a well-dressed man wearing a cowboy hat and boots, who appears to be deeply engaged in a game of poker. Witnesses report seeing him seated at one of the tables, studying his cards and making calculated moves. However, before anyone can approach or interact with him, he mysteriously vanishes into thin air.

The identity of the Gambler remains unknown, but speculation suggests that he may have been one of the many patrons who frequented the Birdcage Theater during its heyday. It is believed that he met a tragic fate during a gambling dispute, possibly involving cheating or an intense altercation that turned deadly. As a result, his spirit is said to remain tied to the place where he met his untimely demise, forever destined to haunt the gambling area of the theater.

Visitors who have encountered the Gambler often describe feeling a sense of heaviness or tension in the air, as if the energy of the intense game he was playing still lingers. Some claim to have seen the cards he was holding or the chips he was betting before he vanished, further adding to the intrigue surrounding his ghostly presence.

The legend of the Gambler at the Birdcage Theater serves as a reminder of the high stakes and sometimes violent nature of the gambling culture that thrived in Tombstone. It offers a glimpse into the past, where fortunes were won and lost, and where disputes could quickly escalate into life-or-death situations.

While the true identity and story of the Gambler may remain shrouded in mystery, his ghostly apparition continues to captivate visitors to the Birdcage Theater. Exploring the gambling area, one can't help but imagine the intense games and the potential tragedies that unfolded there.

The Ghost Light

The ghost light is a prominent fixture and tradition associated with theaters, including the Birdcage Theater. It is a single, illuminated light left on the stage when the theater is empty and dark. The purpose of the ghost light is rooted in superstition and practicality.

Superstitiously, the ghost light is believed to ward off or appease the spirits that may inhabit the theater. It is thought that the light acts as a guiding beacon for the spirits, providing them with a source of illumination so that they do not become restless or mischievous in the darkness. The tradition of leaving a ghost light is rooted in the belief that it helps maintain a harmonious relationship between the living and the supernatural.

Practically, the ghost light serves as a safety measure. In an empty theater, the stage and surrounding areas can be treacherous to navigate in complete darkness. The ghost light helps prevent accidents by providing a small but necessary amount of illumination. It allows anyone entering the theater, be it maintenance personnel or performers, to navigate safely and avoid potential hazards.

In the context of the Birdcage Theater, the tradition of the ghost light takes on a special significance. Given the theater's reputation for being haunted, the presence of the ghost light adds to the ambiance and lore surrounding the venue. Visitors often find comfort in the belief that the light helps maintain a sense of peace and equilibrium within the haunted walls.

The ghost light is a symbolic and practical reminder of the theater's rich history, its connection to the supernatural, and the ongoing preservation of the space. It represents both a nod to tradition and a recognition of the mysteries that lie within the shadows of the Birdcage Theater.

The Crystal Palace Saloon
436 East Allen Street, Tombstone, Arizona

The Crystal Palace Saloon and Hotel, a revered establishment in Tombstone, has etched its name in history as a quintessential relic of the Wild West era. Famed for its ornate Victorian architecture, the Crystal Palace Saloon has welcomed patrons since its construction in 1879, serving as a focal point of the town's social life during the silver mining boom. Its opulent interior, adorned with intricate woodwork and ornate mirrors, witnessed the convergence of diverse characters—miners, cowboys, gamblers, lawmen, and outlaws—each contributing to the saloon's vibrant and storied atmosphere.

Figure 35: The Crystal Palace. Photo by Timothy James Wilson.

The Crystal Palace Saloon's fame stems not only from its architectural splendor but also from its role as a center of entertainment and vice in the Old West. The establishment resonated with the clinking of glasses and the shuffling of cards, as it hosted gambling games like poker and faro that lured professional gamblers and thrill-seekers. Its stage witnessed musical performances, dances, and theatrical events that provided respite from the challenges of frontier life. The saloon's history intertwines with the lives of famous figures like Wyatt Earp, who, along with his brothers, frequented the establishment. It also bore witness to conflicts and rivalries, epitomizing the dynamic and often volatile nature of Tombstone's society.

Notably, the Crystal Palace Saloon underwent restoration efforts to preserve its historical significance, allowing visitors today to step into a living museum that transports them to the heart of the Old West. The saloon's bar, recreated with meticulous attention to detail, invites guests to indulge in libations while surrounded by an authentic ambiance that harks back to a bygone era.

For a dark tourist, the Crystal Palace Saloon and Hotel offers a captivating blend of history, mystery, and intrigue. Beyond its opulence lies a nuanced connection to the shadowy underbelly of the Wild West—a realm teeming with gamblers, outlaws, and secrets. The stories of high-stakes poker games, the whispers of past rivalries, and the echoes of figures like Wyatt Earp create an immersive experience that beckons those with an affinity for the dark corners of history. This historic establishment encapsulates the spirit of the era, making it an irresistible destination for those seeking to embrace the allure of the Wild West's darker and more enigmatic facets.

The Gambler's Presence

The Gambler's Presence is one of the enduring legends within the haunted lore of the Crystal Palace Saloon. This particular story revolves around the ghostly presence of a gambler who is believed to linger within the historic establishment, still drawn to the card tables and the thrill of high-stakes poker games.

According to the legend, the Gambler's Presence is often felt or experienced around the area where the poker tables once stood. Visitors and staff have reported various eerie sensations when near this part of the saloon. Some have described sudden drops in temperature, as if an unseen presence is affecting the environment. Others have shared stories of feeling an unexplainable sensation of being watched or accompanied, even when there's no apparent source for this feeling.

The Gambler's Presence is often associated with the concept of residual energy—the idea that intense emotions and events can leave an imprint on a location, which is then replayed or sensed by those who come afterward. In the case of the Crystal Palace Saloon, this energy might be linked to the intense emotions, rivalries, and high stakes gambling that were part of the saloon's history during the Wild West era.

Legend has it that the Gambler's Presence is particularly strong during certain times, such as evenings or late at night when the saloon's atmosphere harkens back to its heyday. The ambiance of dim lighting, wooden interiors, and perhaps a distant sound of laughter from other patrons might evoke a sense of the past that allows visitors to feel connected to the spirits that supposedly still linger.

The Historic Allen Street
Allen Street, Tombstone, Arizona

Historic Allen Street is the main thoroughfare of Tombstone and stands as a living testament to the storied past of the Old West. Named after E.N. Allen, an early pioneer of Tombstone, Allen Street has preserved much of its 19th-century character and charm, making it a focal point for tourists and history enthusiasts alike.

Allen Street exudes an authentic Wild West ambiance, with its wooden boardwalks, historic facades, and buildings that have stood the test of time. Walking down this iconic street feels like stepping back in time, transporting visitors to the era when Tombstone was a booming silver mining town.

During its heyday, Allen Street was the heart of Tombstone's bustling activity. It was lined with saloons, theaters, general stores, and a wide array of businesses catering to the needs and desires of the town's diverse population. The street was witness to both the triumphs and tribulations of the Old West, including the infamous Gunfight at the O.K. Corral, which occurred just off Allen Street in the vacant lot behind the O.K. Corral.

Figure 36: Allen Street. Photo by Timothy James Wilson.

Allen Street boasts an array of attractions and landmarks that draw visitors from around the world. The O.K. Corral, the site of the famous gunfight, is just a short walk away. The Bird Cage Theatre, a historic theater and saloon, offers guided tours that provide a glimpse into the entertainment and escapades of the past. Additionally, the Tombstone Courthouse State Historic Park offers insights into the history of the town and the region.

Restless Spirits of the Old West

Throughout the year, Historic Allen Street comes alive with events that celebrate Tombstone's heritage. Festivals, reenactments, parades, and other festivities capture the spirit of the Wild West and offer visitors a chance to engage with the town's history in a lively and entertaining way.

For dark tourism enthusiasts, Historic Allen Street offers a unique opportunity to immerse themselves in the history of the Old West, including its tales of outlaws, lawmen, and the often violent conflicts that defined the era. The street's association with the Gunfight at the O.K. Corral and its connection to the legends and lore of the Wild West make it a captivating destination for those interested in the darker and more enigmatic aspects of history.

In essence, Historic Allen Street serves as a living museum, inviting visitors to explore the rich tapestry of the Old West while preserving the legacy of Tombstone's past. Whether strolling along the boardwalks, visiting historic sites, or indulging in local cuisine, this iconic street offers an immersive journey into a bygone era.

Tombstone Courthouse State Historic Park
223 East Toughnut Street, Tombstone, Arizona

Tombstone Courthouse State Historic Park stands as a captivating embodiment of Tombstone's storied past, inviting visitors to delve into the history and legends of the Old West. The building itself, constructed in 1882, is an architectural gem that exudes the charm of the era. Its Victorian-style design, characterized by ornate details and imposing brickwork, offers a visual link to the town's rich history and the iconic events that unfolded within its walls.

The history of the courthouse is deeply intertwined with Tombstone's rise as a silver mining boomtown. This historic edifice served as the Cochise County Courthouse during the turbulent years of the late 19th century, bearing witness to some of the era's most significant legal proceedings, including cases related to mining disputes, property disputes, and the clashes between lawmen and outlaws that epitomized the Wild West.

Figure 37: Tombstone Courthouse State Historic Park. Photo by Timothy James Wilson

For the dark tourism enthusiast, the Tombstone Courthouse State Park holds a unique allure. The courtroom, where justice was meted out and legal battles were waged, becomes a stage for historical exploration. The park's exhibits delve into the lives of infamous characters such as Wyatt Earp and Doc Holliday, who played integral roles in the unfolding drama of Tombstone's history.

While there are no documented accounts of paranormal activity within the courthouse itself, the park is situated within a town renowned for its haunted reputation. Tombstone's dark history, including its gunfights, shootouts, and lawless past, contributes to the allure of the paranormal for those who seek the mysterious and otherworldly. As such, the courthouse becomes part of a broader landscape that tantalizes the imagination of the dark tourist.

Chapter Six: Gold, Ghosts, and Gila Monsters

Wickenburg

Figure 38: Even the street signs embrace the Old West in Wickenburg. Photo taken by Timothy James Wilson.

Amidst the captivating expanse of the Arizona desert, the city of Wickenburg emerges as a fascinating chapter in the intricate tapestry of the American West. Situated a mere 54 miles northwest of Phoenix, Wickenburg is a hidden gem that offers a captivating blend of history, rugged landscapes, and a unique glimpse into the soul of the frontier spirit. With its proximity to the bustling urban hub of Phoenix, Wickenburg stands as a testament to the seamless coexistence of modernity and the untamed allure of the Old West.

Gold, Ghosts, and Gila Monsters

As the sun's rays paint the arid terrain with hues of gold and amber, Wickenburg's geography comes alive in a symphony of contrasts. Rolling desert hills, cacti-studded landscapes, and the meandering waters of the Hassayampa River shape the city's scenic backdrop. The surrounding mountains, including the Vulture Mountains, lend a majestic touch to the horizon, while the stark beauty of the Sonoran Desert invites explorers to venture into its secrets.

Wickenburg's history unfolds like a well-worn map of adventures past. Founded in 1863, it stands as one of Arizona's oldest mining towns, with roots deeply intertwined with the Gold Rush era. The town's very foundations echo with tales of rugged prospectors and determined pioneers who sought their fortunes in the unforgiving landscape. Yet, Wickenburg's history encompasses more than just gold and silver; it's a narrative of resilience, community, and the relentless pursuit of dreams.

Amid our road trip to Wickenburg's history, certain figures emerge as beacons of the city's legacy. Notably, the legendary Henry Wickenburg, after whom the town is named, left an indelible mark. He discovered the Vulture Mine, a symbol of prosperity and the lifeblood of the town during its early days. The legacy of Henry Wickenburg's vision and determination reverberates through the streets and structures that now bear his name.

Join us as we delve into the stories woven into the very fabric of Wickenburg. From its storied past to its vibrant present, this chapter invites you to journey through time and space, exploring a city that stands as a bridge between eras. From its historical landmarks to the whispers of the Old West that linger in the desert breeze, Wickenburg beckons with the promise of discovery and the allure of a world both familiar and unknown.

Henry Wickenburg

Henry Wickenburg, a name immortalized in the history of the American West, was a pivotal figure in the development of Wickenburg. His life's journey was marked by the pursuit of opportunity, the discovery of riches, and the enduring legacy of the town that bears his name.

Born in 1819 in Unterheinriet, Germany, Wickenburg eventually found himself drawn to the allure of the American frontier. In the mid-19th century, he joined the tide of pioneers who sought adventure and prosperity in the western territories. His travels brought him to California during the Gold Rush, where he engaged in various pursuits, including ranching and mining.

However, it was Wickenburg's destiny to find his true fortune in the heart of the Arizona desert. In 1863, while prospecting in the rugged terrain, he made a discovery that would change the course of his life and the history of the region—the rich veins of gold that would become known as the Vulture Mine. This discovery marked the birth of the Vulture Mining District, and the subsequent rush of prospectors and miners transformed the area into a bustling hub of activity.

Henry Wickenburg's determination and leadership were instrumental in establishing a community around the Vulture Mine. He helped create a system of mining operations, bringing in necessary equipment, and even organizing a post office to serve the growing population. The town that grew around the mine naturally took on his name, becoming Wickenburg.

Despite his success, Wickenburg's life was not without its challenges. He faced financial struggles, disputes over mining claims, and the hardships inherent to life in the rugged West. Yet, his enduring legacy lies not just in the riches he unearthed but in his impact on the community. His leadership and vision laid the foundation for Wickenburg's growth, and his legacy is still palpable in the town's historical sites and cultural heritage.

Wickenburg lived out his days as a respected figure, revered by the community he helped shape. He passed away in 1905, leaving behind a town that continues to honor his memory. The Vulture Mine, though now a ghost town, serves as a testament to his legacy and the indomitable spirit of those who sought their fortunes in the untamed landscapes of the American West.

Henry Wickenburg's story is one of adventure, resilience, and the enduring impact of individuals on the course of history. His name is forever intertwined with the town that stands as a testament to his pioneering spirit and his role in shaping the tapestry of the Old West.

The Kay El Bar Guest Ranch
2655 South Kay El Bar Road, Wickenburg, Arizona
Reservations: (928) 684-7593

The Kay El Bar Guest Ranch, in the picturesque town of Wickenburg, stands as a testament to the rich history and allure of the Old West. With its roots traced back to the early 1900s, the ranch's legacy is steeped in the rugged charm of the cowboy era. Offering a genuine Western experience, this historic guest ranch has welcomed visitors for decades, providing a unique glimpse into a bygone era. This guest ranch is not haunted, and no paranormal activity has been reported here.

My reasoning for including this ranch is their accommodations, as well as their efforts to showcase a rustic yet comfortable style that transports guests back in time. Charming cabins, each uniquely adorned to evoke the ambiance of the Old

West, provide a cozy retreat after days filled with adventure. These lodgings offer an authentic slice of Western heritage, ensuring that guests feel immersed in the history and culture that define the region.

For those seeking an authentic cowboy experience, the Kay El Bar Guest Ranch delivers a plethora of activities that pay homage to Western traditions. From horseback riding and guided trail rides to cattle drives that channel the spirit of the ranch's cattle-ranching origins, visitors have the chance to step into the boots of a cowboy and reconnect with the timeless allure of the desert landscape. The ranch creates an environment that encourages guests to disconnect from modern life and embrace the rugged beauty of their surroundings.

What truly sets the Kay El Bar Guest Ranch apart is its dedication to preserving the atmosphere of the Old West. The ranch's history is woven into every corner, and this commitment to authenticity allows guests to experience the Western way of life firsthand. As the sun sets behind the desert horizon, casting an amber glow over the landscape, visitors can almost hear the echoes of past generations and envision a time when cattle ranching and adventure were a way of life.

Vulture Mine
36610 355th Avenue, Wickenburg, Arizona
Information: (877) 425-9229

Our first stop on this weekend's tour is about 21 miles south of our guest ranch, where we will find The Vulture Mine. Situated in the Sonoran Desert, the mine boasts a fascinating history intertwined with tales of prosperity, notorious outlaws, and supernatural occurrences.

Captivated by his find, Henry Wickenburg named the mine after a vulture he spotted perched atop a prominent rock formation, which would later become a recognizable landmark. The discovery of gold sparked a gold rush, attracting hordes of miners and prospectors to the area and leading to the rapid development of Wickenburg as a bustling town centered around mining activities.

Figure 39: Vulture City Mine and Ghost Town. Photo taken by Timothy James Wilson.

The Vulture Mine quickly garnered a reputation as one of Arizona's most prosperous and productive gold mines, yielding substantial amounts of gold and silver. Mining operations involved the excavation of deep shafts, the construction of intricate tunnel networks, and the utilization of heavy machinery, transforming the region into a vibrant mining community. The success of Vulture Mine enticed individuals from various walks of life, including some of the most notorious characters of the Wild West.

Among the intriguing connections between the Vulture Mine and legendary outlaws is the enigmatic figure of Jacob Waltz, known as "The Dutchman." While Waltz was rumored to have been a miner at the Vulture Mine, his true claim to fame derived from his purported knowledge of a secret gold mine in the Superstition Mountains, famously referred to as the Lost Dutchman's Mine (see Chapter Three). While the Vulture Mine thrived, it also epitomized the perilous nature of mining operations during that era. Accidents, violence, and harsh living conditions were common in such environments. Tragic incidents, including cave-ins, disputes over claims, and accidents caused by the treacherous working conditions, claimed the lives of numerous miners. The lawless and rugged atmosphere of the Wild West also drew its fair share of criminal activity, and the Vulture Mine was not exempt from such associations.

Notorious outlaws and bandits sought refuge in the vicinity of the Vulture Mine, further enhancing its connection with lawlessness. One prominent outlaw linked to the area was James "Jim" Addison Reavis, who established a hideout near the mine. Reavis gained infamy for forging land grants and attempting to claim vast regions of Arizona as his own. Eventually, Reavis was apprehended and sentenced for his crimes, but his presence added to the mystique surrounding the mine and its association with legendary outlaws.

However, the history of the Vulture Mine encompasses more than just gold and outlaws. Over the years, reports of paranormal phenomena and ghostly encounters have emerged, infusing the mine with an eerie and chilling dimension. Visitors and employees have shared tales of unexplained footsteps echoing through the corridors, disembodied voices emanating from empty spaces, and shadowy figures seen traversing the premises. Some individuals have even claimed to witness apparitions of miners, their faces caked in dirt and grime, toiling away in spectral form long after their earthly lives had ended.

The paranormal incidents at the Vulture Mine have solidified its reputation as one of Arizona's most haunted locations. As word spread, paranormal investigators and enthusiasts flocked to the area, driven by a desire to capture evidence of the supernatural. Eerie EVP (Electronic Voice Phenomena) recordings, photographs capturing unexplained anomalies, and personal accounts of spectral encounters have fueled the mine's haunted status, attracting those seeking a brush with the otherworldly.

The Lady in White

The legend of the "Lady in White" at Vulture Mine is one of the most enduring and chilling tales associated with this historic location. This spectral figure is said to be a ghostly woman dressed in a white gown or Victorian-era clothing, and her presence has captivated the imagination of visitors and paranormal enthusiasts for years.

The story begins with accounts from various individuals who claim to have encountered the Lady in White while exploring the mine's grounds. According to these reports, witnesses have described seeing a woman of ethereal beauty, her appearance almost luminous against the backdrop of the desert landscape. She is often seen walking silently near the mine's old buildings or wandering through the area.

What sets the Lady in White apart is the sense of melancholy and unease that accompanies her presence. Witnesses often describe feeling a sudden drop in temperature, a feeling of being watched, or an eerie chill that seems to permeate the air. Some have even reported an overwhelming feeling of sadness or a sense of being in the company of something not quite of this world.

As for her identity, the Lady in White remains a mystery. There are no concrete historical records or verifiable accounts that definitively explain who she might have been in life.

Timothy James Wilson

Speculation has ranged from the idea that she could have been a miner's wife who lost her husband in a mining accident, to a woman who lived in the nearby town and had a connection to the mine.

The Phantom Miner

The Phantom Miner is a captivating and eerie tale that has contributed to the mine's reputation as a haunted location. This spectral figure, often described as a miner from a bygone era, is said to appear deep within the mine's tunnels, adding an air of mystery and foreboding to the site.

The story of the Phantom Miner begins with reports from visitors, employees, and paranormal enthusiasts who claim to have witnessed the ghostly apparition while exploring the mine's underground passages. According to these accounts, the Phantom Miner is typically seen wearing traditional miner's clothing, complete with a worn hat, tattered clothing, and carrying a pickaxe and a lantern.

What makes the Phantom Miner particularly chilling is the circumstances under which he is often reported to appear. Witnesses describe encountering him in the dimly lit, narrow passages of the mine, where his figure seems to materialize out of the darkness. Some witnesses report that he appears to be in the midst of performing his mining duties, swinging his pickaxe and moving about the tunnels as if he were still engaged in his labor.

Theories surrounding the identity of the Phantom Miner vary. Some believe that he could be the spirit of a miner who met an untimely or tragic end within the mine's depths. Others suggest that his presence is a testament to the grueling and often perilous conditions that miners endured during the mine's operational years.

175

Gold, Ghosts, and Gila Monsters

Encounters with the Phantom Miner often evoke a sense of unease and trepidation. Witness reports include feelings of being watched, sudden drops in temperature, and an overall sense of foreboding. The appearance of the Phantom Miner serves as a stark reminder of the mine's history and the hardships faced by those who toiled within its tunnels.

Box Canyon
Near Wickenburg, Arizona
GPS Coordinates 34.04924, -112.72364

Box Canyon, nestled near Wickenburg, is a geological wonder that captivates with its rugged beauty and distinctive features. Carved over time by the relentless forces of water and erosion, this natural formation offers an intriguing glimpse into the geological history of the region. Before we get started talking about this amazing place though, I will warn you that this trek involves unpaved, and unmaintained roads. I would highly recommend skipping this sight if you do not have a capable offroad vehicle or renting an off road vehicle for this adventure (it is well worth the cost).

Box Canyon's defining characteristic is its narrow, steep-sided gorge that winds through the landscape. The canyon's walls rise dramatically on either side, forming a literal box shape that gives the site its name. The towering walls are composed of layered rocks, showcasing the geological history of the area.

At the heart of Box Canyon's formation is the Hassayampa River, which has been carving its course through the rock for millennia. Over time, the relentless flow of water gradually chiseled away at the rock layers, creating the distinctive shape and depth of the canyon. The result is a striking visual contrast between the deep shadows cast by the towering walls and the radiant sunlight that illuminates the canyon's floor.

The walls of Box Canyon provide a geological cross-section that exposes a diverse array of rock layers. These layers offer a glimpse into the ancient history of the area, with each stratum representing a different era of deposition and geologic activity.

Sandstones, limestones, and shales are among the types of rock that can be observed in the canyon's walls. The variations in color, texture, and composition reveal the dynamic processes that shaped the landscape over millions of years. Some layers might contain fossils or other clues that offer insights into past environments and ecosystems.

Box Canyon stretches for approximately 3 miles in length, winding through the desert terrain with its narrow passage. The walls of the canyon can reach heights of around 50 feet or more, creating an intimate and awe-inspiring environment for visitors. The relatively compact nature of the canyon enhances the feeling of being enveloped by the landscape and creates a sense of exploration and discovery.

The geological marvel of Box Canyon also plays host to a diverse range of desert plant life. Despite the harsh conditions of the environment, hardy plants such as cacti, desert shrubs, and wildflowers manage to thrive within the protected canyon walls. Visitors might also encounter small wildlife, insects, and birds adapted to the arid surroundings.

Indigenous History of Box Canyon

The presence of Indigenous communities in and around Box Canyon holds a profound and enduring history that spans back for centuries. These indigenous peoples, including the Yavapai and other groups, have established a deep-rooted connection to the land that encompasses Box Canyon. For these communities, the canyon was not merely a geographical location but rather a place of immense cultural and spiritual significance. The indigenous people utilized the resources provided by the area for various purposes, such as hunting, gathering, and engaging in their traditional practices.

One of the most tangible remnants of the Indigenous people presence in Box Canyon is the collection of petroglyphs and rock art that adorns the surfaces of the rocks. These intricate designs offer a window into the spiritual beliefs, rituals, and daily experiences of the indigenous individuals who once inhabited or traversed this region. These etchings may portray animals, humans, symbols, and other elements that held deep cultural or spiritual meanings for these communities.

The unique geological features of Box Canyon might have held a sacred and ceremonial significance for the indigenous peoples. The secluded and enclosed nature of the canyon could have provided a private and reverent space for their ceremonies, gatherings, and other cultural practices.

Archaeological research within the region has also revealed artifacts, tools, and remnants of daily life that offer further insights into the historical activities and lifestyles of these Indigenous people communities. Items like pottery, tools, and implements used for hunting and cooking provide a glimpse into the practical aspects of their existence.

Ghostly Phenomena

While Box Canyon is not specifically haunted, there have been countless reports of weird and strange phenomena occurring in the area. One does not need to have an overactive imagination to dream of Outlaws and Sheriffs shooting it out on the ridges of Box Canyon, or that this might have been a great hiding spot for miners or escaped slaves. Even though we may not have any documented evidence that there was an apprehension of an outlaw here, or some inhumane suffering inflicted upon someone or a group of people by another person.

With this in mind, I turn to a number of things reported about Box Canyon that might make you wonder if we may be missing some pages out of our history books. Hikers, off-roaders, and other outdoors enthusiasts have reported unexplained sounds, eerie feelings, optical illusions, unusual light phenomena, electromagnetic anomalies, and strange apparitions or shapes in the area surrounding Box Canyon for decades.

The area was also considered to be a holy place for the Yavapai people long before the first European stepped foot in Arizona, as we learned earlier. One could imagine that a lot has happened in this area over the centuries that Box Canyon has formed.

The Longest Night

The following is a fictional story that I found online about Box Canyon:

While many people who are not from Arizona do not realize the culture around night-hiking, one only need to spend a few days in the July or August heat to understand why, in the summertime, Arizonians would rather hike at night than during the day. We have already learned in this book just how brutal the Arizona sun can be, and thus we join a group of hikers on an evening hike in Box Canyon.

As the sun began its descent beyond the desert horizon, a group of enthusiastic hikers set out on an evening adventure to explore the mysteries of Box Canyon. Their headlamps cast a feeble glow, illuminating the rocky path ahead as they ventured deeper into the narrowing gorge. Excitement filled the air, accompanied by a sense of anticipation for the unique experience that lay ahead.

As the group hiked further into the heart of the canyon, the walls seemed to close in around them, casting long shadows that danced eerily in the dim light. Unexplained sounds whispered on the desert breeze—soft murmurs that echoed between the rock walls, creating a sense of unease. Laughter and casual chatter faded as the hikers exchanged puzzled glances, questioning the source of the mysterious echoes.

At a bend in the path, the group encountered an optical illusion that played tricks on their perception. The canyon walls appeared to shift and distort, making the path ahead seem to twist and contort in unexpected ways. The hikers, now disoriented, hesitated, unsure of the true direction to follow. Eerie feelings settled over them, like a cool shroud of uncertainty, making them second-guess their every step.

One member of the group consulted a map, attempting to make sense of their surroundings. Yet, the map seemed to be of little use in this twisting labyrinth. GPS systems and other electronics seemed to just all stop working. Despite their best efforts, the hikers found themselves straying from the marked trail, guided only by the unreliable glow of their headlamps.

Hours passed as the group navigated the canyon's confusing passages. The unexplained chatter and laughter grew more persistent, shifting from soft murmurs to indistinct whispers that seemed to come from all directions. The eerie feelings intensified, causing hearts to race and nerves to fray. In the darkness, even familiar features took on sinister shapes, adding to the unsettling atmosphere.

As the night wore on, the hikers realized they were well and truly lost. Panic threatened to take hold, but they rallied their spirits and leaned on one another for support. With the first hints of dawn painting the eastern sky, they stumbled upon a familiar landmark—a rock formation that marked the entrance to Box Canyon. Relief washed over them as they retraced their steps, following the path back to safety.

As the hikers emerged from the canyon at the break of dawn, the desert landscape greeted them with the soft glow of morning light. Exhausted and shaken, they shared their ordeal, recounting the unexplained sounds, eerie feelings, and bewildering optical illusions that had turned their hike into an unexpected adventure.

While they couldn't explain all the mysteries they had encountered, the hikers had a newfound respect for the enigmatic beauty of Box Canyon. As they returned to the trailhead, the first rays of sunlight bathed the desert in warmth, casting aside the shadows of the night. The experience would forever serve as a reminder that even in familiar landscapes, nature has a way of revealing its secrets and testing the limits of human perception.

Stanton
Stanton, Arizona

Stanton is a historic ghost town located 25 miles north of Wickenburg. It was established in the mid-19th century during the Arizona gold rush and played a significant role in the mining history of the region. The town's proximity to the Weaver and Octave mines adds to its historical significance.

I am going to warn that the remains of the town of Stanton are on private land, and when we went there we were met with private property signs, and signs that indicated that the RV park would be closed until October.

Stanton was founded in the 1860s as a gold mining camp, and it quickly became a bustling community as prospectors flocked to the area in search of their fortunes. The town's population reached its peak during the late 1800s, and it boasted amenities such as stores, saloons, hotels, and a post office. As with many mining towns, Stanton's prosperity was closely tied to the success of nearby mines.

Figure 40: Stanton. Photo taken by Timothy James Wilson.

Today, Stanton is considered a ghost town, but some remnants of its past still stand. Visitors can explore the preserved structures, including the schoolhouse, old cabins, and mining equipment. The Stanton Cemetery also offers a glimpse into the lives of those who once called the town home.

Weaver Mine is located near Stanton and was an important gold mining operation during the late 1800s. The mine was named after Pauline Weaver, an early prospector in the region. Weaver Mine produced a substantial amount of gold and contributed to the growth of Stanton as miners flocked to the area. The mine's success led to the establishment of nearby camps and settlements.

Octave Mine is another historic gold mining site situated near Stanton. Founded in the 1860s, Octave Mine became a significant gold producer at its peak. The mine's output contributed to the local economy and the broader growth of the American West. Like Weaver Mine, Octave Mine played a role in attracting prospectors and settlers to the area.

Today, the remnants of Octave Mine include abandoned structures, mining equipment, and other artifacts that offer insight into the challenges and endeavors of the miners who once worked there.

Stanton's history is not only one of prosperity and industry—it's also a tapestry woven with tales of intrigue and darkness. Enter Charles P. Stanton, a man whose name became synonymous with ruthlessness and treachery. Charles P. Stanton changed the town's name from Antelope Station to bear his own name, leaving a mark of his own influence.

Stanton was known as a ruthless figure who orchestrated the deaths of individuals for his own gain. Under his leadership, a murder syndicate claimed up to 50 lives, regardless of age or gender, leaving a trail of fear and devastation. Described by many, including newspapers, as 'the Devil incarnate,' Stanton's legacy remains a chilling reminder of human capacity for malevolence.

The old Stanton store, once a hub of activity, developed a dark reputation for deeds of violence. The echoes of these tragedies seem to linger, as reports of ghostly apparitions and unexplained phenomena abound. The souls of those who met untimely ends, including Charles Stanton himself, are said to haunt the area, their restless spirits roaming the grounds.

Early newspapers reflected the sentiment of an age of ghosts, where the old store stands as a prime spot for those who still wander, unseen but palpably present.

The Martin Family Massacre of 1886
In Arizona's history, one name stands out as a sinister emblem of the lawless frontier: Charles Stanton. Arriving in the territory in 1871, Stanton's dubious beginnings included swindling a friend out of a gold claim. His association with Vega, a notorious figure whose gang was notorious for stagecoach robberies and acts of terror, further solidified Stanton's dark reputation. He manipulated Vega and his gang to carry out his nefarious deeds.

Stanton's sinister rivalry extended to Barney Martin, a competing storekeeper who, weary of the reign of terror, relinquished his business and embarked on a fateful journey with his family in July 1886. En route to meet Charles Genung, a well-known figure, the Martins encountered the Vega gang's ambush. South of Wickenburg, they were coerced to drive to a desolate location near present-day Morristown. There, Vega and Elano Hernandez took their lives with brutal knives. To obscure their crimes, they scalped the victims and set their wagon ablaze, crafting a grim scene.

From a vantage point atop a nearby hill, Stanton watched the massacre unfold, a silent witness to the ruthless act.

As the investigation ensued, the usual suspects—Stanton and Hernandez—were arrested. Strangely, Hernandez's release and Stanton's own exoneration due to lack of evidence only deepened the sense of injustice. Meanwhile, Vega's flight to Mexico ensured his evasion from capture.

Stanton's pride eventually became his downfall when he disrespected Friolana Lucero, a young woman of beauty and grace. A protective brother named Pete Lucero was stirred to action, and on the night of November 13, 1886, he and his companions confronted Stanton in his store. Rifles spoke where the law couldn't, silencing the ruthless crime boss forever. In an ironic twist, Stanton's demise wasn't dealt by the legal system, but by a brother safeguarding his sister's honor.

In the wake of these tragic events, a haunting legacy endures. Many believe that the ghosts of those lost to the violence—the Martin family among them—linger in the town of Stanton, their spectral presence a testament to the profound impact of their untimely deaths. These apparitions, it is said, roam the grounds, a reminder of the dark and often lawless history that has shaped the American West.

The Lawless Frontier

The town of Stanton stands as a stark reflection of the challenges faced by law enforcement and the darker aspects of human nature during the tumultuous era of the late 19th century American West. It is a microcosm of the untamed frontier, where the pursuit of wealth and survival coexisted with lawlessness and violence. Through the lens of Stanton's history, the lack of justice and the intricate web of human behavior during this time period come into focus.

In the late 1800s, the Arizona Territory was a vast and sparsely populated expanse that lacked the robust infrastructure and established legal systems of more developed regions. This made it challenging for law enforcement to effectively maintain order and deliver justice. The remote nature of the frontier meant that crimes could go unpunished, emboldening criminals and fostering an environment of impunity.

The lack of a well-established legal framework and the absence of a strong law enforcement presence in many areas of the frontier contributed to the difficulties in seeking justice. Limited resources, coupled with the vastness of the territory, made it challenging for authorities to investigate crimes thoroughly and apprehend perpetrators.

The absence of a reliable justice system sometimes led to communities taking matters into their own hands. Vigilante justice, where local citizens formed ad hoc groups to punish wrongdoers, was not uncommon. While such actions could provide a semblance of justice, they also had the potential to escalate tensions and result in violence without due process.

Charles P. Stanton's prominence as a ruthless figure in Stanton and its surrounding areas exemplifies the darker aspects of human nature prevalent during this time. His actions, including orchestrating a murder syndicate responsible for numerous deaths, highlighted the lengths to which individuals were willing to go to achieve their goals. Stanton's ability to manipulate and evade justice is indicative of the challenges law enforcement faced in a lawless land.

The history of Stanton is rife with conflicts, rivalries, and personal disputes that often escalated to violence. Whether over disputes about mining claims, romantic entanglements, or personal vendettas, the scarcity of legal recourse often meant that individuals took matters into their own hands, leading to tragic outcomes.

The lack of justice and the presence of violent crime undoubtedly left a profound impact on the communities of Stanton and the surrounding areas. Fear, mistrust, and a sense of vulnerability pervaded daily life, shaping interactions and attitudes within the community. The legacy of lawlessness has left an indelible mark on the collective memory and character of the town.

As visitors explore Stanton today, they are met with a haunting reminder of the complexities of human nature and the challenges of maintaining order in the face of adversity. The town's history serves as a testament to the resilience of those who lived in the frontier, where the pursuit of dreams was coupled with the harsh realities of a world where justice was often elusive, and the darker aspects of humanity were laid bare.

The Wickenburg Massacre
Site GPS Coordinates: 33.9901163773, -112.853027134
Monument: Corner of Wickenburg Way and Flying E Ranch
Road, Wickenburg, Arizona

The Wickenburg Massacre, which occurred on November 5, 1871, is a tragic event that is etched into the history of Arizona and the American West. It was a violent confrontation between a group of Indigenous people and a stagecoach carrying passengers and mail. The incident took place near the town of Wickenburg, which was then a small settlement.

Tensions between settlers and Indigenous peoples were a common feature of the American frontier. As pioneers pushed westward, conflicts over land, resources, and cultural differences often escalated into violence.

Figure 41: The Wickenburg Massacre Memorial. Photo taken by Timothy James Wilson.

On November 5, 1871, a stagecoach operated by the Wickenburg Stage Line was en route from Wickenburg to the settlement of La Paz, which was a significant mining town at the time on the Colorado River. The stagecoach carried passengers, mail, and valuables. The journey was a dangerous one, as the route passed through remote and potentially hostile territory.

As the stagecoach was traveling through the desert landscape, it was ambushed by a group of 15 Indigenous warriors. The warriors were believed to be from the Yavapai and Tonto Apache peoples; however, they were never identified, and officially the case remains unsolved. There is speculation also that the attackers were not Indigenous at all, but rather bandits from Mexico. The attackers, armed with firearms and traditional weapons, surprised the passengers and the driver, opening fire on the stagecoach and its occupants.

The attack resulted in the deaths of at least six people, including the stagecoach driver, Fredrick Wadsworth, and five passengers. Only two people survived the attack, William Kruger, and Mollie Sheppard; however, Sheppard would die a few days later from infection in the wounds she endured in the attack, raising the death toll to seven total. The attackers also managed to seize mail, supplies, and valuables before retreating into the wilderness. The incident sent shockwaves through the region and added to the atmosphere of fear and uncertainty that characterized life on the frontier.

The Wickenburg Massacre had a significant impact on the local communities and the broader Arizona Territory. It highlighted the vulnerability of settlers to attacks from Indigenous groups and underscored the challenges of maintaining law and order in remote areas where resources were limited.

The incident further strained relations between settlers and Indigenous peoples in the region. It contributed to an escalation of tensions and conflicts that would continue to shape the history of the American West.

The Wickenburg Massacre remains a somber reminder of the violence and struggles that marked the era of westward expansion. It is an event that serves as a lens through which we can examine the complex interactions between different cultural groups, the challenges of frontier life, and the clashes between tradition and progress.

The Stagecoach Ghost

The following is a story I found on the internet when doing research for this book:

The moon hung low over the desert landscape as Beth gazed out at the Wickenburg Massacre site. The wind carried a chill that seemed to cut through her, as if the very air held a memory of the tragic events that had transpired there many years ago.

Beth had heard the whispers from the townsfolk, the tales of eerie occurrences and ghostly apparitions that sometimes visited the site after sundown. Skeptical yet curious, she had decided to see for herself what truth lay beneath the legends.

As darkness settled in, Beth found herself standing at the site, her heart racing. The moon cast an ethereal glow over the landscape, illuminating the rocky terrain and the remnants of what once was. The chilling silence was broken only by the distant howl of a coyote.

Suddenly, a soft, mournful whisper carried on the wind reached Beth's ears. She spun around, her eyes scanning the darkness. At first, there was nothing. But then, out of the corner of her eye, she saw a flicker of movement—a shadowy figure standing near the spot where the stagecoach had been ambushed.

Heart pounding, she approached cautiously, the crunch of gravel underfoot echoing in the stillness. The figure seemed to materialize from the darkness—a man, dressed in clothes that harkened back to another era. His face bore a solemn expression, etched with the weight of a tragic past.

"Who are you?" Beth whispered, her voice barely audible above the wind.

The ghostly figure turned toward her, his eyes holding a mixture of sorrow and longing. Without a word, he gestured toward the site—the remnants of the stagecoach, the moonlit desert, the echoes of the past that lingered in the air.

As if in response, the wind seemed to carry faint echoes of voices—a mix of laughter, shouts, and cries. It was as though the very fabric of time had been torn, and Beth found herself transported to that fateful night.

She watched in silence as the events unfolded—the ambush, the chaos, the fear. The figures of the passengers and the attackers moved before her eyes, a ghostly reenactment of the tragedy. And in that moment, she felt a surge of empathy for the lives that had been lost, for the history that had been etched in blood and sorrow.

The ghostly figure turned back to her, his expression a mixture of gratitude and sadness. Without a word, he faded into the darkness, leaving Beth alone with the echoes of the past.

As dawn broke, she stood at the Wickenburg Massacre site, the morning light banishing the shadows of the night. She knew that what she had witnessed was a glimpse into history—a reminder of the lives that had been lost, the pain that had been endured.

And though the ghostly figure had disappeared, she couldn't shake the feeling that the spirits of the past still lingered, their stories etched into the very fabric of the land. The Wickenburg Massacre site had become a place where history and memory converged, where the echoes of the past whispered to those who dared to listen.

The Wickenburg Jail Tree
45 North Tegner Street, Wickenburg, Arizona

Behind a Circle K, in the city of Wickenburg, stands a 200 year old tree with a harrowing tale. The massive mesquite tree, with its dangling chains, and hand cuffs has been the acquaintance of some of Wickenburg's most notorious outlaws. The Wickenburg Jail Tree stands as a unique historical relic that harkens back to a time when unconventional methods were employed for law enforcement in the American West. Jail trees were often used as makeshift holding areas for prisoners before proper jail facilities were established. The Wickenburg Jail Tree is a particularly famous example of this practice.

Figure 42: The Wickenburg Jail Tree. Photo by Timothy James Wilson.

In the early days of settlement in the American West, law enforcement and infrastructure were limited. In many cases, communities resorted to creative solutions to handle those who had broken the law. Jail trees were one such solution. These were living trees with unique configurations of branches that allowed for the temporary confinement of prisoners. The trees served as impromptu jails until proper jail facilities could be built.

191

Gold, Ghosts, and Gila Monsters

The Wickenburg Jail Tree is a mesquite tree with distinct branches that formed a natural cage-like structure. It was utilized by law enforcement in the late 19th century to temporarily confine prisoners, giving rise to its name as the "Jail Tree." It's located in a historic district of Wickenburg, serving as a tangible reminder of the town's Wild West history.

The Wickenburg Jail Tree has drawn attention for alleged paranormal activity. It's said that the spirits of those who were once confined within its branches may linger, leaving an imprint on the site. Visitors and locals have reported experiencing eerie feelings, strange sensations, and even apparitions near the Jail Tree.

Visitors have claimed to hear whispers and faint voices near the Wickenburg Jail Tree, even when there's no one else around. Some have reported glimpses of shadowy figures or apparitions resembling individuals in historical clothing. These accounts often contribute to the sense that the tree is imbued with the energy of the past.

Believers in the paranormal suggest that the intense emotions and experiences associated with confinement and distress may leave a residual energy imprint on a location.

While some visitors interpret these experiences as evidence of paranormal activity, others view them as a reflection of the deep history and emotional weight of the site. The Wickenburg Jail Tree's association with law enforcement, confinement, and the challenges of the frontier contribute to its mystique.

The Wickenburg Jail Tree has become a point of interest for tourists, history enthusiasts, and those intrigued by dark tourism—traveling to sites associated with death, tragedy, or historical adversity. The alleged paranormal activity further adds to the allure of the location for those interested in the unknown and the unexplained.

Gold, Ghosts, and Gila Monsters

Chapter Seven: Whispers in the Shadows

Jerome

Figure 43: Jerome, as seen from Jerome State Historic Park. Photo taken by Timothy James Wilson.

Welcome to our road trip to the most haunted town in Arizona; Jerome. Before we get started, I do have a few recommendations: the first is to consider staying longer in Jerome than just a weekend; this town is packed with history and haunted tales that will stimulate your curious mind.

The second recommendation is to consider who will be coming with you to Jerome, as the town is literally built into the side of a mountain, and thus the twisting road can be very anxiety provoking. There are two ways to get to Jerome, both involve 89A: you can either head southwest on 89A up the mountain from Cottonwood, or you can go over the mountain and drop into Jerome by heading Northeast on 89A from Prescott Valley. I highly recommend that if you have people in your party who may not be able to handle the winding roads, that the road from Prescott Valley might be a little less anxiety provoking. Also, if you have these people with you and they take medication for chronic anxiety, make sure they bring their medication.

I say this because once I was headed to Jerome from Cottonwood with some friends from out of state, and my friend was driving. Halfway up the mountain he stopped and was so terrified he could not continue driving. I convinced him to let me drive his rental car, and we continued our journey.

The third suggestion I might make is to go for a hike at the top of Woodchute Mountain. It is a beautiful place to hike around; however, this is not a hiking book, so I do not go into great detail.

Jerome

The town of Jerome stands as a testament to history, resilience, and the unexplained. With a rich past dating back to the late 19th century, Jerome has earned its reputation as one of the most haunted and intriguing towns in the United States. The intertwining of its storied history and the spectral echoes of the past make it a captivating destination for those seeking a glimpse into the world of the paranormal.

Jerome's story began in the late 1800s when it transformed from a mining camp into a booming copper mining town. Its strategic location atop Cleopatra Hill provided access to valuable copper deposits, and the town quickly grew into a bustling hub of industry and culture. At its peak, Jerome was a thriving community with theaters, saloons, brothels, and all the trappings of a Wild West town.

However, the town's fortunes began to wane in the early 20th century, and by the 1950s, the mines had closed, leaving Jerome a virtual ghost town. In the years that followed, artists, craftsmen, and visionaries moved in, giving the town a new lease on life. Today, Jerome is a designated National Historic Landmark, its streets lined with historic buildings, museums, galleries, and vibrant stories waiting to be told. Wineries and art galleries are scattered throughout the town, and almost the entire town can be navigated on foot.

Jerome's blend of history and hauntings has made it a destination unlike any other. As you wander its streets, exploring its museums and historic sites, you may find yourself wondering about the stories that linger just beyond the visible realm. With its spectral inhabitants and intriguing legends, Jerome invites you to delve into the unknown, to experience a town where history, mystery, and the supernatural converge in a captivating dance.

The Great Fires

As I conducted research for this chapter, one thing that continued to come up was that many of the buildings and other structures of Jerome were rebuilt following a fire in 1899. The fire in 1899 was a significant event in Jerome's history, shaping the town's development and character. For this reason, I wanted to talk about the fire, and its devastation first. There have been several fires of great catastrpohy in the history of Jerome, but the Great Fire of 1899 is considered to be the most devastating.

In April 1899, a devastating fire swept through Jerome, leaving a trail of destruction in its wake. The fire started in the Paul and Jerry's Saloon on the east side of Main Street and quickly spread due to the town's wooden buildings and windy conditions. Despite the efforts of the town's volunteer fire brigade, the fire couldn't be contained and eventually engulfed a large portion of the business district.

The fire destroyed numerous buildings, including saloons, hotels, stores, and more. Many of the wooden structures were quickly consumed by the flames, and the intense heat caused nearby structures to catch fire as well. The fire was particularly destructive because Jerome was built on the steep slopes of Cleopatra Hill, making it difficult to control the blaze.

After the fire was finally extinguished, more than 30 blocks of the town had been reduced to ashes, leaving many residents homeless and without jobs. However, the town's determination and resilience were evident as they began the process of rebuilding almost immediately. Reconstruction efforts were hampered by a lack of water infrastructure, but the community persevered and adapted.

Despite the efforts to prevent another fire of this magnitude, 18 years later history would repeat itself. On April 18, 1917, a fire broke out in the Clarksdale Hotel. The fire started in the hotel, but due to the town's layout and the closeness of its buildings, it quickly spread to other structures in the densely populated business district.

The buildings in Jerome were predominantly made of wood, making them highly susceptible to fires. The flames consumed numerous wooden structures, causing significant damage to the town's infrastructure.

As the fire raged, the townspeople rallied to fight the blaze, but their efforts were hampered by the challenging terrain and strong winds, which caused the fire to spread rapidly. The wooden buildings fueled the fire, creating a daunting challenge for firefighters and volunteers.

Despite their best efforts, the fire continued to advance, destroying a substantial portion of the business district. It is estimated that the fire consumed multiple blocks of buildings and businesses, resulting in extensive damage.

Both fires had a profound impact on Jerome. Many businesses were lost, and the town faced a daunting task of rebuilding once again. In the aftermath of both the fires, Jerome underwent a period of reconstruction, and this event marked a significant chapter in the town's history.

Over time, Jerome managed to rebuild, and the town continued to thrive as a mining community. It would later face economic ups and downs, experiencing multiple transformations, including becoming a ghost town before its resurgence as an artist's colony and tourist destination.

Today, the these fires are remembered as pivotal moments in Jerome's history, and the town's resilience and ability to adapt to adversity have contributed to its enduring appeal as a unique and historic destination.

The fires marked a turning point for Jerome. Instead of rebuilding with wooden structures, the town shifted to constructing buildings with brick and stone, which were more fire-resistant. The architectural style of the town changed as a result, giving Jerome a unique and charming character that still stands today.

A Possible Reason for the Haunting Past

Another interesting tale that I came across when researching for this chapter, is the peculiar method in which many of the buildings were constructed following the Great Fires.

Urban legends say that following the Great Fires, the boom in construction in Jerome cause a high demand for concrete, as prior to the fire most of the structures were constructed of wood, and the people of Jerome did not want a repeat of the devastation, so they opted for a material that was much more resistant: concrete. While this construction method would prevent the entire town from burning, it created a logistical nightmare.

Concrete is generally made of cement, water, and an aggregate such as sand or gravel. While water was readily available in Jerome, cement was not. Thus, all the cement needed to be hauled up a mountain. Additionally, the gravel and crushed rock dug out of mines was used as an aggregate, but it seems that the construction crews were concerned about running out of aggregate, so they looked elsewhere for sources of aggregate. They began cutting the aggregate with the ashes of the burnt city.

In the decades following the rebuild, the United Verde Hospital was built to provide medical care to the residents of the town and treat injured miners. The hospital also operated the only infirmary, and as roads that had been dirt in the past became paved, and sidewalks and steps were constructed out of concrete, the construction companies looked to the United Verde Hospital to provide the ash that they needed to mix with the concrete.

Thus, the legend says that one of the reasons why Jerome is one of the most haunted places in America is because when you walk the streets you are literally walking on the ashes of the dead miners and frontiersmen who once built and founded the city.

The United Verde Hospital was eventually turned into an Asylum, which further perpetuated this legend. Then the Asylum was closed, and the building sat vacant for decades before someone turned it into a hotel in 1994. Today it stands as the Jerome Grand Hotel, which is where you will be staying on this road trip.

The Jerome Grand Hotel
200 Hill Street, Jerome, Arizona
Reservations: (888) 817-6788

The Jerome Grand Hotel is a historic landmark that exudes an air of mystery and intrigue. The building itself stands tall on Cleopatra Hill, overlooking the vast expanse of the Verde Valley. Constructed in 1926, the hotel originally served as the United Verde Hospital, providing medical care to the employees of the United Verde Copper Company and their families.

Figure 44: The Jerome Grand Hotel. Photo taken by Timothy James Wilson.

It is said though by locals that the this was just one of three hospitals built by the mines that had a sinister undertone: as to avoid the perception that the mines were unsafe, the mines would move already dead workers who had succumb to injury or illness in the mine to one of the hospitals so that the mine's injury reports would stay low. This was an inventive method to circumvent safety regulations.

Whispers in the Shadows

The structure is a prime example of Spanish Colonial Revival architecture, featuring a red-brick façade, arched windows, and a prominent bell tower that stands as a symbol of the hotel's rich history. Inside, the hotel maintains its original layout, with long hallways, high ceilings, and vintage décor, evoking a sense of nostalgia for a bygone era.

The Jerome Grand Hotel has witnessed several historically significant events throughout its existence. During its time as a hospital, it played a crucial role in treating miners injured in accidents or suffering from mining-related diseases. Over the years, it gained a reputation for providing excellent medical care and became known as one of the finest hospitals in the region.

Notable individuals associated with the Jerome Grand Hotel include famous American entrepreneur and industrialist, John D. Rockefeller. It is said that Rockefeller himself sought treatment at the hospital during his visits to Jerome.

However, what truly sets the Jerome Grand Hotel apart is its reputation as a hub for paranormal and supernatural occurrences. Many guests and staff members have reported unexplained phenomena within its walls. The hotel is believed to be haunted by the spirits of former patients, doctors, and nurses who once occupied the building. Visitors have claimed to hear disembodied voices, footsteps echoing through empty corridors, and doors opening and closing on their own.

The Young Boy

One particularly troubling ghostly presence often reported is that of a young boy, believed to be a former patient. Witnesses have described seeing him wandering the hallways, playing with toys, or even tugging at their clothing. Others have reported encounters with shadowy figures, eerie whispers, and sudden drops in temperature, indicating the presence of otherworldly entities.

The Legend of the Young Boy is one of the most enduring and intriguing paranormal tales associated with the location. The story revolves around the spirit of a young boy who is said to haunt the hotel's hallways and rooms.

According to local lore, the boy's identity and the circumstances surrounding his presence at the hotel remain a mystery. Some versions of the legend suggest that he was a patient at the hospital when it operated, while others speculate that he may have been the child of a staff member or a visitor.

The boy's spirit is often described as mischievous and playful, engaging with guests and leaving an indelible impression on those who encounter him. Witnesses have reported hearing his laughter echoing through the corridors, seeing him play with toys in empty rooms, or feeling a gentle tug on their clothing as they walk by.

Many guests and staff members have shared their experiences with the young boy's spirit, creating a sense of fascination and intrigue surrounding his presence. Some visitors have even brought toys to leave for him, as if hoping to provide a source of comfort or entertainment in the afterlife.

The exact origin or reason for the boy's ghostly presence remains unknown, leaving room for speculation and personal interpretation. Some believe he may be attached to the hotel due to his untimely death or an unresolved emotional connection to the building. Others view his presence as a residual energy or an echo of the past, forever imprinted on the fabric of the hotel.

Regardless of the specific details, the Legend of the Young Boy has become an integral part of the Jerome Grand Hotel's haunted reputation. His playful nature and interactions

with guests add a touch of charm amidst the eerie ambiance of
the supernatural encounters reported within the historic walls.

Jerome Grand Hotel's Lady in White

The legend of the Lady in White at the Jerome Grand Hotel is
another captivating tale that has added to the hotel's reputation
for paranormal activity. This spectral figure, often associated with
haunted locations around the world, is said to make appearances
within the hotel's corridors and rooms.

According to the legend, the Lady in White is a ghostly
apparition of a woman dressed in a flowing white gown. Her
identity and the circumstances surrounding her presence in the
hotel remain a mystery. Some variations of the story suggest that
she may have been a former patient, a nurse, or even a bride who
met a tragic fate within the hospital or the town of Jerome.

Witnesses who have encountered the Lady in White
describe her as an ethereal figure, appearing suddenly and often
silently. She is sometimes seen wandering the hallways, gliding
gracefully or standing near windows, seemingly lost in her own
world. Her presence is often accompanied by a feeling of sadness
or melancholy, as if carrying the weight of a sorrowful past.

The Lady in White is known to evoke a sense of intrigue
and curiosity among those who encounter her. Some believe that
she may be a residual spirit, forever trapped in a loop, replaying
moments from her past. Others interpret her presence as a sign
of unfinished business or a lingering attachment to the place
where she met her untimely end.

As with many ghost stories, the specifics of the Lady in
White legend vary depending on the storyteller and the accounts
shared by witnesses. Nevertheless, her apparitions and the
emotional impact she leaves on those who see her have become

an integral part of the haunting lore surrounding the Jerome Grand Hotel.

Whether she is a lost soul seeking solace or a spiritual remnant of a bygone era, the presence of the Lady in White adds an air of mystery and melancholy to the already eerie ambiance of the hotel. Visitors who stay at the Jerome Grand Hotel often keep an eye out for her ghostly figure, hoping to catch a glimpse of the ethereal lady who forever wanders its historic halls.

The Tale of the Headless Man

The tale of the Headless Man at the Jerome Grand Hotel is a chilling legend that adds an extra layer of intrigue to the paranormal history of the location. This ghostly figure, as the name suggests, is said to haunt the premises without his head.

The story behind the Headless Man varies, with different versions circulating among locals and visitors. One prevalent account suggests that the man was a former miner who suffered a tragic accident while working in the nearby mines. It is believed that he met his demise in a horrific incident that resulted in the separation of his head from his body.

According to the legend, the Headless Man's spirit continues to wander the halls of the Jerome Grand Hotel, searching for his lost head or seeking closure for the untimely end he suffered. Witnesses who claim to have encountered him describe a chilling apparition—a torso and limbs without a visible head. Despite lacking this essential feature, the entity is said to emit an eerie presence, evoking a sense of fear and unease in those who come across it.

Encounters with the Headless Man are often fleeting, with witnesses reporting glimpses of the spectral figure disappearing into thin air or fading away before their eyes. Some accounts mention disembodied footsteps or the sensation of being watched by an unseen presence, further heightening the spine-tingling nature of the haunting.

The specific origin and details surrounding the Headless Man's story remain steeped in mystery, and it is unclear whether the legend has any historical basis or if it has evolved purely through the tales and experiences of those who have visited the hotel. Nevertheless, the eerie presence of a headless specter roaming the corridors of the Jerome Grand Hotel has become an integral part of its haunted reputation.

For guests and enthusiasts of the supernatural, the potential encounter with the Headless Man adds a macabre element to their visit, keeping them on edge as they explore the historic premises and immerse themselves in the spectral ambiance of the haunted tales surrounding the hotel.

The Phantom Bellboy

The legend of the Phantom Bellboy at the Jerome Grand Hotel is a captivating tale of a helpful and mysterious spirit that is said to assist guests during their stay. This apparition, resembling a bellboy or a hotel staff member from a bygone era, adds an intriguing twist to the paranormal experiences reported within the hotel.

According to the legend, guests have encountered a spectral figure dressed in vintage bellboy attire, complete with a uniform, cap, and a friendly demeanor. The Phantom Bellboy is known to appear unexpectedly, offering assistance to guests with their luggage, guiding them to their rooms, or attending to their needs. Some witnesses have even described interactions where the bellboy engages in polite conversation or provides recommendations for local attractions.

However, what sets the Phantom Bellboy apart is the mysterious nature of his presence. After completing his helpful duties, he vanishes into thin air, leaving guests in awe and questioning the supernatural occurrence they just experienced. Some guests have reported turning away for a moment, only to find the bellboy gone when they looked back. Others have noted a sudden change in the atmosphere, as if an ethereal presence had been momentarily among them.

The origins of the Phantom Bellboy are unclear, and his identity remains a mystery. Some speculate that he may be the spirit of a former hotel employee who dedicated himself to ensuring the comfort of guests during his time on Earth. Others believe that his appearance is a residual energy imprinted on the hotel, a lingering echo of the past hospitality and service that continues to manifest to this day.

While encounters with the Phantom Bellboy are rare, those who have experienced his otherworldly assistance have often felt a sense of gratitude and wonder. His appearance adds an element of nostalgia and charm to the hotel's haunted reputation, reminding guests that even in the realm of the supernatural, acts of kindness and helpfulness endure.

For visitors to the Jerome Grand Hotel, the possibility of an encounter with the Phantom Bellboy adds an extra layer of intrigue, as they anticipate the potential assistance or brief interaction with a friendly spirit from a bygone era. The interesting thing I find with the Phantom Bellboy legend here at the Jerome Grand Hotel is the similarity the story holds with the story of the Phantom Bellboy at the Hotel San Carlos.

Organized Crime

In addition to its supernatural reputation, the Jerome Grand Hotel has a darker side tied to its past. During the 1920s and 1930s, when the town of Jerome was a bustling mining community, it had associations with organized crime. The

Whispers in the Shadows

Prohibition era saw an influx of bootleggers and illicit activities, and it is rumored that the hotel may have been used as a meeting place for underworld figures involved in the smuggling and distribution of alcohol.

The Jerome Grand Hotel has been associated with organized crime due to its historical context and the town of Jerome's connection to illicit activities during the Prohibition era. While specific incidents or crimes directly linked to the hotel are not widely documented, the hotel's proximity to the mining community of Jerome at that time suggests a connection to the organized crime networks of the era.

During the 1920s and 1930s, the United States implemented the Prohibition, a nationwide ban on the production, sale, and distribution of alcoholic beverages. This period gave rise to the illegal production and smuggling of alcohol, leading to the emergence of organized crime syndicates that controlled the underground liquor trade.

Jerome, with its thriving mining industry and transient population, became a hotbed for such illicit activities. The town provided a convenient location for bootleggers to set up operations, hidden amidst the hills and canyons of Arizona. Its proximity to major cities like Phoenix and the Mexican border facilitated the transportation and distribution of illegal alcohol.

While there is no specific evidence linking the Jerome Grand Hotel to any particular crime or gang, it is believed that the hotel may have served as a meeting place or safe haven for those involved in the illicit alcohol trade. The town's notorious reputation as a hub for bootlegging and the presence of underground tunnels and secret passageways in Jerome have fueled speculation about hidden activities taking place within the hotel's walls.

It is worth noting that the association of the Jerome Grand Hotel with organized crime during the Prohibition era is based on historical context and the reputation of the town at that time. The exact extent of the hotel's involvement or specific incidents related to organized crime may be difficult to ascertain due to limited historical records and the secretive nature of such activities.

Nonetheless, the connection to the Prohibition era and its association with the illicit liquor trade add an intriguing element to the hotel's history and contribute to its allure as a place with a storied past, blending both supernatural and his

Today, the Jerome Grand Hotel stands as a testament to the town's rich past. It continues to welcome guests who seek an unforgettable experience, blending history, charm, and the possibility of encounters with the supernatural. Whether one is drawn to its haunted reputation, its architectural splendor, or its historical significance, the Jerome Grand Hotel remains a captivating destination that invites visitors to step back in time and explore the mysteries within its walls.

Arizona Copper Art Museum
849 Main Street, Clarkdale, Arizona
Information: (928) 649-1858

Sitting at the base of Woodchuck Mountain (the mountain that Jerome is situated on), the Arizona Copper Art Museum in Clarkdale, is a captivating establishment that showcases the rich history and artistic significance of copper in the region. I am going to note here, that if anyone in your party has a fear of heights or fear of cliff-side roads, that you visit Clarkdale either on your way to Jerome, or your way back, as the road up Woodchuck Mountain to Jerome can be a little anxiety provoking.

209

The building of the Arizona Copper Art Museum is a testament to the town's heritage, with its rustic charm and architectural elements reminiscent of the early 20th century. Originally constructed in 1928, the museum building was initially the Clarkdale Bank. Designed by renowned architect Robert T. Evans, it features a unique blend of Spanish Colonial Revival and Mission Revival styles. Its exterior boasts a stunning façade with intricate details, including decorative tile work and wrought-iron accents. The interior showcases high ceilings adorned with ornate chandeliers and grand arched windows that allow natural light to illuminate the space.

Figure 45: Arizona Copper Art Museum. Photo by Timothy James Wilson.

Throughout its history, the Copper Art Museum has witnessed Clarkdale's growth and contraction. The once thriving copper mining town played a crucial role in the state's mining industry. The museum itself stands as a tribute to this heritage, documenting the impact of copper mining on the region's economy and culture.

As for alleged paranormal or supernatural occurrences, the Copper Art Museum has gained a reputation for being a site of ghostly encounters. Numerous visitors and staff members have reported eerie sensations, unexplained sounds, and sightings of apparitions throughout the building.

If you really want a treat, show up across the street for breakfast at Violette's Bakery Café. Their Belgian Waffles will keep you fueled up for the walking involved with exploring both Clarksdale and Jerome.

The Phantom Teller

One prevalent paranormal account revolves around the ghostly figure of a woman believed to be a former bank employee, possibly a teller. The accounts of her presence within the museum are primarily based on eyewitness reports and local legends. Since her identity and background remain shrouded in mystery.

According to the stories, witnesses have described her as a figure dressed in vintage attire, usually wearing a white dress or clothing reminiscent of the early 20th century. She appears to be lost or disoriented, sometimes wandering the halls or standing in specific areas of the museum.

The exact origins and circumstances surrounding the ghostly woman are unclear, as there are no specific historical records or confirmed accounts linking her to any specific person who worked at the bank during its operation. Some speculate that she may have been a former employee who experienced a tragic event or suffered a personal loss, which could explain her lingering presence within the building.

Over time, the stories of the ghostly woman have become part of the local lore surrounding the Copper Art Museum. Visitors and staff members have shared their encounters, contributing to the museum's reputation as a site of paranormal activity. However, it is important to note that these accounts are based on personal experiences and should be considered as part of the museum's folklore rather than established historical fact.

The Lost Treasure

The legend of the Lost Treasure associated with the Copper Art Museum has captured the imagination of treasure hunters and enthusiasts for many years. The story goes that during the peak of the copper mining era, a wealthy miner or a group of miners supposedly hid a significant fortune in gold and valuable gemstones somewhere near the museum.

According to the legend, the precise location of the treasure remains a mystery, with various theories and speculations circulating among those intrigued by the tale. Some believe that the treasure might be buried deep within the surrounding landscape, hidden in a remote canyon or perhaps concealed within an abandoned mine shaft. Others speculate that it could be located within the town itself, possibly within a secret compartment or beneath a significant landmark.

While the exact origins and details of the treasure's existence are uncertain, the allure of discovering such a cache of wealth has enticed many individuals to embark on treasure-hunting expeditions in the area. Over the years, countless adventurers have explored the desert landscape surrounding Clarkdale, hoping to uncover clues or stumble upon the long-lost treasure. Some have even dedicated their lives to the pursuit, employing various methods such as conducting research, utilizing metal detectors, or following historical records and local legends.

Despite the efforts made by treasure hunters, no concrete evidence of the treasure's existence has been found to date. The Lost Treasure of the Copper Art Museum remains an enigma, heightening the mystery and fascination surrounding the museum and the history of copper mining in the region.

While it's essential to approach the legend with skepticism and acknowledge that the existence of the treasure is unverified, the tale adds an element of adventure and intrigue to the lore of the Copper Art Museum and continues to capture the imagination of those drawn to the possibility of discovering a hidden fortune.

The Mysterious Tunnel

The legend of the Mysterious Tunnel associated with the Copper Art Museum adds an element of intrigue and adventure to the museum's history. According to the tale, a secret underground tunnel once existed, connecting the museum to various locations within the town.

The specifics of the tunnel's purpose and routes vary in different versions of the legend. Some accounts suggest that the tunnel served as an escape route for miners during times of danger or emergencies. It was said to provide a hidden passage from the mines to the museum, allowing miners to quickly evacuate or seek shelter. This would have been especially useful during times of mine collapses, cave-ins, or other hazardous incidents.

In other versions, the tunnel is believed to have served as a means of transporting valuable copper ore discreetly. It is said that the tunnel connected the museum to nearby mines, businesses, or even a train station. Miners could allegedly move the copper ore through the tunnel, avoiding public attention and potential theft or sabotage.

While the legend of the Mysterious Tunnel adds an element of mystery to the museum's history, no concrete evidence has been found to substantiate its existence. Exploration attempts and investigations have not uncovered any physical traces of such a tunnel.

It's important to note that underground tunnels were not uncommon in mining towns like Clarkdale, as they provided practical transportation and safety measures. However, whether a secret tunnel specifically connected the Copper Art Museum to other locations remains a topic of speculation and folklore.

Despite the lack of verifiable evidence, the legend of the Mysterious Tunnel adds an air of excitement and adventure to the historical narrative of the Copper Art Museum. It sparks the imagination, prompting visitors to envision hidden passages and secret connections beneath the town's surface, contributing to the fascination surrounding the museum's rich copper mining heritage.

Other paranormal tale associated with the museum involves inexplicable temperature drops, disembodied voices, and the sound of footsteps echoing through empty corridors. Visitors have reported feeling a sense of unease or being watched while exploring the exhibits.

The Douglas Mansion
100 Douglas Road, Jerome, Arizona
Park Information: (928) 634-5381

Jerome State Historic Park and the Douglas Mansion is a historic site and museum located in Jerome. It offers visitors a glimpse into the town's rich mining history and provides insights into the lives of the people who lived and worked in the area during its heyday as a booming copper mining town.

Figure 46: The Douglas Mansion at Jerome State Historic Park. Photo by Timothy James Wilson.

The park is situated on a hill overlooking the town of Jerome and the picturesque Verde Valley. The Douglas Mansion itself was once the home of James S. Douglas, a prominent mining magnate. The mansion, built in 1916, is an impressive Spanish Colonial Revival-style building that stands as a testament to the wealth and influence of its former owner.

The Douglas Mansion serves as a museum that educates visitors about the history of Jerome and the mining industry that shaped the town's development. Inside the museum, you can find a variety of exhibits that showcase artifacts, photographs, and interactive displays related to the town's history. The exhibits cover topics such as mining techniques, the lives of miners and their families, and the challenges faced by the community.

The museum provides a detailed overview of the mining operations that drove Jerome's growth in the late 19th and early

20th centuries. Copper mining was the primary industry in the area, and the town played a significant role in meeting the demand for copper during World War I.

James S. Douglas, the mansion's original owner, was a prominent figure in the mining industry. He was involved in several successful mining ventures and played a key role in the development of the Jerome area. The mansion, which he used as a retreat, reflects his influence and the prosperity he enjoyed during his career.

In addition to the historical aspects, visitors to the park can enjoy stunning views of the town of Jerome, the Verde Valley, and the surrounding landscape. The elevated location of the mansion provides an excellent vantage point for appreciating the beauty of the area.

James S. Douglas

James S. Douglas was a distinguished mining engineer and entrepreneur whose impact on the mining industry of the late 19th and early 20th centuries remains significant. Born in Quebec, Canada, in 1837, Douglas embarked on a journey of mining knowledge, studying engineering at McGill University and further honing his skills at the Freiberg Mining Academy in Germany. His career soared when he joined the engineering staff of the Phoenix Mine in Nevada, where his innovative ideas and expertise gained him recognition. However, it was his association with the Copper Queen Mine in Bisbee, that solidified his legacy.

As part of the Copper Queen Consolidated Mining Company, Douglas modernized and expanded the mine's operations, leading to increased copper production and profitability. His influence extended to Jerome, where he spearheaded the development of the United Verde Copper Company and the United Verde Mine, transforming the town into a thriving mining hub. Beyond his business acumen, Douglas was known for his philanthropic efforts and support for educational initiatives. James S. Douglas passed away in 1918, leaving behind a lasting impact on mining technology and the communities he touched.

Inextricably tied to the legacy of James S. Douglas and the Jerome State Historic Park, the Douglas Mansion has garnered a reputation for being haunted, steeped in stories of supernatural encounters. Locals and visitors alike have reported witnessing the ghostly figure of James S. Douglas himself, with descriptions often matching his appearance during his lifetime. Some claim to have seen him wandering the mansion's halls, perhaps still overseeing the operations he once managed. Alongside Douglas, various other ghostly tales have woven a tapestry of haunting: the mysterious lady in white ascending the grand staircase, phantom footsteps echoing across wooden floors, doors opening and closing without explanation, and unexplained music filling the air. These chilling phenomena have spurred interest in ghost tours and paranormal investigations, inviting the curious to delve into the mansion's spectral history. While skepticism lingers, the legends of hauntings add a layer of intrigue to the mansion's already rich history, leaving visitors to ponder the enigmatic stories that shroud this historic site.

The Mysterious Lady in White at Douglas Mansion
The folklore of the mysterious lady in white at the Douglas Mansion is one of the many haunting tales that have added an air of mystery to the historic site. Legend has it that a ghostly woman dressed in white roams the mansion's corridors and rooms, captivating the imagination of those who hear her tale.

This mysterious woman in white is believed to be the ghost of a former resident or visitor to the mansion. Her identity and the circumstances of her presence are often shrouded in ambiguity, adding to the eerie allure of the story. Some versions of the legend suggest that she may have been a previous owner of the mansion, a family member, or even a guest who met a tragic fate within the mansion's walls.

Visitors report sightings of the woman in white regularly, often catching fleeting glimpses of her figure as she moves through the building. Some witnesses claim to have seen her ascending the grand staircase, her white dress flowing behind her. Others recount encountering her in various rooms, her presence leaving a chilling imprint on their memories.

The woman in white is often associated with an aura of sadness or mystery. Some interpretations of the legend speculate that she may be a lost soul, or a spirit bound to the mansion due to unfinished business or a tragic event. Her appearances are sometimes accompanied by cold spots, unexplained sounds, or other paranormal phenomena, adding to the sense of otherworldly presence.

While the true origins of the woman in white remain uncertain, her story has become an integral part of the mansion's haunted reputation. As with all legends of this nature, the tale has evolved over time, with each retelling adding its own nuances and interpretations. Whether a product of overactive imaginations or a reflection of something unexplainable, the woman in white at the Douglas Mansion continues to captivate those who are drawn to the mysteries of the paranormal.

The Jerome (Hogback) Cemetery
Jerome-Perkinsville Road, Jerome, Arizona

Perched atop Cleopatra Hill, the Jerome Cemetery, also known as the Hogback Cemetery, is a resting place that intertwines the past with the mysterious. Reverberating with whispers of history and local folklore, the cemetery has garnered a reputation for being haunted. Allegations of paranormal activity have woven a shroud of intrigue around the site, drawing those intrigued by the supernatural. Stories of eerie encounters and ghostly phenomena have emerged, including sightings of shadowy figures gliding among the headstones, full-bodied apparitions appearing briefly before fading, and even orbs of light captured in photographs. Such reports contribute to the cemetery's reputation as a place where the boundary between the living and the ethereal might blur.

Adding to its mystique, the Jerome Cemetery is said to house the final resting places of individuals who were integral to the mining era that defined Jerome's history. While specific legends of hauntings and documented apparitions are often shared through local lore, the cemetery's most famous residents are the everyday people who played a role in shaping the town. Though not necessarily famous in the traditional sense, the individuals buried here represent the tapestry of Jerome's past—a community of miners, families, and individuals who carved out their lives in the heart of the Arizona wilderness.

The Haunted Hamburger
410 Clark Street, Jerome, Arizona
Phone: (928) 634-0554

Maybe it's just me, but in my opinion, there is nothing better than a juicy hamburger, unless of course that hamburger is in a haunted building, in one of the most haunted towns in Arizona. So, whenever I am in Jerome, I stop by the Haunted Hamburger for some Chipotle Deviled eggs, a Haunted Burger and Jalapeño Coleslaw. It's a very Arizonan take on the American classics, but don't think that I would have sent you to a restaurant that wouldn't have a ghost story on the menu, as the name says, you might be eating your dinner with an unexpected guest, like the Miner's Ghost.

Figure 47: The Haunted Hamburger. Photo taken by Timothy James Wilson.

When planning to go to the Haunted Hamburger, especially on a weekend, I recommend stopping by the restaurant a few hours prior to when you plan on eating and getting your name on the list. This place is pretty popular, so it may behoove smart travelers to check in early, as often times the line can be pretty long; however, they do have a texting system, so you could stop in at 3:30 PM and get your name on the list, go explore town and return 6:00 PM when your table is ready. Yes, I have personally seen the line get to 2 ½ hours more than once.

The Miner's Ghost

One of the most prominent haunting legends involves the presence of the Miner's Ghost who is believed to linger within the building. According to the legend, the miner was a former resident of the building dating back to the days when it functioned as a boarding house for miners. The miner's apparition is said to be seen wearing typical clothing from the mining era, which includes a hat, boots, and sometimes carrying mining tools. Some accounts suggest that he might appear at the bar area or in corners of the restaurant.

In connection with the miner's presence, there have been reports of the distinct scent of tobacco smoke wafting through the air without any visible source. This phenomenon is often interpreted as the miner's way of making his presence known, as smoking was a common habit among miners in the past.

Beyond just being seen or sensed, some accounts claim that the miner's ghost is interactive. Staff and visitors have reported feeling as though they are being watched, or they've experienced strange touches or sensations that they attribute to the miner's presence.

Many patrons, including my wife and I, have experienced a general feeling of cold spots in the building. One summer evening a few years ago, we sat on the patio, where it was about 80 degrees out, and soon we were both shivering to stay warm, while other patrons seemed to be fine in typical summer attire. This can be complimented with a since of unease or being watched while inside the restaurant.

Alongside the miner's presence, disembodied voices and unexplained sounds have been reported. Some have claimed to hear faint whispers or conversations that cannot be attributed to any visible individuals.

There have been instances where the lights inside the restaurant have flickered or dimmed momentarily, even when there have been no apparent electrical issues. This phenomenon is sometimes attributed to the presence of spirits attempting to communicate.

The Cornish Pasty Company
403 Clark Street, Jerome, Arizona
Information: (928) 267-6474

The Cornish Pasty Company is kind of a local phenomenon to Arizona. I know they have a few restaurants out of state, but most of their restaurants are in Arizona. I first became familiar with this eatery in Jerome while literally traveling to this city to take photos for this book. Their food was so amazing, and at first bite I knew I had to include this place in my book.

The Cornish Pasty Company serves something called a Cornish Pasty, or Cornish Knocker as they are known across the pond where they originated in a small mining town called Cornwall in Southwest England. There is an entire haunted history to the Cornish Pasty, that we will need to travel to England to understand.

Cornish Knockers, also known as Tommyknockers in American Western mining lore, are legendary spirits originating from the tin mines. These mischievous entities earned their moniker "Knockers" due to the distinctive knocking sounds they made within the depths of the tin mines.

Residing in the darkest recesses of these mines, these spectral beings were often described as slight in stature, standing at just two feet tall, with long hooked noses. They had a peculiar habit of appearing to miners they favored, donning miniature replicas of miners' attire.

Figure 48: The Cornish Pasty Company. Photo Taken by Shirley Marie Wilson.

Miners in Cornwall had a tradition of sharing a portion of their meals with these spirits as an attempt to appease them. Cornish miners typically consumed pasties, a delectable mixture of spiced meat and potatoes enclosed in pastry, often featuring an apple filling at one end, rendering it a complete meal.

To prevent soiling the rest of their meal, miners would touch only the crimped edge of the pasty with their dirty hands, discarding the soiled portion for the Knockers.

When it was time to dine, a maiden above the mine shaft would shout "Oggy Oggy Oggy," and the miners would respond with "Oi Oi Oi." "Oggy" referred to the pasty.

The sound of Knockers knocking within the mine was seen as a favorable omen, signaling the presence of rich new veins or warning of impending danger.

One notable tale tells of a man who purchased a home in the mining district. He was startled by the sound of heavy boots ascending and descending his staircase. However, when he investigated, no one was to be found. A young maid eventually explained that the noises were the work of the Knockers, indicating a valuable tin lode beneath his house. This proved true, as his home concealed one of the most abundant tin mines ever discovered.

In another incident, a miner deep within a tin mine heard a mysterious voice calling his name between each strike of his hammer. He followed the voice, and as he moved away, a substantial rockfall occurred in the area where he had been working.

One superstition held that hearing Knockers outside a mine was an ominous sign of an impending death.

In the village of Breage in West Cornwall, a night watchman reported hearing distinctive knocking sounds followed by what seemed like the overturning of a trash bin. Despite finding no evidence of disturbance outside, he fell seriously ill and passed away shortly after sharing his experience with friends.

Although encounters with Knockers have dwindled with the decline of tin mining, many believe that these spirits still dwell in the deepest recesses of abandoned mines to this day.

The Connor Hotel
160 Main Street, Jerome, Arizona
Reservations: (928) 634-5006

Nestled within the rugged landscape of Jerome, the Connor Hotel stands as a timeless testament to the town's storied past and its connection to the mining industry that once fueled its prosperity. Erected in 1898 during the peak of the copper boom, the Connor Hotel served as luxurious accommodations for travelers, mine investors, and dignitaries who ventured to the bustling mining town. With its striking Victorian architecture, ornate detailing, and historic charm, the hotel transported guests to an era of opulence and grandeur. Over the years, the hotel's walls have borne witness to countless stories, from the dreams of fortune seekers to the tragedies and triumphs of a mining community that weathered the challenges of its time.

Figure 49: The Connor Hotel. Photo taken by Timothy James Wilson.

Yet, within the walls of the Connor Hotel, history has converged with tales of the supernatural, weaving an air of mystery that adds an extra layer of fascination. Accounts of paranormal activity have swirled around the hotel, capturing the attention of visitors and enthusiasts alike. Guests have reported hearing phantom footsteps echo through hallways in the dead of night, as if the spirits of past patrons continue to roam the corridors. Doors have been said to open and close of their own accord, a peculiar occurrence that defies explanation. The temperature within rooms and hallways has been known to fluctuate unexpectedly, leaving a chill in the air that evokes the presence of unseen entities.

Whispers in the Shadows

But it is the spectral figures that capture the imagination most profoundly. Some have shared stories of glimpsing shadowy figures moving just beyond the periphery of vision, while others claim to have seen apparitions that materialize and dissipate in the blink of an eye. The apparitions, often described as wearing clothing reminiscent of the hotel's heyday, evoke a sense of timelessness that blurs the boundaries between the past and the present.

As patrons dine in the hotel's restaurant, they may find themselves in the company of unseen companions, as whispered conversations and unexplained sounds linger in the air. The Connor Hotel has become a haven for those intrigued by the unexplained, drawing paranormal enthusiasts, curious visitors, and history aficionados alike. With its rich history and spectral stories, the Connor Hotel is a destination that invites guests to step back in time and perhaps catch a fleeting glimpse of the mysterious forces that continue to inhabit its halls.

Anna Hospkins: Jealous Hauntings

In the early 1920s, the quiet mining town of Jerome, was rocked by a shocking and violent incident at the Connor Hotel that would forever change the lives of those involved. The central characters in this gripping tale were Anna Irene Hopkins and Lucille Gallagher, both schoolteachers in the town.

Anna Hopkins, a woman marked by jealousy and suspicions of her husband Clarence's infidelity, reached a breaking point on March 31, 1921. Seated in the dining room of the Connor Hotel, Anna launched a vicious and premeditated attack on Lucille Gallagher. Without warning, she threw a tumbler filled with carbolic acid into Lucille's face, causing severe burns and excruciating pain.

Figure 50: The Connor Hotel. Photo taken by Shirley Marie Wilson.

The trial that followed revealed the depths of Anna's emotional instability. Witnesses shared stories of her erratic behavior, jealousy, and a long-standing feud with Lucille. Anna's defense argued that her mental state was compromised, while the prosecution contended that her attack was a result of uncontrolled anger and an undisciplined temper.

The jury's verdict on May 19, 1921, found Anna guilty of her crime. She was sentenced to serve 5 to 14 years in the state prison in Florence. Anna's life took several unexpected turns as her parole was granted, revoked, and then reinstated. Along the way, she faced personal tragedies, including the death of her son Robert P. Hopkins in a car crash in 1931.

Whispers in the Shadows

Today, the Connor Hotel, where the violent attack occurred, still stands as a historical landmark in Jerome. The Connor Hotel's dark history has given rise to stories of paranormal activity, with rumors that Anna's spirit continues to haunt the premises. Some believe that her intense emotions and the violence she unleashed have left an indelible mark on the hotel.

Visitors to the Connor Hotel have reported eerie experiences, such as sudden drops in temperature, unexplained sounds, and even apparitions believed to be Anna herself. The hotel's reputation as a haunted location has drawn the curious and the brave, eager to experience the ghostly presence for themselves.

Despite the passage of time, the tale of Anna Hopkins and Lucille Gallagher remains an enigmatic and haunting story. The complex motivations behind Anna's attack, the enduring rumors of her ghostly presence, and the indelible impact on the history of Jerome continue to captivate and intrigue those who delve into its history.

Liberty Theatre
110 Jerome Avenue, Jerome, Arizona
Information: (928) 649-9016

The Liberty Theatre, directly north of the Connor Hotel, stands as a silent witness to a bygone era of entertainment and a repository of enigmatic tales. This historic building boasts a storied past that blends the allure of the silver screen with the eerie whispers of paranormal activity.

Constructed in the early 20th century, the Liberty Theatre initially opened its doors to the eager audiences of Jerome in 1918. It quickly became a hub of cultural activity, offering a space for movies, live performances, and social gatherings. The building itself exudes an old-world charm, with its vintage marquee, ornate facade, and classic Art Deco architectural elements.

Figure 51: The Liberty Theatre (right) and the Connor Hotel (left). Photo by Timothy James Wilson.

Beyond its historical significance, the Liberty Theatre has gained notoriety for the whispers of the supernatural that seem to linger within its walls. Many visitors have reported an uncanny feeling upon entering the theater, as if they are stepping back in time to an era of grand cinematic experiences.

Over the years, numerous witnesses have claimed to have seen ghostly figures moving through the darkened theater. These apparitions are often described as shadowy forms or fleeting glimpses of people in vintage attire. Some believe that these specters could be remnants of patrons who once enjoyed films within the Liberty Theatre's walls.

Unexplained sounds echo through the theater, captivating those who are attuned to the supernatural. Visitors have reported hearing phantom footsteps, whispered conversations, and the faint rustling of seats when no one is around. The origins of these sounds remain a mystery, adding to the eerie ambiance of the venue.

Some accounts go beyond passive apparitions, describing encounters with entities that seem to interact with the living. Cold spots, sudden temperature drops, and gentle touches have left attendees perplexed and intrigued. It's as if the spirits of the past are trying to communicate with those who dare to venture into their realm.

The projection room of the Liberty Theatre holds a reputation as a focal point for paranormal activity. Projectionists have reported feeling an otherworldly presence while working alone in the dimly lit room. Some claim to have experienced unexplained equipment malfunctions or sensed an unseen observer watching them.

Given the persistent accounts of supernatural encounters, the Liberty Theatre has become a focal point for those interested in the paranormal. Allegations of hauntings have drawn investigators, mediums, and thrill-seekers to the site. Some visitors even speculate that the spirits of former theatergoers or performers might be drawn to the nostalgic atmosphere, refusing to relinquish their connection to the place that once brought them joy.

As the Liberty Theatre continues to stand as both a historical landmark and a source of ghostly tales, its mystique endures. Whether one believes in the paranormal or not, there is no denying the magnetic allure of a building that blends the allure of vintage entertainment with the shroud of the unknown. For those who step inside, the past and the present converge, and the line between reality and the ethereal becomes delightfully blurred.

The Projectionist is Dead

Deep within the historic Liberty Theatre, a chilling legend has taken root—the tale of the Ghostly Projectionist. This mysterious figure, shrouded in tragedy, is said to haunt the theater's projection room, forever bound to the place where he once operated the machinery that brought films to life.

The young man who was once a diligent and passionate projectionist at the Liberty Theatre during its bustling heyday, was known for his dedication to his craft, ensuring that every film was flawlessly presented to the eager audiences. However, fate took a sinister turn one fateful night.

On a stormy evening when the theater was aglow with the glow of the silver screen, disaster struck. A catastrophic mishap occurred in the projection room—a fire broke out, engulfing the room in flames before anyone could react. Trapped amidst the inferno, the projectionist lost his life, his dreams, and his earthly ties to the theater.

Yet, it seems that death did not sever his connection to the place he loved. Over the years, reports from employees, visitors, and paranormal enthusiasts have recounted eerie encounters in the projection room. Those who dare to step into this spectral domain have described a palpable sense of unease, as if they were not alone. Cold drafts and inexplicable chills often accompany this sensation, even on the warmest of days.

The most unsettling accounts involve encounters with a shadowy figure, standing silently amidst the flickering lights and projection equipment. Witnesses have reported feeling as though they were being watched by an unseen presence, a feeling that persists even when they turn to face the empty room.

But it's not just the sensation of being watched that has fueled the legend. Some visitors have reported hearing the faint sound of footsteps pacing across the floor, as if the ghostly projectionist is continuing his work in the afterlife. Others have claimed to hear faint whispers, as if the spirit is attempting to communicate or share his passion for the art of projection.

Whether this ghostly figure is a residual echo of the young projectionist's dedication, or a restless spirit tied to the projection room, the legend of the Ghostly Projectionist has woven itself into the fabric of the Liberty Theatre's history.

The Lady in Red

One of the most enduring legends surrounding the Liberty Theatre centers around the ethereal figure of the Lady in Red. As the tale goes, a glamorous woman dressed in a striking red gown is said to make periodic appearances, her presence felt as a flicker of movement, a fleeting glimpse, and an overwhelming sensation of otherworldly beauty.

The Lady in Red is believed to have lived during the theater's vibrant era, a time when elegance and grandeur graced the halls. Some versions of the legend suggest that she was an actress, or a performer associated with the theater, while others romanticize her as a theatergoer who enjoyed the performances in her resplendent red attire.

Witnesses who have encountered the Lady in Red often describe feeling a mix of awe and melancholy. She's said to appear near the stage or in the grand lobby, her presence marked by a gentle rustle of fabric and a faint scent of roses that lingers in the air before fading away. Some have even claimed to catch a glimpse of her form, elegant and timeless, before she vanishes into the shadows.

The origin of the Lady in Red and her connection to the Liberty Theatre remain unknown, but her lingering presence adds a touch of elegance and romance to the theater's haunted lore.

The Ghostly Audience Members

As the lights dim and the curtain rises, the Liberty Theatre's stage seems to come alive not only with living performers but also with the specters of an unseen audience. The legend of the Ghostly Audience Members tells of apparitions that materialize during performances, blending seamlessly with the living attendees as they watch the show.

Eyewitnesses have reported unusual occurrences during performances—faint whispers and laughter from empty seats, the sensation of someone brushing past them in the aisle, and even the sight of shadowy figures occupying seats that should be unoccupied. Some describe feeling as though they are part of a dual audience, sharing the experience with those from another time.

Perhaps the most haunting aspect of the Ghostly Audience Members legend is the sense of shared enjoyment. Some witnesses have reported feeling a palpable energy of appreciation and applause emanating from the spectral guests, as if they are reliving the joy of the performances they once attended.

While skeptics may attribute these experiences to the vivid imagination of theatergoers or the atmospheric qualities of an old building, those who have encountered the Ghostly Audience Members are convinced that the lines between past and present blur within the Liberty Theatre, allowing the echoes of long-gone audiences to join in the ongoing celebration of the performing arts.

As these legends continue to weave their mysterious threads through the history of the Liberty Theatre, they remind us that the past is never truly gone, and the spirits of those who once graced its stage and attended its performances may still linger, finding solace and connection in the world of the living.

The United Verde Mine
Jerome-Perkinsville Road, Jerome, Arizona

The United Verde Mine stands as a tangible relic of the town's mining heyday. To this day it is still one of the most productive Gold and Copper mines in the United States. Established in 1883, the mine's history is a blend of triumphs, tragedies, and the lingering mysteries of the past. As visitors venture into the depths of this historic mine, they are not only met with the echoes of pickaxes and the rumbling of carts but also with whispers of the paranormal that seem to traverse time itself.

The United Verde Mine, once a thriving copper behemoth, holds tales of arduous labor, strikes, and technological advancements that shaped the destiny of Jerome. Copper extracted from these tunnels fueled industries across the nation, leaving an indelible mark on the town and the mining landscape.

As visitors traverse the mine's passages, they can't help but feel the weight of history bearing down on them. However, it's not just the echoes of the past that reverberate through these tunnels. Reports of paranormal activity have lent an air of mystique to the United Verde Mine, captivating the imagination of those who dare to explore its depths.

Among the spectral phenomena reported, the mine is said to be haunted by the specter of a former miner, forever toiling in the dark corridors. Witnesses have described encountering an ethereal figure, dressed in old-fashioned mining attire, moving through the shadows as if still engaged in his labor. Some claim to have heard phantom footsteps, as if a miner's boots were still echoing through the chambers.

Visitors have reported an unsettling feeling of being watched or followed, even when alone in the mine's tunnels. Cold spots, inexplicable drafts, and sudden drops in temperature have left many wondering if they share the tunnels with unseen entities. These eerie occurrences often defy rational explanation, fueling beliefs that the mine is a conduit for the otherworldly.

The United Verde Mine and its haunting legends are a testament to the layers of history that lie beneath the surface of Jerome. Beyond the captivating tales of mineral riches and industrial labor, the mine offers a portal into the world of the unknown. Whether visitors come seeking the history of mining or the thrill of encountering the unexplainable, the United Verde Mine stands as a timeless enigma, bridging the gap between past and present, reality and the supernatural.

The Legend of Headless Charlie

The chilling legend of Headless Charlie at the United Verde Mine has captured the imagination of locals and visitors alike, infusing the mine's history with a haunting air of mystery. This macabre tale revolves around a tragic mining accident that purportedly led to the restless spirit of a miner forever known as Headless Charlie.

Headless Charlie was a miner who toiled deep within the bowels of the United Verde Mine during its heyday. One fateful day, tragedy struck when a catastrophic accident—be it a cave-in, an explosion, or some other calamity—claimed Charlie's life in the most gruesome manner imaginable: by severing his head from his body. This ghastly incident left an indelible mark on the mine's history, giving rise to the legend that endures to this day.

According to those who have ventured into the mine's dark tunnels, the apparition of Headless Charlie is said to roam the passages, a spectral figure devoid of a head but unmistakably human in form. Witnesses describe a faint, ethereal glow surrounding his body, casting an eerie light that stands out against the inky darkness of the mine. His headless form is often reported to be in a state of perpetual motion, as if eternally searching for something that has eluded him.

Visitors and miners alike have reported eerie encounters with Headless Charlie. Some claim to have caught fleeting glimpses of his figure, while others have been unnerved by the sensation of being followed through the labyrinthine tunnels. The sound of disembodied footsteps echoing in the distance and the sudden drop in temperature have left many with the uncanny feeling of being in the presence of a supernatural force.

Cold spots—areas where the temperature inexplicably drops—have been reported in the mine, often accompanying encounters with Headless Charlie. Some brave souls have even claimed to hear faint whispers emanating from the shadows, as if the ghostly miner is trying to communicate from beyond the veil of death.

The legend of Headless Charlie serves as a poignant reminder of the perilous and often tragic conditions that miners faced in their pursuit of precious metals. While historical records may not substantiate the specific incident, the tale endures as a testament to the dangers of mining and the indomitable spirit of those who worked these treacherous mines.

For those who dare to venture into the United Verde Mine, the legend of Headless Charlie adds an extra layer of anticipation and dread. As flashlight beams cut through the darkness, explorers may find themselves bracing for the chilling sight of a headless apparition lurking just beyond their line of sight.

Whether a product of imagination, folklore, or an actual encounter with the paranormal, the legend of Headless Charlie continues to captivate the hearts and minds of those who delve into the United Verde Mine's history. It stands as a testament to the power of local legends to transform a place, weaving together fact and fiction into a tapestry that transcends time, haunting the halls and tunnels of the mine for generations to come.

The Miner's Lament

Deep within the labyrinthine passages of the various mines in Jerome, but especially at the United Verde Mine, a haunting legend echoes through the tunnels—a tale known as the Miner's Lament. The story speaks of restless spirits, anguished cries, and the sorrowful echoes of those who met untimely ends in the pursuit of copper riches.

It is said that on certain moonless nights, when the mine is cloaked in a profound darkness, a mournful chorus rises from the depths. The Miner's Lament begins as a distant, ethereal sound, like a faint whisper carried on a gentle breeze. But as it drifts through the tunnels, it gains strength and clarity, evolving into heart-wrenching cries and soulful moans that reverberate off the walls.

The legend tells of miners who lost their lives in the mine's treacherous conditions—men who were trapped by cave-ins, overcome by toxic gases, or crushed beneath heavy machinery. Their spirits, unable to find rest, are said to gather in the darkest corners of the mine, their voices intertwining in a sorrowful chorus of despair.

As the tale goes, these spectral miners are forever trapped in a state of limbo, condemned to relive the final moments of their lives in a perpetual cycle of torment. The Miner's Lament is a poignant reminder of the sacrifices made by those who braved the dangers of the mine, hoping to secure a better future for themselves and their families.

Whispers in the Shadows

Many who have ventured into the United Verde Mine claim to have heard these ghostly cries—the haunting echoes of men who toiled in the depths and met tragic fates. Some say the sounds are most haunting during the stillness of the night, when the mine's passages are shrouded in darkness and the weight of history hangs heavily in the air.

Visitors report that the Miner's Lament starts as a distant, indistinct murmur, growing steadily louder and more distinct as they venture deeper into the mine. The cries seem to surround them, as if the walls themselves are bearing witness to the miners' anguish. Some claim to have felt an overwhelming sense of sadness and empathy, as if they were sharing in the miners' grief and suffering.

As the legend of the Miner's Lament continues to be shared, it serves as a powerful reminder of the human cost of mining and the enduring legacy of those who worked in the United Verde Mine. The haunting cries that echo through its tunnels are a testament to the resilience and spirit of those who came before, etching their stories into the very fabric of the mine's history.

Gold King Mine and Ghost Town
Perkinsville Road, Jerome, Arizona
Information: (928) 634-0053

The Gold King Mine Museum and Ghost Town, nestled in the picturesque hills of Jerome, stands as a fascinating blend of history, nostalgia, and eerie tales of the supernatural. This unique attraction offers visitors a glimpse into the past with its meticulously preserved buildings, vintage mining equipment, and the allure of a once-thriving mining community.

Figure 52: Gold King Mine and Ghost Town. Photo taken by Timothy James Wilson.

The Gold King Mine Museum and Ghost Town is a living testament to Arizona's mining heritage. Founded by Don Robertson in the 1960s, the site began as a labor of love—an endeavor to preserve the history of the area and share it with future generations. Today, it's a popular tourist destination that transports visitors back in time to experience the life of a mining town.

Amid the rustic buildings, antique cars, and vintage machinery, the site offers a comprehensive view of the mining industry's evolution and the challenges faced by those who lived and worked in these rugged landscapes. The museum houses an impressive collection of artifacts, including mining tools, vehicles, and household items, all contributing to a vivid portrayal of daily life during the mining boom.

Yet, beyond its historical significance, the Gold King Mine Museum and Ghost Town is also known for another facet of its allure—paranormal tales that have woven themselves into the fabric of the place.

Visitors and staff alike have reported eerie sightings of ghostly figures in period clothing wandering through the buildings and streets of the ghost town. These apparitions, often glimpsed from the corner of one's eye, vanish upon closer inspection, leaving an air of intrigue and uncertainty.

On certain quiet nights, whispers and faint voices are said to drift through the ghost town. These eerie murmurs are often untraceable, giving rise to speculation about the spirits that might still linger among the abandoned buildings.

The Haunted Bunkhouse

The old bunkhouse at the Gold King Mine Museum and Ghost Town is not just a relic of the past—it's a place where the echoes of history seem to linger a little too closely. Employees and visitors have shared chilling encounters within its walls that have solidified its reputation as a hotspot for paranormal activity.

Reports of doors slamming shut on their own, footsteps echoing down empty hallways, and the sensation of being watched have all been linked to the bunkhouse. In some instances, objects have moved or vanished without explanation, leaving behind an eerie sense that something beyond the realm of the living is at play.

One particularly unsettling story involves a staff member who entered the bunkhouse alone to retrieve some equipment. As they moved through the building, they suddenly heard the distinct sound of footsteps following them, even though they were certain they were the only person inside. When they turned around, the footsteps ceased, and an overwhelming feeling of unease settled over them. The incident left a lasting impression and added another layer of intrigue to the bunkhouse's reputation.

The Lingering Presence

As visitors stroll through the Gold King Mine Museum and Ghost Town, many have reported an inexplicable sensation of being watched or accompanied by an unseen presence. These experiences often occur in various parts of the ghost town and seem to transcend mere imagination.

Some visitors have described encountering sudden, inexplicable cold spots that seem to drift past them. Others have reported feeling a distinct change in the atmosphere, as if they've crossed an invisible threshold into a different realm. These lingering sensations have led many to believe that the spirits of those who once inhabited the town are still observing and guarding their former domain.

One visitor shared an account of feeling a gentle touch on their shoulder while standing in front of an old, weathered building. They turned around, expecting to see a fellow guest, but found themselves alone. The sensation was undeniable and left them pondering the possibility of contact with a presence from beyond.

The Old Mine Tunnel

The mine tunnel at the Gold King Mine Museum and Ghost Town is a portal to the past, a passage that once echoed with the sounds of miners hard at work. Today, it echoes with whispers of a different kind—whispers of the supernatural.

As visitors venture into the tunnel, some have reported hearing faint footsteps and shuffling sounds that seem to come from within the earth itself. These sounds defy logical explanation, as the tunnel is now empty and devoid of any living presence. Yet, those who have experienced these auditory anomalies are left with a sense that the past is not as distant as it may seem.

One account tells of a group of friends exploring the tunnel when they suddenly heard the sound of pickaxes striking rock and distant chatter. Believing that there must be another group of visitors ahead, they continued on, only to find the tunnel empty and silent. The mystery of those phantom sounds continues to intrigue and bewilder those who dare to venture into the depths.

These stories of the haunted bunkhouse, the lingering presence, and the old mine tunnel weave a tapestry of the paranormal at the Gold King Mine Museum and Ghost Town. Whether these experiences are a product of vivid imaginations, echoes of history, or something else entirely, they add a layer of mystery and allure to an already captivating destination. As visitors explore the site's rich history and engage with the unexplained, they become part of a narrative that bridges the gap between the living and the beyond.

Husband's Alley
154 Main Street, Jerome, Arizona

On the front of the Bolshevita Boutique, in the western most corner of the building you will find a Historic Marker that marks the location of Husband's Alley, the narrow walking alleyway between the Bolshevita Boutique and the Puscifer Store (140 Main Street). First glance might disregard this walkway, as just another walkway between buildings, but I assure you that it is not. Wives may want to make sure their husbands don't wander down this alleyway.

It was here, during Jerome's vibrant years that a district known as the old Cribs District, or "Husband's Alley," emerged.

This alleyway was notorious for its proximity to saloons, where patrons could effortlessly slip away from their revelry to engage in another form of diversion.

Figure 53: Husband's Alley. Photo taken by Timothy James Wilson.

The legends of Husband's Alley weave a tapestry of the macabre, intertwining tales of the human experience, tragedy, and a touch of the supernatural.

In days gone by, Jerome was a town where sex workers were scattered throughout, and brothels coexisted with saloons. As history unfurled, the businesses of pleasure were discreetly relocated to the streets behind Main, becoming the notorious Cribs District. This district was named after the small wooden structures that the ladies lived in, and entertained clients, that were called "cribs." This shift birthed the legends of women who once traversed these cobblestones, advertising their trade while men sought their services behind closed doors.

As the sun dips below the horizon, the alley casts long shadows that seem to conceal the stories of countless women who endured hardships and heartaches in the pursuit of survival. The cries of those who suffered in silence, their bodies and spirits scarred by the trials of the cribs, may still resonate within the shadows that dance across the cobblestones.

Visitors and those who tend to the alley have reported hearing faint whispers and laughter—a spectral echo of the women who once walked these paths. Shadowy figures sometimes emerge, their presence fleeting yet unmistakable, perhaps a glimpse into the past that refuses to fade away. Cold spots materialize out of nowhere, seemingly triggered by the passage of unseen forces, leaving behind a chilling reminder of the alley's haunted history.

Husband's Alley is more than just a physical space; it's a portal to a bygone era where the hierarchy of sex work played out against the backdrop of a mining town's bustling energy. The allure of companionship and the shadows of desperation converge, leaving an indelible mark on the present. As visitors traverse the cobblestones, they tread upon layers of history and sorrow, their steps echoing the ghostly footfalls of women who once walked this same path.

Husband's Alley stands as a testament to the complexities of human experiences—both the highs and the depths. As the wind carries whispers of forgotten tales, the alley becomes a living history, an ever-present reminder of the lives lived and lost in its shadows. Through the legends of hauntings and the echoes of the past, Husband's Alley beckons those who dare to explore its history—a haunting melody that lingers on, forever entwined with the souls who once called it home.

The Haunting of Sammie Dean

In the heart of Husband's Alley lies a haunting story that echoes through time—a tale of tragedy, violence, and a restless spirit named Sammie Dean. Born in the early 20th century, Sammie's life would take a dark turn, forever binding her to the alley's cobblestones.

Sammie Dean was a woman of her era, navigating the tumultuous landscape of Jerome's Cribs District. In 1931, Sammie's life was tragically cut short in a chilling act of violence. The perpetrator of her untimely demise was the son of a powerful and influential member of the community. Strangled and silenced, Sammie's death sent shockwaves through the town, casting a somber pall over the alley where she once walked.

Yet, death did not sever Sammie's connection to the place that had been both her livelihood and her prison. In the years following her tragic passing, numerous accounts emerged of Sammie's ghostly presence lingering in the alley's shadows.

Those who have encountered Sammie's spirit describe unsettling experiences—a presence felt even when the alley appears deserted. Witnesses have reported hearing footsteps echoing in the silence, as if someone is walking unseen beside them. Whispers of laughter, soft and ethereal, have been heard when no living soul is around. Some visitors claim to have caught glimpses of a fleeting figure, Sammie's apparition perhaps, moving as if lost between this world and the next.

The building where Sammie once resided is said to be particularly haunted. Visitors have reported sudden drops in temperature, as if an icy breath brushes against their skin. Eerie apparitions have been witnessed, manifesting as shadowy figures that seem to materialize and fade away like wraiths in the night.

Despite the passage of time, Sammie's story refuses to fade away. Her spirit's lingering presence stands as a reminder of the injustices faced by women of her time, trapped in a cycle of exploitation and violence. Her story is a chilling testament to the power of tragedy and the resilience of the human spirit, as well as a haunting reminder of the darkness that still lingers in the alleys of Jerome.

As the wind whispers through Husband's Alley, it carries with it the echoes of Sammie's tale—a tale that transcends death, giving voice to a woman whose spirit still walks among us, seeking solace and perhaps justice in the afterlife.

Jennie's Place
136 Main Street, Jerome, Arizona

Jennie's Place, also known as the "Jennings Hotel," is a historic building located on Main Street, near Husband's Alley. Originally constructed in 1924, it was built as a boardinghouse to accommodate single miners who worked in the nearby United Verde Mine. It has since been converted to shops along Main Street. Over the years, the building has undergone various transformations and renovations, and today it stands as a distinctive artist-in-residence hotel, where each room is uniquely designed by different artists.

The building's history is rooted in its association with the mining industry that once thrived in Jerome. During the early 20th century, Jerome was a bustling mining town known for its rich copper deposits. The boardinghouse provided lodging for the men who toiled in the United Verde Mine, offering a place to rest and recuperate after long shifts underground.

As for its reputation for being haunted, Jennie's Place has become a focal point for tales of paranormal activity. Visitors, guests, and even some artists who have stayed at the hotel have reported experiencing eerie phenomena that they attribute to spirits from the past. The stories of hauntings at Jennie's Place include:

guests have reported hearing unexplained noises, such as footsteps, whispers, and doors opening and closing on their own. Cold spots, where the temperature suddenly drops, have also been reported in various areas of the building.

Some individuals have claimed to have seen shadowy figures or apparitions dressed in period clothing, reminiscent of the early 20th century. These sightings are often attributed to the spirits of former miners or residents who may still roam the premises.

There have been accounts of objects moving without explanation or being displaced from their original positions. Some guests have described instances where items were seemingly moved by an unseen presence.

Jennie Bauters

Jennie Bauters was a historical figure who is connected to the history of Jennie's Place. While not much is known about her personal background, she gained notoriety due to her tragic and untimely death. Her story has become intertwined with the lore of the haunted Jennie's Place.

Jennie Bauters was a young woman who lived during the early 20th century. She worked as a sex worker in Husband's Alley. The circumstances of Jennie Bauters' murder are full of mystery and speculation. According to local legends, Jennie was allegedly murdered by the son of a prominent and influential member of the town. The exact details of the murder and the identity of the murderer vary in different versions of the story. Some say that she was strangled to death, while others suggest that she was stabbed. The motivation behind the murder is often attributed to a dispute or altercation, possibly related to her profession or personal matters.

Jennie Bauters' untimely death is believed by some to be the reason for her lingering spirit at Jennie's Place, formerly known as the Jennings Hotel. Visitors and guests have reported experiencing paranormal activity that they associate with Jennie's ghost. Common phenomena attributed to her presence include footsteps, whispers, cold spots, and even sightings of an apparition resembling a woman from the early 20th century.

The name "Jennie" associated with the hotel is likely a reference to Jennie Bauters, who was a part of the town's history during a tumultuous era. Her tragic fate and the circumstances surrounding her death have contributed to the building's reputation as a haunted location. The stories of her spirit wandering the hotel's corridors add to the allure and mystique of the establishment.

Chapter Eight: Ghostly Encounters on Route 66

Kingman

Figure 54: Kingman's display of classic cars and trucks is very extensive on Route 66. Photo taken by Timothy James Wilson.

Kingman is, as I feel, the most forgotten city in Arizona. The city of just 33,000 people remains one of the last remnants of Route 66. Unfortunately, though, Kingman is often just thought of as a place to fill up your gas tank on the way to Las Vegas for most Arizonians. I am optimistic though that this chapter will change your feelings about the city that traverses' eras, from the wild days of the Old West to the iconic era of Route 66. Kingman is a place where history is alive, and the so are some of the historic spirits that founded the area.

Before we get into the history and geography of the town, there are a few things that I want to say. Of all the road trips that I have included in this book, Kingman can be one of the most frugal, as the biggest expense on this trip is probably going to be gas to get there. The motel and other sights listed here are really inexpensive, and in the town of Kingman a dollar can go a long way. At the time that I am writing this book, a room at the El Travatore Motel is running $109.00 per night, and it is a nice roadside motel.

As far as dining goes, the town is broke up into two distinct areas: the historical district on Andy Devine Avenue and Beale Street, which offers a fair share of places to eat that all kind of revolve around the idea of a 1950's diner. The other area that you can look is on Stockton Hill, where you will find the more modern dining options. Unfortunately, in our travels to Kingman, my wife and I have never found a restraint that stands out to us, we have however found a restaurant that serves a chicken sandwich that is medium rare and will awaken you in the middle of the night with haunting stomach issues (that's called food poisoning), but at the very least will keep you safe from the ghosts in the motel.

The history of Kingman is a mosaic of cultures, industries, and stories that have converged over the years. Once a vital stop along the Santa Fe Railroad, Kingman's roots run deep, shaped by Indigenous communities, Spanish explorers, and pioneers who sought to tame the wild frontier. The city's strategic location at the crossroads of historic trails and highways has made it a melting pot of influences, a hub of commerce, and a bridge between the past and the present.

Today, the city is a popular destination to visit due to the allure of Route 66. Additionally, the Disney movie Cars was inspired by Kingman, Peach Springs, and Oatman. The area has a number of really interesting places to visit, and a rather remarkable landscape.

El Travatore Motel
1440 East Andy Devine Avenue, Kingman, Arizona
Reservations: (928) 753-6520

Nestled along the outskirts of a quaint southwestern town, the El Trovatore Motel stands as a silent sentinel, capturing the essence of a bygone era. Its vibrant adobe façade, adorned with hand-painted murals depicting desert landscapes and Spanish motifs, invokes a sense of nostalgia. The motel's layout is centered around a sun-dappled courtyard with a trickling fountain, creating an oasis of serenity amid the arid landscape. Each room boasts a unique blend of vintage furnishings and modern amenities, preserving the essence of mid-20th-century motel culture.

The El Trovatore Motel, born in the post-World War II era, emerged as a beacon for weary travelers seeking respite from the endless stretches of desert highway. Established in 1950 by the visionary entrepreneur Carlos Ramirez, the motel quickly gained renown for its warm hospitality and eye-catching exterior. Over the decades, it became a cherished stopover for travelers exploring the southwestern United States, a living testament to the region's rich history.

Amid the colorful history of El Trovatore Motel, whispers of spectral visitors and eerie occurrences have woven a tapestry of paranormal intrigue. Guests and staff alike have reported inexplicable footsteps echoing through empty hallways, cold spots that seem to defy the desert heat, and fleeting glimpses of shadowy figures. The most enduring legend centers around the tragic tale of Maria Gonzales, a young woman whose love was torn apart by circumstances beyond her control. It is said that her restless spirit still roams the courtyard, pining for her lost love.

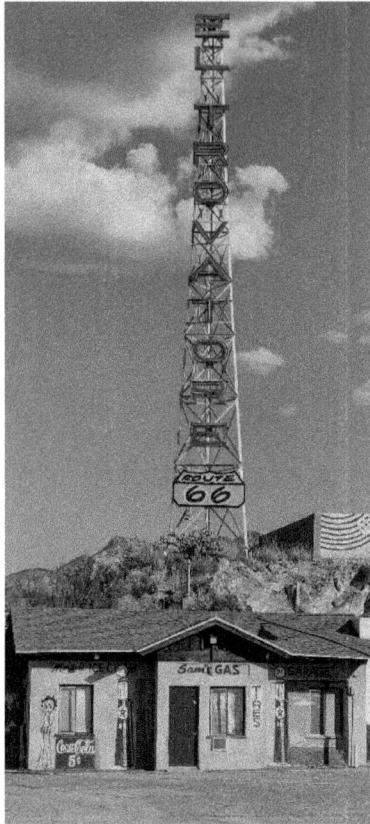

Figure 55: The El Trovatore Motel on Route 66. Photo by Timothy James Wilson.

While El Trovatore Motel predominantly exudes an air of nostalgia and mystique, it also bears witness to a darker underbelly of history. In the late 1970s, the motel inadvertently found itself linked to a notorious criminal escapade. A gang of bank robbers, seeking a hideout, took refuge within the motel's rooms, leaving behind a trail of fear and uncertainty. The ensuing standoff with law enforcement unfolded in a tense 48-hour period, etching another layer of intrigue into El Trovatore's history.

Timothy James Wilson

Oddities, too, find their place in the motel's story. Whimsical artifacts, accumulated over the decades, decorate the lobby—a mishmash of trinkets and relics left behind by travelers from all walks of life. A taxidermy collection of regional wildlife sits next to antique radios, vintage travel posters, and a collection of mismatched keys that once opened doors to memories long past.

The El Trovatore Motel stands as a testament to the interwoven threads of history, hauntings, and oddities. Its adobe walls have borne witness to the ebb and flow of time, from the heyday of road trips to the digital age of travel. With its captivating legends and whispers of the otherworldly, the motel offers not just a place to lay one's head, but an opportunity to traverse the corridors of time, experiencing the layers of stories that have shaped this desert oasis.

Additionally, the murals on the walls of the motel are quite remarkable, and the motel has a fair share of themed rooms, including a Marylin Monroe room.

The Fantasma of Maria Gonzales

The tale of Maria Gonzales, a haunting and tragic narrative, has become an integral part of the El Trovatore Motel's mystique. Legend has it that Maria's story unfolds in the midst of the motel's courtyard, where her presence is said to linger to this day.

In the mid-20th century, during the heyday of the motel, Maria Gonzales was a young woman whose heart was captivated by a dashing musician passing through the southwestern town. Their love blossomed against the backdrop of the desert sunsets, the strains of his guitar serenading her under the starlit skies. Their bond seemed unbreakable, an oasis of happiness in an otherwise arid existence.

However, fate has a way of casting shadows even on the most vibrant of romances. The musician's journey was marked by an itinerant spirit that could not be tethered. He was drawn by the allure of distant stages, melodies that whispered his name in cities far beyond the horizon. Duty to his craft tore him away from Maria's side, leaving her behind with a heart heavy with longing.

As the days turned into weeks, and the weeks into months, Maria's hope began to wane. News of her lover's exploits reached her ears through the whispers of passing travelers. Rumors painted a picture of fame and fortune, but the distance between them only grew. Her letters went unanswered, and her dreams of reuniting seemed to evaporate like mirages in the desert.

Despair took hold of Maria's heart, and in her anguish, she penned a final letter, confessing her enduring love and the depths of her sorrow. Clutching the letter to her chest, she retreated to the courtyard of El Trovatore Motel one moonlit night, beneath the very fountain where the waters had once laughed with joy.

It is said that Maria's spirit never left that courtyard. Her ghostly figure has been glimpsed by many over the years— dressed in a flowing gown, her face a mask of sorrow and yearning. Some claim to have heard the faint strains of a guitar carried on the wind, as if the musician's melodies were still trying to reach her.

Her presence is both a poignant reminder of lost love and a haunting tale that has become intertwined with the motel's history. To this day, visitors and guests who step into the courtyard of El Trovatore Motel might feel a shiver down their spine, as if the echoes of Maria's heartache still reverberate through the desert air. Whether a tale of true love or a figment of the imagination, Maria Gonzales has become an eternal resident in the collective consciousness of those who wander through the motel's adobe corridors.

The Standoff

The notorious chapter of the El Trovatore Motel's history involving a gang of bank robbers and a tense standoff is a tale that has left an indelible mark on the motel's legacy. The events took place during the late 1970s, casting a shadow over the peaceful facade of the desert retreat.

In those days, the motel still retained its reputation as a favored stop for travelers traversing the desert highways. However, fate took a dark turn when a gang of seasoned bank robbers sought refuge within the El Trovatore Motel's rooms after a daring heist. They were on the run, desperate to evade the law enforcement agencies that were hot on their trail.

The gang's sudden arrival sent shockwaves through the quiet community, and a sense of unease permeated the once-tranquil atmosphere. As authorities closed in, the situation escalated into a tense standoff that would test the nerves of both law enforcement officers and the criminals holed up within the motel.

For two harrowing days, the motel became the center of a high-stakes confrontation. Law enforcement cordoned off the area, barricading roads and establishing a perimeter around the El Trovatore Motel. Negotiators attempted to establish communication with the robbers, while residents and curious onlookers gathered at a distance, anxiously awaiting the resolution of the standoff.

The situation reached a climax on the second night, as negotiations broke down and gunfire erupted. The ensuing exchange of bullets shattered the stillness of the desert night, punctuated by the glare of flashing lights and the wailing of sirens. Eventually, the gang members were apprehended, though not without further violence and chaos.

The aftermath of the standoff left an indelible impact on both the motel and the community. While the scars of that dark period have gradually faded, the echoes of the past remain. Visitors and locals sometimes speak in hushed tones about the incident, as if the memory of those tense days still lingers in the desert winds.

The tale of the gang of bank robbers and the subsequent standoff serves as a reminder that even amid the peaceful vistas of the desert, stories of crime and desperation can take root. The El Trovatore Motel's history is a tapestry woven with threads of both tranquility and turmoil, showcasing the multifaceted nature of the human experience.

The Route 66 Museum
120 West Andy Devine Ave, Kingman, Arizona
Information: (928) 753-9889

In the middle of Historic Kingman, right on Route 66, the Route 66 Museum stands as a captivating tribute to the iconic highway that once connected the Chicago and West Coasts of the United States. As you step through its doors, you embark on a journey through time, immersing yourself in the vibrant history of Route 66 and the communities it touched.

Once heralded as the "Main Street of America," Route 66 emerged as a lifeline for travelers during the early 20th century. Stretching from Chicago to the Pacific Ocean, this highway traversed diverse landscapes and countless towns, serving as a symbol of American exploration and ambition. From the Dust Bowl migrants seeking refuge during the Great Depression to the post-war road trippers chasing adventure, Route 66 bore witness to a kaleidoscope of stories and experiences.

Figure 56: The Route Museum and Vister Center Gift Shop in Kingman. Photo taken by Timothy James Wilson.

The Route 66 Museum in Kingman serves as a time capsule, preserving the spirit of the legendary highway. Housed within a restored railway depot, the museum boasts an eclectic collection of artifacts, photographs, and interactive exhibits that chronicle the road's evolution. Vintage automobiles, neon signs, and retro gas station memorabilia transport visitors to an era when the highway was a lifeline and a symbol of freedom.

Interactive displays invite guests to experience the nostalgia of the open road, allowing them to listen to radio broadcasts of the past, sit behind the wheel of a classic car, and explore the quintessential diners that dotted the route. A replica of a 1950s drive-in theater, complete with a vintage car, offers a glimpse into the entertainment culture that flourished along the highway.

The history of Route 66 is intertwined with tales of the paranormal, and the Route 66 Museum in Kingman is no exception. The Route 66 Museum in Kingman, is steeped in legends of paranormal activity, adding an extra layer of intrigue to its historical significance. While these stories are not officially substantiated, they have become part of the local lore and contribute to the mystique of the museum.

One of the most commonly shared tales involves the sound of phantom footsteps echoing through the museum's corridors during the quiet hours of the night. Visitors and staff have reported hearing distinct, unexplained footsteps that seem to move through the exhibits, as if retracing the paths of travelers from the past.

Another chilling account centers around a night security guard who allegedly encountered a translucent figure near the museum's collection of vintage cars. According to the story, the guard was conducting a routine check when they noticed a faint, ghostly silhouette moving among the vehicles. The figure reportedly vanished as the guard approached, leaving behind a sense of unease.

Some visitors have claimed to witness shadowy figures moving among the exhibits, their forms darting in and out of view. These figures are often described as fleeting and indistinct, leaving observers with a sense that they might be catching glimpses of spirits from another era.

Accounts of objects moving on their own or items being rearranged within the museum have also contributed to the eerie reputation. While these occurrences might have logical explanations, they have added to the atmosphere of mystery and speculation.

Cold spots, areas where the temperature inexplicably drops, have been reported within the museum. These sudden drops in temperature are often associated with paranormal activity and are believed by some to be a sign of spiritual presence.

The Route 66 Museum bridges the tangible past with the spectral mysteries of the present. As visitors explore the artifacts and stories of the iconic highway, they might find themselves wondering whether the spirits of travelers past continue to journey alongside those who pay homage to the road that captured the American imagination.

The Haunted Motel on Route 66

In this legend, travelers come across a seemingly ordinary motel while driving along Route 66. As the sun sets and darkness falls, the motel's neon sign begins to flicker to life, casting an eerie glow that seems to emanate from within the walls.

Curious and tired from the road, travelers decide to check in for the night. Inside, they find a vintage interior frozen in time, reminiscent of a bygone era. The rooms are well-maintained, but there's an unsettling feeling in the air—an inexplicable chill that seems to follow them.

During the night, strange things occur. Guests report hearing whispers in the hallways, doors creaking open and shut on their own, and even glimpsing shadowy figures moving about. Some claim to have seen objects move on their own or to have felt an otherworldly presence at the foot of their beds.

The most chilling aspect of the legend is the persistent glow that emanates from certain rooms, even when the lights are turned off. The source of this eerie illumination remains a mystery, and no amount of investigation can explain why these rooms seem to be bathed in an otherworldly light.

In the morning, as the sun rises and the glow fades, travelers check out of the motel with a mixture of relief and unease. The legend lives on, as those who have experienced the "Glowing Motel" on Route 66 recount their eerie encounters and speculate about the origins of the supernatural phenomena.

This legend taps into the fascination with the unknown and the uncanny, reminding us that even the most mundane places can hold secrets beyond our comprehension. It's a tale that invites travelers to contemplate the mysteries that exist just beneath the surface of the familiar, adding an extra layer of intrigue to their journeys along the historic highway.

Locomotive Park
310 East Beale Street, Kingman, Arizona

Across the street from the Route 66 museum is Locomotive Park, a captivating destination for history enthusiasts and railroad aficionados. This park offers a fascinating glimpse into the region's rich railroad heritage. At its heart lies the magnificent Santa Fe steam locomotive, Engine 3759, a true relic from the past. This majestic locomotive, built in 1927, stands proudly as a symbol of the era when railroads played a pivotal role in shaping the American West.

Figure 57: Locomotive Park. Photo taken by Timothy James Wilson.

Visitors can explore the intricacies of this historic locomotive, gaining insights into its workings and the bygone era it represents. Locomotive Park provides a serene and shaded environment, making it a delightful spot for picnics and relaxation, while also serving as a point of interest for those traversing the iconic Route 66. It's a must-visit destination for anyone looking to immerse themselves in the history of Kingman and the significance of railroads in its development.

However, the locomotive has a history, as it is said that on a full moon, in the middle of the night you can look into the cab and see the ghost of the locomotive's engineer, still monitoring the controls of the locomotive.

The Hotel Brunswick
315 East Andy Devine Avenue, Kingman, Arizona
Reservations: (928) 377-5461

The Hotel Brunswick, a three-story structure, boasts a charming exterior characterized by its decorative wooden balconies, arched windows, and intricate trim work. The lobby, adorned with period furniture and vintage decor, evokes a sense of nostalgia for a bygone era. The hotel's 36 rooms, while updated for modern comfort, still retain elements of their historical charm.

Figure 58: The Hotel Brunswick on Route 66. Photo taken by Timothy James Wilson.

Over the years, the Hotel Brunswick has garnered a reputation for more than just its historical significance—it's also become known for its purported paranormal activity. Guests, staff, and visitors have shared stories of strange occurrences that have both intrigued and unsettled those who have experienced them.

One of the most enduring legends involves a spectral woman dressed in a flowing white gown. This apparition is often seen walking the halls or standing at the foot of beds before vanishing into thin air. Some believe she may have been a former guest or staff member who met a tragic fate within the hotel.

Many individuals have reported hearing phantom footsteps echoing through the hotel's corridors, particularly during the quiet hours of the night. The sound of footsteps on hardwood floors has been heard even when there's no visible source for the sounds.

Visitors have spoken of mysterious knocking, rapping, and tapping sounds emanating from empty rooms or corridors. These noises are often attributed to the building's haunted reputation.

Cold spots—areas where the temperature suddenly drops—have been experienced by guests and staff in various parts of the hotel. Some believe that these temperature fluctuations might be indicative of paranormal presence.

Reports of objects moving without any apparent cause have added to the tales of paranormal activity. Doors opening and closing by themselves and items shifting position have been recounted by multiple witnesses.

Some guests have described waking in the middle of the night to find a spectral figure standing near the foot of their bed. These figures are often described as ethereal and translucent, leaving individuals with an eerie feeling of being watched.

Unfortunately, the Hotel Brunswick no longer operates as a hotel, but has been converted into a high-end luxury apartment building. There are rumors that occasionally a room or two becomes available on a popular vacation rental website, but I have not found it.

The Ghost Town of Chloride
Chloride, Arizona

From Kingman, the drive to Chloride is about 18 miles to Grasshopper Junction, where you will drive east until you reach Chloride, approximately 4 miles down the 125. Chloride is a well-preserved ghost town that provides a fascinating window into the history of the American West. Founded in the late 1800s, Chloride experienced its heyday during the silver mining boom of the late 19th century. At its peak, it boasted a thriving population and numerous businesses that catered to the needs of miners and settlers.

Figure 59: Chloride. Photo taken by Timothy James Wilson.

Today, Chloride is a quiet and picturesque ghost town that retains much of its historic charm. Visitors can explore the remnants of the town's past, including old mining structures, abandoned buildings, and artifacts from its mining days. The town's location in the Cerbat Mountains adds to its rugged and scenic appeal.

Chloride is not only known for its historical significance but also for its reputation as a place of paranormal activity. Over the years, visitors and locals have shared stories of ghostly encounters and unexplained phenomena that have contributed to Chloride's mystique.

The Ghostly Bride at the Pioneer Cemetery

In the heart of the Cerbat Mountains, nestled among the whispering pines, lies the Haunted Pioneer Cemetery. Its weathered tombstones stand as silent sentinels to a bygone era, a testament to the lives of those who once called this rugged land their home. Among the stories whispered among the winds, one tale rises above the rest—the legend of the Ghostly Bride.

Long ago, in the days of the Arizona frontier, a love story unfolded that would leave an indelible mark on the land and the hearts of those who hear its echoes. The protagonist of this tale was a radiant young woman named Eliza, a vision of beauty and innocence. Her heart belonged to Samuel, a dashing young miner with dreams as vast as the desert sky.

As their love blossomed, the couple dreamed of a future together, a life of happiness and companionship. The promise of marriage hung in the air, and preparations for their wedding day were underway. Eliza's eyes sparkled with anticipation, her heart brimming with joy.

But fate, as it so often does, had other plans. On the eve of their wedding, tragedy struck. Eliza's life was cut short by a sudden and devastating illness, leaving Samuel devastated and the entire community in mourning. The town wept for the loss of a bright star extinguished all too soon.

On the day that was meant to unite their souls forever, Samuel stood before an empty altar, his heart heavy with grief. The wedding bells tolled mournfully, a poignant reminder of the love that was never fully realized. With the sun setting behind the Cerbat Mountains, Samuel made a solemn vow—a promise that transcended life and death itself.

In the years that followed, visitors to the Haunted Pioneer Cemetery would speak of a vision—a ghostly apparition in a flowing white gown, her form radiant against the moonlit night. It was said that she wandered among the tombstones, her presence a mix of melancholy and ethereal grace. Some claimed to have glimpsed her near the tombstone that bore her name, her eyes holding a timeless sadness.

Witnesses recounted encounters filled with unexplained phenomena. Eerie sounds would fill the air, whispers carried by the wind, and footsteps that echoed as if from another realm. The air would grow chilly, and a feeling of being watched would settle upon those who dared to linger after dark.

But the most haunting aspect of the legend was the bride's affinity for the living. Some who visited the cemetery reported experiencing an overwhelming surge of emotion—an intense sadness, a deep sense of longing, or even an unexpected joy that defied explanation.

While skeptics dismissed these stories as mere tales, believers saw in them a testament to the enduring power of love, a connection that transcended the boundaries between life and death. To them, the Ghostly Bride was a symbol of a love that defied time, a reminder that even in the realm of the supernatural, the heart's yearnings remained steadfast.

And so, the story of the Ghostly Bride of the Haunted Pioneer Cemetery continues to captivate those who visit the site. As they walk among the tombstones and feel the winds carry echoes of the past, they can't help but wonder if Eliza's spirit still roams the land, seeking the love that was so tragically cut short—

a love that endures beyond the veil that separates the living from the beyond.

The Silver Bell Mine

The Silver Bell Mine, a remnant of Chloride's mining history, has also been the site of reported paranormal activity. Visitors have claimed to see ghostly figures around the mine entrances and have heard mysterious voices echoing within its passages.

The Silver Bell Mine, like many mines in the American West, played a pivotal role in the mining boom of the late 19th and early 20th centuries. Mining in the area was primarily focused on silver and other valuable minerals. The mine provided employment opportunities and contributed to the growth and development of the local community.

The mine is a physical reminder of the challenges and triumphs of those who worked the land in pursuit of precious minerals. Though its operation has long ceased, the structures that remain evoke a sense of the industry that once thrived in the area. Mine entrances, shafts, and other remnants are testaments to the labor and determination of the miners who toiled beneath the earth's surface.

In addition to its historical significance, the Silver Bell Mine has become known for stories of paranormal occurrences, contributing to its mystique including stories of ghostly figures, unexplained voices, mysterious lights, and sensations of a presence.

A Ghost Town with Wild Western Charm: Oatman
20 County Highway 10, Oatman, Arizona

The trip from Kingman to Oatman will take you a little less than an hour; just head south on I-40 for about 6 miles, then take the

County Highway 10 southwest about 23 miles. There will be a parking lot at 20 County Highway 10 that you can park at for this expedition. Just make sure to watch out for burros (donkeys).

Figure 60: Oatman. Photo by Timothy James Wilson.

The road is known for its twists and turns and along the way you will find a small roadside business called the Cool Spring Cabins. If you are a fan of the Disney movie Cars, you will immediately recognize the two old cars sitting outside the building as Nater and Doc Hudson. This is the place that actually inspired Radiator Springs in the series.

Oatman is a once-thriving mining town that has transformed into a popular tourist destination known for its wild west charm and historical significance. The town's history is deeply intertwined with the mining industry and the rugged spirit of the American frontier.

Oatman's story began in the early 20th century when gold was discovered in the nearby Black Mountains. The town rapidly grew as miners flocked to the area in search of fortune. At its peak, Oatman was a bustling mining camp with numerous businesses, saloons, and hotels catering to the needs of the miners.

While the mining boom eventually faded, Oatman found a new lease on life through tourism. The town is famous for its population of burros that roam freely on its streets. These burros are descendants of the animals used by early prospectors and have become a beloved symbol of Oatman's history. Visitors often enjoy feeding and interacting with these friendly creatures.

Oatman has retained its Old West atmosphere, with wooden boardwalks, historic buildings, and mock gunfights that reenact the lawless days of the past. The town's architecture and ambiance transport visitors back to the era of saloons, gold prospectors, and rugged individualism.

Figure 61: Beware, the road to Oatman is plagued with sharp turns and cliffs. Photo taken by Shirley Marie Wilson.

One of Oatman's most famous landmarks is the Oatman Hotel. Built in 1902, it's the oldest two-story adobe structure in Mojave County. The hotel's interior retains its historic charm, and visitors can even dine in the restaurant where Clark Gable and Carole Lombard reportedly stayed on their honeymoon.

Oatman hosts various annual events that celebrate its history and culture, such as the Oatman Bed Races, which is a quirky and entertaining tradition that adds to the town's unique charm every January.

Oatman's location along the iconic Route 66 has further contributed to its popularity among travelers seeking to experience the nostalgia of this historic highway. Tourists from around the world visit Oatman to witness its authentic Wild West ambiance and take part in the unique attractions it offers.

A Haunting Name

The town Oatman has a name of a rather haunting page of Arizona history, as the town was named for Olive Oatman. Olive Oatman was a historical figure known for her remarkable survival story during the mid-19th century in what is now Arizona. Her tale is often referred to as the "Oatman Massacre" and is a notable episode in the history of American settlers and Indigenous encounters.

Olive Oatman was born in 1837 in Illinois. In 1851, when she was 14 years old, her family embarked on a journey to California with hopes of finding a better life. They, along with a small group of other settlers, followed a wagon trail through the southwestern United States.

While traveling through what is now southwestern Arizona, about 25 miles west of Gila Bend, the Oatman family encountered a group of Native Americans, believed to be members of the Tolkepayas tribe (part of the Yavapai people). In February 1851, the Oatman family was attacked by this group. Most of the family members were killed in the attack, including Olive's parents and four of her siblings.

Olive and her younger sister, Mary Ann, were captured by the Tolkepayas. They were enslaved by the tribe and subjected to difficult conditions, including forced labor and harsh treatment. The two where then traded to another tribe of Indigenous people. With this second tribe, the younger sister died, but Olive managed to gain acceptance into the tribe.

After several years in captivity, Olive was eventually released in 1856, following negotiations between the United States government and the Native American tribe. Their release was facilitated by the efforts of a U.S. Army officer named Royal Stratton.

Olive Oatman, now a young woman, returned to white society and became famous for her story. She was often seen with a distinctive blue tattoo on her chin.. Her story generated considerable interest and curiosity among the general public.

Olive went on to marry John B. Fairchild and had a family of her own. She lived in various places, including Illinois and Oregon, and her life was marked by both hardship and resilience. She published her autobiography, "Life Among the Indians," in 1857, which recounted her experiences.

Olive Oatman's story serves as a historical reminder of the challenges faced by pioneers and the complex interactions between different cultures during westward expansion in the United States. Her distinctive chin tattoo, which she chose to keep throughout her life, became a symbol of her unique and tragic journey.

The Legend of Oatie Hauser

In the heart of the Black Mountains, nestled within the windswept town of Oatman, there existed a tale as old as the desert itself—a story whispered through the wooden boardwalks and carried on the whispers of the wind. It was the story of Oatie Hauser, a woman whose spirit lingered in the corners of the Oatman Hotel, forever binding her to the town that bore her name.

Long ago, during the town's heyday as a bustling mining camp, Oatie Hauser was a name that echoed through the saloons and alleyways. With raven-black hair and eyes that held secrets, Oatie was a woman who had carved a path of independence in a world dominated by men. She was a soiled dove, as they called her—a term that hinted at the shadows of her life but failed to capture her spirit.

Amid the clinking of glasses and the laughter of miners, Oatie moved through the Oatman Hotel like a tempest, her presence both captivating and enigmatic. But behind the façade of laughter, there was a sadness that haunted her eyes, a pain buried deep within that few dared to inquire about.

It was a fateful night, a night when the desert stars painted the sky with their brilliant glow, that Oatie's life took a tragic turn. A love that had bloomed amid the dust and gold was cut short by violence—a life taken too soon, a story unfinished. The town was gripped by shock, and Oatman bore witness to a grief that could not be measured in tears alone.

As the years rolled on, Oatie's presence endured, her essence intertwined with the very timbers of the Oatman Hotel. Guests who stayed within its historic walls spoke of encounters that went beyond the realm of the living. Footsteps echoed in empty hallways, a whisper of laughter danced on the breeze, and doors would creak open without a touch.

It was said that Oatie's spirit remained bound to the hotel, a guardian of sorts. She watched over the guests who entered her domain, offering a gentle touch to the lost and the weary. Some guests claimed to have felt a fleeting touch, a brush of cool air that carried with it a sense of comfort.

But it was in the old room, Room 15, that Oatie's presence was most strongly felt. Guests who stayed there spoke of an otherworldly atmosphere, a feeling that they were not truly alone. Some reported seeing the faint outline of a figure—an apparition with dark hair and eyes that held both sorrow and kindness.

And so, the legend of Oatie Hauser lived on, a tale woven into the fabric of Oatman's history. Her story was a reminder that even in the passage of time, the spirits of those who once walked the earth could linger, their presence an echo of love and tragedy. To this day, visitors to the Oatman Hotel venture into Room 15, not just seeking a night's rest, but perhaps a connection—a moment when the past and the present converged, bridging the gap between the world of the living and the world beyond.

Domestic Terrorism

April 19, 1995 started like any other day in America. The sun came up, and people all over the world started their day not knowing the epiphany that would surround this day for history. That all changed at about 9:02 AM, when the disgruntled Army veteran, Timothy McVeigh, detonated a powerful homemade bomb inside a rental truck parked in front of the Alfred P. Murrah Federal Building in Oklahoma City. The explosion resulted in the tragic deaths of 168 people, including 19 children, and caused extensive damage to surrounding buildings. The bombing remains one of the deadliest acts of terrorism on U.S. soil and had a profound impact on the nation, leading to increased security measures and anti-terrorism efforts.

In the weeks that followed, the American people would become very familiar with the small town of Kingman, Arizona. The national media would dub the town as a lawless wild western town where anti-government conspirators like McVeigh congregated. This was because, the small town was not only where McVeigh's had lived, but also where McVeigh hatched the entire plan to begin with. Additionally, in the weeks following the attacks the FBI arrested two of McVeigh's co-conspirators in the area of Kingman; Michael Fortier, who had been McVeigh's roommate in Kingman for most of the year prior to the bombing.

The second of McVeigh's co-conspirators arrested in the Kingman area was Steven Garrett Colbern. Colbern was hiding out at the Oatman Hotel when the manager of the hotel recognized him and called the authorities. Colbern was arrested for providing McVeigh with weapons.

Unfortunately, the scars of this attack have long haunted the small town of Kingman's reputation for almost three decades. This is unfortunate, because the town, as well as the surrounding area, has so much to offer, and can really be a delightful place to visit, especially if you are on a budget.

Ghostly Encounters on Route 66

Chapter Nine: High Society Hauntings

Scottsdale, Tempe, and Paradise Valley

Figure 62: Mill Avenue in Tempe. Photo taken by Timothy James Wilson.

Amidst the sun-kissed landscapes and cerulean skies of Arizona lies a trio of cities that beckon to those with a penchant for the mysterious and the unconventional. Scottsdale, Paradise Valley, and Tempe are more than just picturesque destinations; they are enigmatic realms where history intertwines with legends, and the allure of the past dances with the contemporary. In this exploration, we invite you to delve beyond the tourist brochures and immerse yourself in the hidden histories, whispered tales, and peculiar facets that make these cities unique.

High Society Hauntings

From the artistic tapestry of Scottsdale, where creative inspiration and Western heritage converge, to the luxurious enclaves of Paradise Valley, where opulence masks intriguing stories waiting to be uncovered, and finally to the spirited vitality of Tempe, where education and urban life intersect with legends of the past – each city holds a distinctive narrative that dark tourists will find irresistibly alluring.

As we venture into the heart of these Arizona gems, prepare to discover the tales of those who walked these streets long before us and the echoes of their presence that linger still. Join us on a journey where the ordinary gives way to the extraordinary, and where the allure of the unknown takes center stage. Welcome to Scottsdale, Paradise Valley, and Tempe – a triad of cities that offer an invitation to explore the enigmatic.

Scottsdale: Where Art, Luxury, and Desert Beauty Converge

Nestled in the Sonoran Desert, Scottsdale has evolved from its rugged Wild West origins into a sophisticated oasis known for its vibrant arts scene, luxurious resorts, and captivating natural landscapes. Its history dates back to prehistoric times when Indigenous cultures inhabited the region, leaving behind fascinating petroglyphs and artifacts. Fast forward to the mid-20th century, Scottsdale transformed from a modest farming community into a hub for artists seeking inspiration in its sweeping desert vistas.

Today, Scottsdale boasts a thriving arts district, home to galleries showcasing contemporary and traditional works. The city's historic Old Town district retains its Western charm, offering a glimpse into the area's past through its preserved buildings and saloons. The city also thrives as being known for its extensive fashion boutiques, luxury resorts and spas, and its numerous golf courses.

For the dark tourist, stories of the area's rumored hauntings and the prospect of exploring its preserved Western heritage might hold a unique appeal.

Paradise Valley: A Luxurious Oasis with Hidden Histories

Nestled within the heart of the Phoenix metropolitan area, Paradise Valley is a perfect example of wealth, luxury, and exclusivity. Historically, the land was used for farming, cattle ranching, and as a retreat for wealthy visitors seeking respite from city life. The transformation into an enclave of upscale residences and resorts began in earnest during the mid-20th century.

Paradise Valley is the wealthiest city in Arizona, and the names of some of the city's residents include rock stars, world class athletes, a former vice president of the United States, and some of the most well-known and powerful business and political figures in Arizona's history.

While Paradise Valley exudes luxury, beneath its glossy surface lie fascinating tales waiting to be uncovered by dark tourism enthusiasts. The lavish estates that now dot the landscape may have intriguing histories, and the stories of the individuals who shaped the region's rise to prominence could reveal unexpected facets of its allure.

Tempe: A Blend of History, Education, and Urban Spirit

The city of Tempe, situated on the banks of the Salt River, offers a multifaceted experience that embraces its historical roots and vibrant modernity. Originally inhabited by the Ancient Sonoran Peoples, the region saw agricultural prosperity due to their intricate canal system. The establishment of Arizona State University in the late 19th century infused Tempe with an intellectual and cultural vitality that endures to this day.

High Society Hauntings

For dark tourism enthusiasts, Tempe's history of urban development presents a rich tapestry to explore. The iconic Hayden Butte, or "A" Mountain, features Indigenous petroglyphs and symbolizes the city's indigenous past. Tales of urban legends, rumored paranormal encounters, and even glimpses into the seedy underbelly of the city's past could captivate those drawn to the enigmatic and obscure.

Each of these cities offers a distinctive perspective on Arizona's diverse heritage, from Scottsdale's artistic evolution to Paradise Valley's hidden narratives and Tempe's blend of history and urban vibrancy. For dark tourists seeking to uncover the layers of history beneath the surface, these cities hold promises of intriguing tales waiting to be unraveled.

The Hermosa Inn
5532 North Palo Cristi Road, Paradise Valley, Arizona
Reservations: (602) 955-8614

Figure 63: The Hermosa Inn. Photo taken by Timothy James Wilson.

Situated within the affluent Paradise Valley, The Hermosa Inn stands as one of the area's most esteemed and highly rated hotels. This Phoenix suburb boasts an array of opulent hotel resorts and opulent million-dollar mansions, contributing to its status as one of Arizona's most prosperous locales. However, what sets The

Hermosa Inn apart from its luxury counterparts in Paradise Valley? A captivating history is at the heart of its distinctiveness. Crafted by the hand of cowboy artist Alonzo "Lon" Megargee in 1935, the establishment known as 'Casa Hermosa' encompassed roles as Lon's personal residence, an art haven, and even an underground gambling hideaway. It's been whispered that secret tunnels were ingeniously constructed to offer a means of evasion from the law during attempts to thwart his illicit gambling gatherings. Presently, The Hermosa Inn envelopes Lon's former abode and artistic workspace, the original edifice now christened Lon's, an affectionate reference to its visionary founder.

Reports persist that the spirit of Alonzo Megargee lingers on within The Hermosa Inn. Accounts from both guests and staff recount glimpses of Lon's towering, slender figure adorned with a classic cowboy hat. Some assert that he delights in disrupting the silence of late nights by shattering glassware and beer bottles, while also playfully engaging in toilet flushing across the premises.

Alonzo Megargee's personal narrative unveils a path that diverges remarkably from his later renown as a Southwest cowboy artist. Hailing from a well-to-do Scottish lineage in Philadelphia, he embarked on a journey of artistic expression after overcoming an upbringing marked by rebellion and hardship. Aided by exposure to operas, art galleries, and museums through his father's sporadic presence, Alonzo's innate artistic tendencies began to flourish. Yet, a pattern of defiance and adventure culminated in his departure from formal education and pursuit of a cowboy lifestyle in Arizona.

Megargee's transition from a champion bronc buster to an accomplished artist unfolds as a tale of resilience. He weathered challenges, from a profound drought to a personal tragedy that catapulted him into the realm of artistry. Under the patronage of Arizona's first governor, he undertook monumental mural commissions, infusing Arizona's cultural narrative into the walls of its state capitol. Throughout his journeys in Mexico, Spain, France, and Tahiti, Alonzo Megargee cultivated an artistic and architectural acumen that would later contribute to the conception of The Hermosa Inn.

The culmination of his artistic journey, La Casa Hermosa, emerged from the desert landscape. Employing architectural techniques gleaned from his travels, he employed adobe bricks and distinctive fireplaces to realize his vision. Amidst the allure of the luxury resort, Lon's lingering presence imparts an ethereal quality. His restless spirit, as reported by witnesses, interweaves into the inn's story, manifesting as enigmatic shadows, unexplained incidents, and even solitary toilet flushes.

The tale of Lon Megargee and The Hermosa Inn is one where the artistic soul of a cowboy converged with the spirit of the Southwest, leaving an indelible mark on both a physical establishment and the fabric of its legends.

Old Town Scottsdale
Near North Scottdale Road and Indian School Road, Scottsdale

Figure 64: Old Town Scottsdale. Photo taken by Timothy James Wilson.

Old Town Scottsdale is a vibrant and historic district. Known for its unique charm and Western ambiance, this area offers a delightful blend of culture, history, and entertainment. The streets of Old Town are lined with an array of quaint buildings that showcase architectural styles from the late 19th and early 20th centuries, giving visitors a sense of stepping back in time.

The history of Old Town Scottsdale dates back to the late 1800s when the area was initially settled. Originally known as Orangedale, the town served as an agricultural community, primarily cultivating citrus fruits and cotton. Over time, it transformed into a prominent trade center and grew into the bustling hub that it is today.

One significant event that shaped Old Town Scottsdale's history was the construction of the Arizona Canal in 1885. The canal played a pivotal role in the region's development by providing irrigation to the arid land, facilitating further growth and prosperity. This expansion attracted prominent individuals, including George Washington Scott, who later became the town's namesake.

Old Town Scottsdale has also been associated with famous and historically significant people. One notable figure is Frank Lloyd Wright, the renowned architect. Wright established his winter home and architecture school, Taliesin West, in the nearby desert. His presence influenced the local architectural scene and contributed to the region's artistic and creative atmosphere.

The Goldwater Mercantile

The Goldwater Mercantile Ghost is a legendary ghost associated with the historic Goldwater Mercantile building in Old Town Scottsdale. The building, now home to the Old Town Tavern, has gained a reputation for alleged paranormal activity and is said to be haunted by a restless spirit.

The Goldwater Mercantile building holds historical significance as it was once a thriving mercantile store, established by the Goldwater family, who played a prominent role in the early development of Scottsdale. Over the years, reports and stories have emerged of strange occurrences and eerie experiences within the building, leading to the belief in a ghostly presence.

Visitors and staff members have claimed to witness a range of paranormal phenomena within the Goldwater Mercantile building. These reports include hearing phantom footsteps, disembodied voices, and objects moving without explanation. Some have even described a feeling of being watched or an unexplainable chill in certain areas of the building.

While the origins of the alleged haunting remain uncertain, local legends and speculation have attempted to explain the ghostly presence. Some believe that the ghost could be tied to the building's rich history, perhaps connected to past employees, customers, or even members of the Goldwater family themselves.

The tales of the Goldwater Mercantile Ghost have contributed to the building's mystique and draw curiosity from those interested in the supernatural and the unknown. Whether one believes in the existence of the Goldwater Mercantile Ghost or not, the legends and stories associated with the alleged haunting add an extra layer of fascination to the history and character of Old Town Scottsdale. Visitors can't help but be intrigued by the idea of a ghostly presence lingering within the walls of this historic building.

The Ghost of Winfield Scott

The Ghost of Winfield Scott is a legendary figure associated with Old Town Scottsdale. Winfield Scott, the town's namesake, was a prominent figure in the early settlement of the area and is believed to have left a lingering presence even after his passing.

Winfield Scott was a Civil War veteran who settled in the region in the late 19th century. He played a significant role in the development of Scottsdale and was known for his contributions to agriculture and community-building. According to local legends, after his death, his spirit continued to wander the streets of Old Town Scottsdale.

Reports of the Ghost of Winfield Scott vary, but common accounts describe a spectral figure resembling a man dressed in old-fashioned attire, often seen near the Arizona Canal or around his former residence. Witnesses have claimed to see him walking along the canal banks, sometimes carrying a lantern or a cane. Others have reported catching glimpses of him near the Winfield Scott Plaza, which stands as a tribute to his legacy.

These sightings and encounters with the Ghost of Winfield Scott have been shared among locals and visitors for several decades. The legend of the Ghost of Winfield Scott adds an element of mystery and intrigue to the history of Old Town Scottsdale, captivating those who are interested in the supernatural and the region's rich past.

Organized Crime

During the mid-20th century, Old Town Scottsdale experienced a surge in tourism and entertainment, attracting individuals involved in organized crime. While it is important to note that the criminal activities in Old Town Scottsdale were not as notorious or pervasive as in some other cities, there were instances of organized crime that left an indelible mark on the area's history.

Old Town Scottsdale's proximity to larger cities like Phoenix, coupled with its growing reputation as a tourist destination, made it an attractive target for criminal enterprises. The region's flourishing nightlife, vibrant casinos, and abundance of entertainment venues provided ample opportunities for illicit activities to flourish.

One of the notable figures associated with organized crime in Old Town Scottsdale was Gus Greenbaum, a high-ranking member of the Mafia. In the 1940s and 1950s, Greenbaum operated and owned several gambling establishments in the area, including the infamous Jockey Club and the Turf Club. These establishments, known for their opulence and extravagant entertainment, became hotbeds of illegal gambling, prostitution, and other vices.

The Jockey Club was a renowned hotspot where high-stakes gambling took place. Patrons would indulge in games of chance while rubbing shoulders with influential mobsters and other criminal figures. The club's luxurious atmosphere and discreet nature made it a popular destination for both locals and out-of-town visitors seeking excitement and anonymity.

However, the criminal activities in Old Town Scottsdale took a sinister turn in 1958 when Gus Greenbaum and his wife were found brutally murdered in their Phoenix home. This shocking incident sent shockwaves through the criminal underworld and marked a significant turning point in organized crime activities in the region. The exact motives and culprits behind the murders remain unsolved to this day, adding an air of mystery to the case.

The murders of Gus Greenbaum and his wife had a profound impact on the criminal landscape of Old Town Scottsdale. The incident sent a clear message that even high-ranking mobsters were not immune to violence and that law enforcement would not tolerate criminal activities within their jurisdiction. As a result, organized crime's influence in the area began to decline.

In subsequent years, law enforcement agencies, bolstered by community support, intensified their efforts to combat criminal activities in Old Town Scottsdale. Increased surveillance, strict regulations, and close collaboration with federal authorities aimed to dismantle organized crime networks and prevent the resurgence of illicit operations.

The collective determination of the community and law enforcement to maintain law and order paid off. Old Town Scottsdale gradually transformed into a thriving and safe district, focused on promoting tourism, cultural activities, and preserving its rich history. The remnants of the once-infamous gambling establishments have been repurposed into legitimate businesses that contribute to the area's charm and character.

While the organized crime activities in Old Town Scottsdale may not have reached the scale or notoriety of other cities, such as Chicago, they remain a part of the area's history. The legacy of organized crime serves as a reminder of the challenges faced by the community in the past and highlights the resilience and dedication to maintaining a safe and vibrant neighborhood. Today, Old Town Scottsdale stands as a testament to the community's resolve to overcome its dark past and create a thriving, law-abiding district for residents and visitors to enjoy.

Despite the occasional criminal incidents, Old Town Scottsdale remains a beloved destination for locals and tourists alike. Its rich history, charming architecture, and lively atmosphere continue to draw visitors who are captivated by its unique blend of the past and present. Whether you're strolling through the art galleries, savoring delicious cuisine at the numerous restaurants, or exploring the various boutiques and shops, Old Town Scottsdale offers a delightful experience that is sure to leave a lasting impression.

Robert William Fisher

Robert William Fisher gained national attention for the heinous act of killing his family and subsequently setting fire to his house in Scottsdale. This tragic event occurred on April 10, 2001, just a few miles from Old Town Scottsdale.

Fisher was born on April 13, 1961, in Brooklyn, New York. He served in the United States Navy and later worked as a surgical catheter technician. Fisher was married to Mary Fisher, and they had two children, Brittany and Bobby. The family resided in Scottsdale, where they lived a seemingly ordinary life.

However, in 2001, Robert Fisher carried out a horrifying act: he slaughtered his wife and children, then set fire to the family's home in an attempt to destroy evidence and cover up his crimes.

When authorities discovered the scene, they were confronted with the heartbreaking aftermath of the tragedy. However, Robert Fisher was nowhere to be found, as he fled the area immediately following the murders.

Fisher was quickly placed on the FBI's Ten Most Wanted Fugitives list, which thrust him into the national spotlight. Despite extensive efforts by law enforcement agencies and numerous leads, Fisher has managed to evade capture for over two decades, becoming one of the most wanted fugitives in the United States.

Over the years, there have been sporadic sightings and reported leads, but none have led to his apprehension. Fisher's case has been featured on various television shows, documentaries, and true crime programs, which have helped keep the public aware of his ongoing status as a fugitive.

The Robert William Fisher case remains open, and law enforcement agencies continue to pursue leads and investigate possible sightings. The search for Fisher serves as a reminder of the devastating consequences of his actions and the importance of holding those responsible for such heinous crimes accountable.

Robert William Fisher's truck was discovered the day after the crimes were committed, abandoned along with the family dog in the Tonto National Forest near the town of Young (approximately three hours away).

The discovery of the abandoned truck initially led authorities to believe that Fisher had taken his own life, as they found no trace of him at the scene. However, as the investigation progressed, it became apparent that Fisher had intentionally staged the scene to divert attention and facilitate his escape.

Robert William Fisher remains at large. His disappearance and ability to evade capture have made him one of the most sought-after fugitives in the United States. The case remains open, and law enforcement agencies continue their efforts to locate and apprehend him.

Over the years, several theories have emerged regarding the whereabouts and fate of Robert William Fisher, the fugitive who killed his family and set fire to his house in Scottsdale. While these theories remain speculative, they offer possible explanations for his disappearance:

One theory suggests that Fisher carefully planned his escape and has been able to remain in hiding all these years. This theory posits that he may have assumed a new identity, possibly using fraudulent identification documents, and has been living under the radar, possibly outside of the United States.

Another theory proposes that Fisher, overwhelmed by guilt or the fear of being captured, may have taken his own life. Despite extensive searches conducted in the wilderness areas near his abandoned truck, his body has never been found, leaving open the possibility that he ended his own life in an undiscovered location.

Some believe that Fisher may have received assistance from an underground network or individuals sympathetic to his cause. This theory suggests that he may have been aided in creating a new identity, acquiring resources, and maintaining a low profile, making it difficult for law enforcement to track him down.

Speculation also exists that Fisher may have fled to another country, utilizing connections or resources to leave the United States. This theory suggests that he may have taken advantage of his Navy background or engaged in illegal activities to finance his escape and start a new life abroad.

It is important to note that these theories remain speculative, and there is no definitive evidence to confirm any of them. The case of Robert William Fisher continues to be actively investigated, with law enforcement agencies and the public urged to provide any relevant information that could lead to his capture.

"A" Mountain
Trailhead: 201 South Packard Drive, Tempe, Arizona

High above the bustling city of Tempe stands A" Mountain, a sentinel guarding the secrets of ages past. Among its weathered rocks lie ancient petroglyphs, etched by the hands of Indigenous ancestors who once inhabited these lands. Yet, as twilight casts long shadows across the desert landscape, whispers of another presence emerge - the spirits of those who once called this mountain home.

Local legend tells of encounters with shadowy figures that materialize from the rocks, their forms shifting like desert sands in the wind. Those who have ventured to A" Mountain after dark speak of feeling an unexplainable chill in the air, a sensation that lingers long after they descend. Footsteps echo in the quiet night, even when no one is around, and murmurs carried by the breeze hint at stories untold.

Figure 65: A Mountain. Photo taken by Timothy James Wilson.

Some say the ancient ones return to the mountain, unable to part from the land that nurtured them for generations. As the moon rises over the desert, A" Mountain's ancient petroglyphs seem to come to life, weaving a tapestry that connects the past to the present. It is a reminder that history, both tangible and ethereal, continues to echo through the ages.

Tempe Town Lake and Rolling Hills Golf Course
1415 North Mill Avenue, Tempe, Arizona

Beyond the urban hustle of Tempe, Tempe Town Lake and the nearby Rolling Hills Golf Course hold secrets whispered through the reeds and ripples of water. The serenity of the lake belies a reputation for strange happenings, leaving both locals and visitors pondering the mysteries that lie beneath its tranquil surface.

As the sun dips below the horizon, some have reported unexplained ripples disturbing the lake's still waters, as if caused by unseen hands. Others speak of ghostly apparitions that emerge from the shadows, their forms fleeting and ethereal. The air carries an air of anticipation, and a sense that the natural world isn't the only inhabitant of this serene space.

Figure 66: The Rolling Hills Golf Course. Photo taken by Timothy James Wilson.

Adjacent to Tempe Town Lake, the Rolling Hills Golf Course seems to harbor its own enigmatic presence. The darkened fairways and quiet greens are said to come alive with whispers and rustling leaves that defy the stillness of the night. Whether it's the spirit of those who once walked these grounds or the echoes of something more elusive, the tales of Tempe Town Lake and the surrounding area continue to captivate those who seek out the uncanny.

Old Hayden Flour Mill
119 South Mill Avenue, Tempe, Arizona
Information: (480) 350-4311

The Old Hayden Flour Mill is a historic landmark that holds a rich history and is steeped in the culture of the area. The building itself stands as a testament to the industrial past of the region and has become an iconic symbol of the community.

Figure 67: The Old Hayden Flour Mill. Photo taken by Timothy James Wilson.

The mill was originally constructed in 1874 by Charles Trumbull Hayden, a prominent figure in the development of Tempe and the surrounding area. The mill played a crucial role in the agricultural economy of the region, processing locally grown wheat into flour. The Hayden Flour Mill, as it was known, became a vital center for trade and commerce, attracting farmers and merchants from far and wide.

Over the years, the mill underwent several expansions and renovations, adapting to changing technology and increasing demands. The imposing red brick structure that stands today reflects the building's early 20th-century design, showcasing elements of the industrial architecture of the time. It stands as a symbol of the prosperity and progress that accompanied the growth of Tempe.

High Society Hauntings

The Old Hayden Flour Mill also holds historical significance due to its associations with notable individuals. Charles Trumbull Hayden himself was a prominent figure in the area, known for his contributions to the development of Tempe. Additionally, Hayden's son, Carl T. Hayden, was a distinguished politician who served as Arizona's first representative in the United States Senate. The Hayden family's legacy is deeply intertwined with the mill and the community it served.

As for paranormal or supernatural occurrences, the Old Hayden Flour Mill has gained a reputation for being a site of various unexplained phenomena. Reports of ghostly sightings, strange noises, and eerie sensations have circulated among locals and visitors. Some claim to have encountered the spirits of former mill workers or even the apparition of Charles Trumbull Hayden himself. These accounts, though not scientifically proven, have contributed to the mill's aura of mystery and intrigue.

The Ghostly Mill Worker

The legend of the Ghostly Mill Worker at the Old Hayden Flour Mill is a tale that has been passed down through generations. According to the legend, there have been numerous sightings and encounters with the spirit of a former mill worker who roams the premises.

The Ghostly Mill Worker is believed to be the apparition of a laborer who worked at the mill during its operational years. Witnesses have described seeing a figure dressed in old-fashioned clothing, often wearing tattered work clothes or a worn-out apron. The ghostly presence is said to appear in various areas of the mill, sometimes seen walking through the hallways, near the old machinery, or in the storage rooms.

Visitors and employees have reported eerie experiences associated with the Ghostly Mill Worker. Some claim to have heard unexplained footsteps echoing through the corridors, accompanied by the sound of creaking floorboards. Others have reported feeling a sudden drop in temperature or a peculiar chill in the air when encountering the apparition. Some witnesses have even claimed to have engaged in brief conversations with the spirit, only to have it vanish without a trace.

The legend suggests that the spirit of the Ghostly Mill Worker may be tied to the mill's history and the laborers who toiled within its walls. It is said that the ghostly presence is restless, perhaps still bound to the mill due to unfinished business or a deep attachment to the place where they once worked.

Charles Trumbull Hayden's Ghost

The legend of Charles Trumbull Hayden's Ghost is a captivating tale associated with the Old Hayden Flour Mill in Tempe. According to local folklore, the spirit of the mill's original founder, Charles Trumbull Hayden, is said to linger within the historic building.

Charles Trumbull Hayden was a prominent figure in the development of Tempe and the surrounding region. He played a vital role in establishing the Hayden Flour Mill as a cornerstone of the local economy. The legend suggests that Hayden's deep connection to the mill and his significant impact on the community may have bound his spirit to the place he once called his own.

Witnesses claim to have encountered the ghostly apparition of Charles Trumbull Hayden within the mill's premises. Descriptions often depict an elderly man, dressed in attire reminiscent of the time in which he lived, including a hat and a long coat. The ghostly presence is believed to roam various areas of the mill, sometimes appearing near the old machinery or overlooking the operations from a vantage point.

High Society Hauntings

Encounters with Hayden's ghost are said to evoke a sense of awe and reverence. Witnesses have reported feeling a profound presence, as if being observed by an otherworldly figure. Some accounts speak of brief conversations with the spectral manifestation, with the ghostly Hayden imparting wisdom or sharing stories from the mill's past before dissipating into thin air.

Haunted Basement

The legend of the haunted basement at the Old Hayden Flour Mill in Tempe, is a chilling tale that has captured the imagination of locals and visitors alike. According to the legend, the mill's basement holds a particularly active and eerie presence, making it a hotspot for paranormal activity.

The basement of the Old Hayden Flour Mill is rumored to be a place where unexplained phenomena occur. Those who have ventured into the depths of the mill have reported encountering strange sounds, disembodied voices, and an overwhelming sense of unease. The atmosphere is said to be heavy and oppressive, with an unsettling energy that permeates the air.

Visitors to the basement have described hearing inexplicable whispers or murmurs, as if unseen entities are engaged in conversation. Some accounts speak of echoing footsteps that seem to manifest from nowhere, adding to the sense of a spectral presence. The darkness and labyrinthine layout of the basement contribute to a feeling of being watched or followed, heightening the spine-chilling experience.

The legends surrounding the haunted basement suggest that the spirits of former mill workers may still inhabit the area, continuing their work even in the afterlife. Some believe that the residual energy of the toil and labor performed in the mill over

Timothy James Wilson

the years has left an imprint, resulting in the paranormal occurrences witnessed by those who dare to explore the basement's depths.

In recent years, the Old Hayden Flour Mill has undergone restoration efforts to preserve its historical significance. It now stands as a testament to Tempe's past and serves as a venue for events, exhibitions, and community gatherings. The surrounding area has also been transformed into a vibrant park, offering a picturesque setting for leisure activities and providing a link between the city's history and its present.

Whether one is captivated by its architectural grandeur, fascinated by its historical significance, or intrigued by the tales of the supernatural, the Old Hayden Flour Mill continues to hold a special place in the hearts and minds of the people of Tempe.

Gammage Auditorium at Arizona State University
1200 South Forest Avenue, Tempe, Arizona
Information: (480) 965-3434

Figure 68: Gammage Auditorium at Arizona State University. Photo taken by Timothy James Wilson.

Nestled within the heart of Arizona State University looms a foreboding structure that has stood the test of time—the Gammage Auditorium. Named after the renowned architect Frank Lloyd Wright, who envisioned its majestic design, this imposing edifice rises from the ground like a monolithic sentinel, exuding an eerie grandeur that belies its dark secrets.

Constructed in the mid-1960s, Gammage Auditorium was intended to be a beacon of culture and artistic expression, a hallowed space where performances of theater, music, and dance would enrapture audiences for generations to come. Its architectural splendor, with its sweeping curves and geometric patterns, is said to be an homage to the natural landscapes of the surrounding Sonoran Desert.

Yet, behind its gleaming façade lies a shadowed history, a tale whispered among those who have witnessed the unexplained phenomena that permeate the very essence of the auditorium. Whispers carried on the wind speak of ghostly apparitions that materialize upon the stage, spectral performers forever trapped in the liminal space between life and death.

Audience members have reported eerie encounters with phantom figures, their ethereal forms gliding across the stage during performances, seemingly unaware of the living world around them. Witnesses speak of the chilling sensation that creeps up their spines as unseen eyes bore into their souls, evoking a palpable sense of dread that lingers long after the final curtain falls.

A Haunting Melody: The Ghostly Pianist

Within the dimly lit confines of Gammage Auditorium, a legend of tragic brilliance and eternal music unfolds—a tale whispered among those who have witnessed the ethereal presence that lingers upon the stage. It is the legend of the Ghostly Pianist, a spectral musician forever bound to the ivory keys, captivating both the living and the afterlife with his haunting melodies.

Long ago, in the heyday of Gammage Auditorium, there was a pianist of unparalleled talent whose skill knew no bounds.

Timothy James Wilson

His fingers danced across the keys with a supernatural grace, conjuring melodies that transcended the mortal realm and evoked a profound range of emotions in his listeners. Night after night, enthralled audiences were enraptured by his performances, as if transported to realms of enchantment and melancholy.

Yet, tragedy fell upon this musical prodigy, shrouding his once-illuminated path in darkness. The details of his untimely demise remain obscured by time, lost within the shadowy depths of the auditorium's history. Some say he met his end in a tumultuous love affair, while others whisper that he bargained with Lucifer who exacted a dire price for his otherworldly talent. Whatever the cause, his life was cut short, leaving his soul forever bound to the stage that had been witness to his musical brilliance.

Since that fateful day, the ghostly presence of the pianist has haunted the hallowed halls of Gammage Auditorium. When darkness blankets the auditorium, a somber melody emanates from the grand piano, notes echoing through the empty space as if played by an invisible hand. The melancholic strains weave through the air, carrying the weight of the pianist's unfulfilled aspirations and eternal longing.

Witnesses fortunate—or perhaps unfortunate—enough to be present during these spectral performances describe a mesmerizing spectacle. An otherworldly glow casts an ethereal sheen upon the stage as the piano keys depress and release, seemingly of their own accord. The ivories respond to the phantom touch, their melancholic notes filling the void, evoking a haunting mixture of joy and sorrow that tugs at the very core of one's being.

The Ghostly Pianist's presence is not confined to his ethereal performances alone. He is said to wander the corridors of Gammage Auditorium, his ghostly figure glimpsed fleetingly by those who dare to venture into the depths of the building

297

after dusk. Witnesses speak of a figure draped in darkness, his form hazy and indistinct, drifting through the shadows with a melancholic air. Some claim to have heard whispers of a lost love, a mournful lament that permeates the air, leaving a lingering sense of heartache in its wake.

The legend of the Ghostly Pianist has become an integral part of Gammage Auditorium's enigmatic aura, an inseparable piece of its haunted tapestry. His spectral presence continues to captivate and enchant, drawing those with a penchant for the supernatural to witness the eternal performance that unfolds in the dead of night.

So, should you find yourself within the atmospheric embrace of Gammage Auditorium, listen closely. Amidst the silence, you may catch the faint strains of a spectral melody, an elegy composed by the ghostly pianist. But beware, for his ethereal music carries a bittersweet allure that can ensnare the unwary soul, forever binding them to the haunting legacy of the enigmatic musician who resides within the very heart of the auditorium.

The Vanishing Actress: A Haunting Enigma

Within the echoes of Gammage Auditorium resides the enigmatic legend of the Vanishing Actress—a tragic figure forever entwined with the ethereal fabric of the theater. Her story whispers through the shadows, captivating those who dare to unravel the mysteries hidden within the grand stage.

Long ago, during the zenith of Gammage's theatrical glory, there was an actress of extraordinary talent. Her performances were the stuff of legend, captivating audiences with her enchanting presence and captivating performances. Night after night, she graced the stage, breathing life into the characters she portrayed and leaving audiences spellbound in her wake.

Yet, behind her radiant façade lay a life steeped in shadows and secrets. Whispers swirled through the theater's backstage corridors, hinting at a troubled existence and a mysterious past. Some claimed she had made a pact with otherworldly forces to obtain her extraordinary acting abilities, while others speculated that her immense talent had come at a grave personal cost.

Tragedy struck swiftly and without warning, forever altering the actress's destiny. The details of her demise are lost in the pages of history. Some speculate foul play, while others speak of an accidental fall from the grand stage, sealing her fate within the theater's spectral embrace.

Since that fateful day, witnesses have reported encounters with the ghostly presence of the Vanishing Actress. Her apparition materializes during twilight hours, her visage adorned in the costumes of bygone eras. The ethereal figure rehearses lines, gliding across the stage as if lost in a world between the realms of the living and the dead.

Those who have crossed paths with her ghostly form speak of her mesmerizing presence. They describe her as a vision of ethereal beauty, her eyes filled with longing and a lingering sorrow that transcends the boundaries of time. Her spectral performances are said to rival those of her living days, captivating the hearts and souls of those fortunate enough to witness her ephemeral encore.

The Vanishing Actress is not confined to the stage alone; she wanders the labyrinthine corridors of Gammage Auditorium, her phantom presence felt by those who dare to explore the theater after nightfall. She is known to make her presence known to actors, stagehands, and visitors alike, evoking a sense of reverence and awe. It is even said that she once appeared on stage during a performance in the early 1980's.

Although her motives remain obscured, some believe that the Vanishing Actress seeks solace or redemption within the theater's spectral realm. Her ghostly apparition, forever tied to the stage that once ignited her spirit, continues to roam the theater, yearning to complete performances that were tragically cut short.

As twilight settles upon Gammage Auditorium, be watchful for the spectral form of the Vanishing Actress. Perhaps you will glimpse her melancholic figure, draped in the garments of another era, and witness the echoes of her past brilliance. But be cautious, for her ethereal allure may entice you into the labyrinth of her haunting tale, where the line between reality and the supernatural is forever blurred.

Haunted Spectators at Gammage Auditorium

Deep within the enigmatic embrace of Gammage Auditorium, there exists a chilling legend that haunts the balcony—the tale of the Shadowy Figures. These elusive apparitions, veiled in darkness, cast an eerie presence upon the theater, their spectral forms stirring whispers of mystery and trepidation among those who dare to tread its haunted halls.

The origins of the Shadowy Figures are shrouded in ambiguity, their true identities concealed within the veils of time. Some speculate that they were avid theatergoers, eternally bound to the auditorium they once adored. Others believe they may be residual echoes of performers, forever reliving their ethereal audience's reactions. Whatever their true nature, their spectral existence adds an unsettling layer to the theater's haunted tapestry.

Witnesses who have glimpsed the Shadowy Figures describe their spectral forms as wisps of darkness, blending seamlessly with the dimly lit balcony seats. Their silhouettes remain indistinct, yet their presence exudes an aura of haunting familiarity. They manifest during performances, their attention transfixed upon the stage as if captivated by the unfolding drama, though their expressions remain forever concealed within the ethereal void.

Those who have encountered these phantom spectators speak of an overwhelming sense of being observed, as if the weight of their spectral gaze lingers upon them. Some claim to have felt a palpable chill in the air, an icy reminder of the spectral presence lingering in the shadows. The atmosphere becomes charged with an inexplicable energy, heightening the senses and instilling a profound unease in those who dare to venture into their domain.

In the depths of the night, as the spotlight fades and darkness envelops Gammage Auditorium, be vigilant for the appearance of the Shadowy Figures. Peer into the balcony seats, where the border between the living and the spectral is at its thinnest. Should you encounter these ethereal onlookers, know that you are in the presence of an enigmatic legacy—one that transcends time and whispers of the eternal fascination the theater holds for both the living and the ghostly alike.

Illuminating the Supernatural

Within the darkened expanse of Gammage Auditorium, a spectral phenomenon flickers and dances, captivating all who bear witness. The legend of the Phantom Lights, an ethereal illumination that defies rational explanation, weaves a tale of intrigue and mystique within the haunted corridors of this revered theater.

As the curtains draw close and the stage is engulfed in darkness, whispers circulate among the theater's denizens—

whispers of spectral lights that manifest with an otherworldly presence. Technicians and stage crew members recount eerie encounters with these enigmatic illuminations, setting the stage for an ethereal performance like no other.

The Phantom Lights materialize unpredictably, casting an ethereal glow that defies the laws of conventional illumination. They flicker and shimmer, morphing between colors with a fluidity that seems almost sentient. Witnesses have observed these spectral lights emanating from seemingly empty fixtures, as if guided by an invisible hand or a supernatural force beyond human comprehension.

The behavior of the Phantom Lights is as perplexing as their existence. They may intensify with a sudden brilliance, bathing the stage in an ethereal radiance that surpasses the power of any conventional lighting equipment. In other instances, they may dim and fade, casting an eerie glow that barely illuminates the shadows, leaving the theater in an unsettling semi-darkness.

Some who have witnessed these supernatural illuminations claim to have felt an inexplicable energy in their presence—a tingling sensation that prickles the skin, leaving an indelible impression upon their psyche. The Phantom Lights seem to possess a consciousness of their own, reacting to the ebb and flow of the theater's energy and performances.

Theories abound regarding the origin of these phantom illuminations. Some suggest that they are echoes of performances past, the residual energy of theatrical brilliance imbuing the lights with a spectral glow. Others propose that they are manifestations of otherworldly entities—beings that are drawn to the creative energy that permeates Gammage Auditorium, using the lights as a conduit to interact with the mortal realm.

The Phantom Lights not only mesmerize and perplex but also add an extra layer of intrigue to the theater's ambiance. Their ethereal presence imbues performances with an otherworldly quality, as if the spirits of past artists are joining in the production, casting their spectral radiance upon the stage. The theater becomes a vessel for supernatural energy, blurring the lines between the physical and the metaphysical.

Stagehands and technicians have reported peculiar anomalies during their late-night shifts. Lights flicker and dim without cause, props mysteriously shift positions overnight, and unexplained footsteps echo through empty corridors. Some even claim to have heard disembodied whispers, as if the very walls of the auditorium were whispering secrets from ages past.

The Gammage Auditorium has become a magnet for paranormal investigators, each seeking to unlock the enigmatic mysteries that shroud the venue. Electronic voice phenomena recordings have captured spectral whispers, evoking names of long-forgotten performers and echoes of forgotten applause. Photographs taken within the auditorium have revealed ethereal apparitions, their semi-transparent forms a haunting testament to the specters that roam its hallowed halls.

As the sun sets and casts long shadows upon the Gammage Auditorium, an air of foreboding descends upon its hallowed grounds. It becomes a place where the boundary between the living and the dead blurs, where the echoes of applause intertwine with the spectral whispers of those who have passed beyond the veil.

Dare you venture into the realm of the Gammage Auditorium, where the phantoms of performers continue their eternal encore, and where the sinister secrets of the stage reveal themselves to those who are brave enough to confront the shadows that lurk within? The choice is yours, but be warned— for once you step foot into the ghostly enclave of the Gammage

High Society Hauntings

Auditorium, you may find yourself forever ensnared by its dark and enigmatic charm.

Chapter Ten: Haunted Highways

Route 85 from Buckeye to Ajo

Figure 69: A roadside stop along Route 85. Photo taken by Timothy James Wilson.

This road trip is going to be a little different from the other road trips that we have taken in this book, as with this road trip the road is part of the story. We will be traveling along Route 85, starting in Buckeye, through Gila Bend, down to Ajo, and conclude at the Organ Pipe Cactus National Monument in this trip, and these three small towns will be sharing their haunted secrets along the way.

This trip begins Buckeye, at the intersection of Interstate 10 and State Route 85, about 40 miles west of downtown Phoenix. I recommend breaking this trip into three segments, the first is to explore Route 85 between Buckeye and Gila Bend, the second to explore Route 85 between Gila Bend and Ajo, and the third to investigate the area south of Ajo, especially Organ Pipe National Monument.

Essentially, for this trip I would recommend a one-night stay at The Best Western Space Age Lodge in Gila Bend, and two nights at La Siesta Cabins in Ajo. Additionally, this trip will be taking you to some interesting desert areas, so wearing sturdy hiking boots, taking an adequate supply of water, and hiking essentials are key. Additionally, please remember that regardless of the time of the year the Arizona sun can be brutal, please dress accordingly, and bring plenty of sunscreen. I recommend also a wide brimmed hat.

Route 85
From Buckeye to Gila Bend

Route 85 in Arizona unveils a unique and eerie journey, steeped in unsettling stories and a chilling history. This enigmatic highway spans 123 miles, that will lead you through landscapes that conceal dark secrets and the lingering echoes of history. Route 85 is rumored to be a repository of haunted structures and sites, each housing its own unsettling legends and phantoms. As you embark on this mysterious highway, you may stumble upon several locations that bear the weight of their haunting narratives.

Our initial leg of the journey covers the 35 miles from Interstate 10 to Gila Bend, a stretch that encompasses the mysteries of the Sonoran Desert as well as its beauty.

As you set forth on this desolate desert highway, its rugged terrain and unforgiving heat serving as a stark reminder of nature's indifference to human existence. Beneath the relentless sun, the arid expanse of the Sonoran Desert stretches endlessly, a vast emptiness of some of the most beautiful, yet deadly, desert that seems to extend beyond the horizon.

Figure 70: Route 85. Photo taken by Timothy James Wilson.

Continuing along the route, the Gila River Indian Reservation unveils its haunting past. Now home to the Akimel O'odham and Pee Posh people, the very ground upon which the highway now lays was once the backdrop for tales of conflict and bloodshed. It's said that the spirits of fallen indigenous warriors still linger here, their anguished whispers carried by the desert winds. The fertile farmlands, once a source of sustenance, now bear witness to the haunting legacy of those who suffered and perished in long-forgotten battles.

Throughout history, Route 85 has claimed several victims. Locals whisper that the road itself hungers for souls, enticing unsuspecting travelers into its sinister embrace. Abandoned vehicles, twisted wrecks of metal, serve as solemn reminders of past accidents—scenes of horror and tragedy that unfolded along this desolate highway. The spirits of those who met their untimely demise are said to haunt the road, their restless souls trapped in a purgatory of eternal torment.

Route 85 transcends being just a highway; it's a conduit for the spectral spirits and grim tales of a troubled past. It beckons those daring enough to traverse its path, challenging them to confront the horrors that lie dormant within. However,

be forewarned, for the road cares not for the living or the dead—
it hungers only to consume, to perpetuate its grim legacy. Venture
forth at your own peril, for the road's insatiable appetite knows
no limits, and those who dare to journey along its ominous
course may find themselves ensnared in a fate with no escape.

Robbins Butte Wildlife Area
Buckeye, Arizona

Hidden, just 7 miles to the south of Interstate 10, you'll discover
the amazing preservation of land known as the Robbin's Butte
Wildlife Area. Within its vast expanse of 1681 acres, a realm of
uncanny ambiance and eerie beauty thrives. This shadowy
wilderness, ensnared by dense, entangled vegetation, conceals
secrets murmured by rustling leaves and ever-shifting shadows.

Figure 71: Robins Butte Wildlife Preservation Area. Photo taken by Timothy James Wilson.

To the north, the ghostly Gila River marks its boundary,
offering wildlife enthusiasts open ponds veiled in marshy cattails.
Alongside these spectral waters, vast stretches beckon, thickets of
impenetrable tamarisk—salt cedar—seeming to reach out with
gnarled fingers to ensnare curious wanderers. Native willows,

cottonwoods, and mesquites stand as haunting sentinels amidst this twilight undergrowth.

Within this captivating realm, a diverse array of life flourishes. Mountain lions roam like silent phantoms, their gleaming golden eyes concealing feral secrets. Javelina, resembling shadows emerging from an ethereal realm, traverse the mysterious landscape. And under the moonlight's pallor, the slithering coils of rattlesnakes intertwine with the spectral glow of desert flora.

However, it's the cacti that possess the most haunting allure. Their spiny silhouettes stand as guardians, seemingly protecting the enigmatic stories passed down through generations. Amidst their prickly embrace, scorpions emerge as enigmatic apparitions, their sting a venomous reminder of the darkness that can lurk beneath beauty.

In the heart of this land, the past lingers like a ghostly echo. Ruins, like whispers from ages long past, hint at the souls who once inhabited this eerie sanctuary. Petroglyphs etched into stone serve as ancient scripts, enigmatic symbols resonating with stories of life and lore spanning centuries.

Today, Robbins Butte remains a realm not only of the living but also of the otherworldly. It's whispered that amidst the thorny thickets and desolate waters, restless spirits find solace in the veiled embrace of twilight. The remote and foreboding brush conceals secrets yearning to be told, perhaps illuminated by the flicker of a campfire's glow as night settles in.

A few years ago, my wife and I hiked in this this area, exploring this wilderness. In the heart of this wilderness, we stumbled upon an opening in the thick brush to the Gila River. This is where we encountered a peculiar insect congregation— Velvet Ants. Also known as Cow killers, these creatures seemed like vengeful phantoms, their territorial nature a harbinger of spectral warnings.

These Velvet Ants, with hues as dark as the secrets whispered by the wind, are bearers of pain. Their stings, like talons, can induce an agony that feels like flames licking at the soul, a pain echoing in the night, lingering like a haunting melody.

Born of a parasitic dance, these ants engage in a ritualistic symbiosis with other insects—bees and wasps—conjuring echoes of shared fates. Female Velvet Ants, wingless and enigmatically robust, wield stingers more potent than the curses of the ancients, delivering torment as powerful as the whispers that drift through the tenebrous air.

Within this wilderness of shadow and secrets, the life cycle of the Velvet Ants unfolds. A parasitic rite, woven into the fabric of life, intertwines them with other insects—a sinister masquerade. Female Velvet Ants navigate the realm, seeking out the nests of unwitting hosts, laying eggs and weaving webs of dread that ensnare the larvae and pupae of their hosts. It's a tale of otherworldly cannibalism, a dark symphony of life and death.

The sting of these otherworldly specters is etched into the fabric of pain, its tale told through the cries of those who ventured too close. The unleashed agony is like a malevolent spirit clawing at the senses, searing the soul with its touch—an intensity transcending the mortal realm, its echoes rippling through the fabric of time and existence.

This venomous sting is the haunt of the Velvet Ants—a spectral defense, a spectral curse. Despite their seemingly ephemeral nature, these enigmatic creatures wield a stinger infused with the essence of the uncanny. Their venom, a sinister potion, laden with special tinctures that craft the essence of pain, each droplet akin to a whisper from hell.

As the shadows deepen and the night's cloak descends, a cautionary tale reverberates through the darkness. It speaks of phantoms concealed beneath the veil of flora and fang, a tale of pain borne from the otherworldly kiss of the Velvet Ants. Should you traverse this realm, heed the spectral warnings and let the shadows guide your steps. In the dance between twilight and darkness, the secrets of the Robbin's Butte Wildlife Area are woven—a tapestry of the eerie and the unknown.

Now, let's resume our journey on Route 85.

A Ghostly Hitchhiker

The eerie tale of the ghostly hitchhiker along Route 85 casts a chilling shadow, along this highway it is advised that you not stop for hitchhikers.

Route 85, a desolate stretch of highway, meanders through forsaken lands, where a malevolent presence holds sway. As the moon casts eerie silhouettes across the land, a specter emerges from the ethereal realm. The ghostly hitchhiker materializes, a phantom draped in a ghastly glow, luring unsuspecting travelers towards their impending doom.

This otherworldly hitchhiker isn't your run-of-the-mill traveler; she's an apparition trapped in perpetual unrest. Draped in tattered garments of a bygone era, she takes the form of a young woman, her eyes brimming with eternal sorrow.

Her phantom presence appears before weary drivers, abrupt and unsettling, as if conjured from the depths of the night. Her echoing voice pleads for a ride to a nearby town, spinning tales of desperate reunions or urgent destinations. Some drivers, moved by compassion for her plight, succumb to her ethereal entreaty.

As the ill-fated journey unfolds, an oppressive chill descends upon the vehicle, seeping into the very bones of the driver. An unexplainable unease grips their senses, constricting like a suffocating vice. Nervous glances into the rearview mirror reveal the hitchhiker's transformation; a grotesque metamorphosis that sends shivers down their spine.

Once-captivating eyes become hollow voids, devoid of all humanity. Her visage contorts with anguish and despair, a ghastly mask that defies all reason. Panic ensnares the driver, an instinctual urge to escape the unholy presence within their car. Desperate to be rid of this malevolence, they swerve to the roadside and come to an abrupt halt, their heart racing.

Turning to confront the nightmarish entity in their backseat, terror reaches its peak. Yet, in a cruel twist, the hitchhiker has vanished, leaving only an empty void where her spectral form once haunted. A mocking emptiness lingers, a cold reminder of their brush with the supernatural.

The legend whispers of a tragedy that befell this tormented spirit, her soul forever doomed to wander Route 85. Some claim a tragic car accident claimed her life, while others insist she fell victim to a brutal murder, her quest for justice unfulfilled. Regardless, her spectral apparition serves as an ominous omen, a macabre reminder of the perils concealed within the darkness.

Thus, the legend of the ghostly hitchhiker of Route 85 endures, weaving its web of terror and captivating the imaginations of both locals and wanderers alike. Let this cautionary tale resonate in your mind as you traverse these desolate roads, for the mournful cries of the specter still echo in the darkest corners of the night.

Lewis State Prison
26700 AZ-85, Buckeye, Arizona

Beyond the confines of the Robbins Butte Wildlife Area, a few miles down the road, a cautionary tale awaits on the right side of Route 85—a stark reminder of why apprehension lingers around hitchhikers: the Lewis State Prison complex, comprised of eight distinct units, each varying in security levels, ranging from level 2 to the highest security level, MAX. This modern penitentiary is a sentinel of confinement, its walls etching stories of caution and confinement into the landscape.

Figure 72: Lewis State Prison. Photo by Timothy James Wilson.

While no successful jailbreaks have been reported from within the prison's confines, one endeavor stands as a testament to the challenges of such an escape. An incident in 2004 etched an enduring chapter, the longest prison standoff in United States history. It unfolded within the Morey Unit, a segment of the Lewis complex.

Across a span of 15 days, commencing on January 18 and concluding on February 2, a chilling ordeal unfolded. Two officers, a male and a female, found themselves unwilling captives in the clutches of two inmates, Ricky Wassenaar and Steven Coy. Their desperate bid for escape devolved into an unforeseen crisis—a hostage situation. Amidst this grim predicament, a narrative of terror and resilience unfurled.

313

The plight of these officers took an even darker turn, as the inmates subjected them to unspeakable horrors. Sexual assault stained the already bleak canvas of captivity, inflicting trauma that would forever mark this lamentable chapter. The very structures that were meant to confine became witnesses to an excruciating saga of powerlessness and fear.

As the standoff reached its tumultuous end, the names Ricky Wassenaar and Steven Coy etched themselves into the collective memory. Wassenaar was eventually convicted and sentenced to 16 life sentences for the standoff.

This chilling narrative of captivity, resilience, and darkness serves as a somber reminder of the complex interplay between confinement and the human spirit. The Lewis State Prison complex stands not only as a bastion of containment but also as a silent sentinel bearing witness to the unfolding tales of lives intertwined in a symphony of crime and consequence.

The Historic Gillespie Dam Bridge
South Old US Highway 80, Arlington, Arizona

Just past the Lewis State Prison, turn right at South Woods Road, and then right again on South Old US Route 80. About 14 miles up you will come to the Historic Gillespie Dam Bridge. There is a small parking area on the southbound side of the road, where you can get out and walk around.

The bridge is an older truss-style bridge that spans the Gila River. Construction on the bridge was completed in 1927, and the rust and wear shows its age.

The remarkable thing about the bridge though, for us is the countless stories about the bridge. Locals and visitors to the area tell tales of ghostly figures encountered on the bridge, chasing them off the bridge. Many describe the bridge as making them feel uneasy on the bridge, as if someone or something is watching them on the bridge.

Figure 73: The Historic Gillespie Dam Bridge. Photo by Timothy James Wilson.

When I first encountered stories about this bridge I disregarded them as folklore, until 2021. My wife on the other hand has always regarded the bridge with cautious anxiety.

In early October 2021, I was in the area before sunrise, exploring a few notable duck hunting areas that I was planning to hunt later that year, with my dog Annie. Annie was a very intuitive Pitbull, and probably the best dog I have ever had. We crossed the bridge, and Annie started to stir in the back seat of my truck.

Noticing her stir, I pulled over in the parking area south of the bridge, as I thought she was signaling that she needed to go to the bathroom. I grabbed her leash and walked her along the road expecting that she would do her business and we would be back on the road.

As I let her out of the truck, I noticed some movement that I thought to be odd on the bridge. I walked her toward the bridge when she became noticeably agitated, the hair on the back of her neck stood up and she began growling and backing at the bridge. I pulled on the leash to get her to come with me, but she refused to advance towards the bridge at all.

Finally, after what seemed like a 20-minute ordeal, I finally took her back to the truck, and we drove away. As I pulled out, she barked and growled at the bridge.

This was all very confusing to me, as Annie was always a very passive dog, and I had never experienced anything like that with her.

Gila Bend, Arizona

Figure 74: A Roadside sculpture in Casa Grande. Photo by Timothy James Wilson.

Gila Bend is a small town located approximately 70 miles southwest of Phoenix, at the meeting point of Route 85 and Interstate 8.

Gila Bend has a rich history dating back to ancient times when it was inhabited by indigenous peoples, including the Ancestral Sonoran Desert Peoples and Tohono O'odham Nation.

The area is characterized by its fertile soil and access to the Gila River, making it an attractive location for agriculture and settlement.

The town's name comes from the nearby Gila River, which played a vital role in the region's development. In the late 19th century, Gila Bend became a key stop along the Southern Pacific Railroad route, facilitating trade and transportation in the area. It was officially incorporated as a town in 1962.

The town is characterized by its flat terrain, with the Gila River running nearby. It is surrounded by vast stretches of desert, providing residents and visitors with opportunities for outdoor activities such as hiking, birdwatching, and off-roading.

The nearby Barry M. Goldwater Air Force Range, which covers a vast area of desert, is an essential part of the town's geography. This range is used for military training and testing, and Gila Bend has a close relationship with the U.S. military.

If you are a backpacker looking to achieve the ultimate solace, the Barry M. Goldwater Air Force Range might be the ultimate adventure, as 1.9 million acres of uninhabited, and untouched Sonoran desert lays near Gila Bend, and all you need to do is get a permit from the DOD.

Gila Bend has a small-town, close-knit community feel. The culture of the town is influenced by its history, with a mix of Native American, Mexican, and American traditions. Residents often participate in local events and festivals that celebrate the region's cultural diversity and history.

The town's economy has traditionally been linked to agriculture, with farming and ranching playing a significant role. In recent years, tourism has also become important due to its proximity to popular attractions like the Organ Pipe Cactus National Monument and the Sonoran Desert National

Monument. Gila Bend's culture reflects the importance of these natural treasures.

Gila Bend is also known for being a popular stop for travelers along Interstate 8, with various restaurants and services catering to tourists passing through the area.

The Best Western Space Age Lodge
401 East Pima Street, Gila Bend, Arizona
Reservations: (928) 683-2273

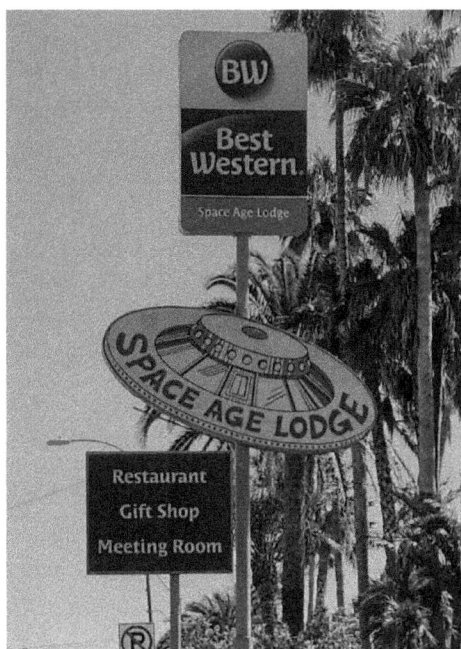

Figure 75: The Space Age Lodge in Casa Grande. Photo by Timothy James Wilson.

While I have tried to direct you throughout this book to locally owned hotels and other establishments, this hotel is an exception, because of its uniqueness. The Best Western Space Age Lodge is a unique and iconic hotel located in Gila Bend. This mid-century motor lodge captures the spirit of America's fascination with space exploration during the Space Race era. With its distinctive space-themed architecture, the Best Western Space Age Lodge offers guests a nostalgic journey into the past while providing modern comforts.

The Space Age Lodge's architecture stands out due to its space-themed design elements. The exterior of the motel features rocket-like structures, a flying saucer-shaped lobby, and a satellite-shaped observation deck. The space-age aesthetics pay homage to the optimism and enthusiasm of the mid-20th century's fascination with space travel and exploration.

Step into the lobby, and you'll be greeted by a retro-futuristic interior that transports you to the era when the Space Race was in full swing. The décor includes space-themed artwork, vintage furnishings, and memorabilia that captures the excitement of the time when humanity was reaching for the stars.

The Space Age Lodge offers a variety of amenities, including a heated pool, hot tub, and a restaurant with a space-themed menu. The guest rooms are designed with comfort in mind, featuring modern conveniences while retaining a touch of the motel's nostalgic charm.

A Cosmic Encounter

Standing as a time capsule of an era when the world's gaze turned to the stars, you will find the Best Western Space Age Lodge. Among the retro-futuristic architecture and space-themed décor, there's a tale that whispers of a cosmic encounter that defies explanation.

In the dead of night, a lone traveler checked into the Space Age Lodge, seeking respite after a long journey. The desert breeze carried an eerie stillness, and the stars above seemed to twinkle with an uncanny intensity. Little did the traveler know that the motel's space-inspired ambiance was about to manifest in ways beyond imagination.

As the traveler settled into their room, an otherworldly presence began to make itself felt. Strange lights danced outside the window, casting an ethereal glow across the room. The air hummed with a palpable energy, and a sensation of being watched settled over the traveler like a shroud.

Suddenly, the room was bathed in an otherworldly blue light. Startled, the traveler rose from the bed and stepped to the window, heart racing. What they saw defied all reason—a figure stood beyond the glass; its form indistinct yet somehow familiar. With a voice that seemed to resonate within the traveler's mind, the figure conveyed a message of peace and unity across the cosmos.

Overwhelmed by a mixture of fear and fascination, the traveler hesitated for a moment, then summoned the courage to step outside. In the crisp desert air, they found themselves face to face with an entity that defied earthly description. The figure emanated a sense of wisdom and benevolence, speaking in a language that transcended words.

As quickly as the encounter had begun, it faded away, leaving the traveler standing alone under the starlit sky. When morning broke, they found themselves questioning the reality of what had transpired. Was it a dream, a trick of the mind, or a genuine encounter with beings from beyond the stars?

The tale of the cosmic encounter at the Best Western Space Age Lodge remains shrouded in mystery, shared in hushed conversations among those who dare to explore the depths of the unknown. Some believe the motel's space-themed ambiance somehow opened a portal to another realm, while others chalk it up to the boundless imagination that space inspires.

Timothy James Wilson

In the heart of the desert, the Space Age Lodge continues to stand as a reminder that the universe holds secrets beyond our comprehension, waiting to be uncovered by those who dare to seek the truth among the stars.

Oatman Flat
South Oatman Road, Dateland, Arizona

Every single place that I have listed in this book is a place that I have personally been, with the exception of Oatman Flat, and Oatman Family Gravesight. This is the same Oatman family that we talked about in Chapter 9, and the sight of both the massacre and the family graves is about 35 miles west of Gila Bend.

I don't know much about this sight, as I have never been there, but as I was writing chapter 9 of this book realized that it could work as a nice little side trek for this chapter. I plan on going there someday, and maybe will include a little bit more about it in a future volume of this book.

I also cannot find any evidence that the sight is haunted, or that any paranormal activity has ever taken place there. It is however a grave so if you decide to go, I think midnight on a night with a full moon should be a safe bet.

Back on Route 85
From Gila Bend to Ajo

As we embark on a captivating second leg of this 55-mile journey from the vibrant town of Gila Bend to the charming oasis of Ajo, along the scenic Route 85. This stretch of desert highway weaves through the Sonoran landscape, offering travelers a blend of raw natural beauty and glimpses into the region's history and culture.

As you depart Gila Bend, the desert's vastness stretches before you, a canvas of muted hues and towering saguaro cacti that stand like ancient sentinels. The road winds through the desert expanse, inviting contemplation and solitude as you navigate the sun-soaked horizon.

Figure 76: Desert landscapes as seen from Route 85. Photo taken by Timothy James Wilson.

Keep an eye out for the incredible variety of desert flora and fauna that call this landscape home. From barrel cacti and cholla to the elusive roadrunner darting across the road, the Sonoran Desert reveals its inhabitants with every turn. The stark beauty of this arid environment contrasts with the vibrant life it sustains.

As you journey along Route 85, the Gila Bend Mountains rise in the distance, their rugged profiles etching the sky. The contrast of earth and sky as the sun rises creates a sense of awe as you traverse this landscape that has seen the passage of time for millennia. The route carries you through valleys and over gentle rises, revealing the desert's subtle shifts in elevation. Ancient rock formations, sculpted by wind and time, serve as reminders of the forces that have shaped this terrain over countless ages.

Timothy James Wilson
The Phantom Truck Driver

On moonless nights, when darkness engulfs the land, a specter emerges from the depths of the forsaken highway. The legend speaks of an ancient, rust-ridden truck, its once vibrant colors faded to a morose palette of decay. Its towering frame rumbles with an ominous resonance, a sound that reverberates through the fabric of existence, heralding the approach of doom.

The phantom truck materializes out of thin air, defying the laws of the mortal realm. Its spectral form glides along the desolate road, its headlights casting an ethereal glow that penetrates the night. The truck bears no license plates, no markings of any discernible origin. It is a vessel of the damned, forever condemned to traverse Route 85, an emissary from the netherworld.

Those who have the grave misfortune of crossing paths with this spectral juggernaut speak of an otherworldly terror that seizes their very core. The air thickens with an haunting mist, suffocating the senses and heralding the impending arrival of the phantom driver. It is said that the truck moves with unholy swiftness, careening through the darkness like a demon on wheels, its tires screeching against the asphalt as if in defiance of the natural order.

The phantom truck driver himself remains veiled in mystery, hidden beneath a cloak of shadow and malevolence. Witnesses catch but fleeting glimpses of his spectral form, a twisted figure draped in tattered raiment, his face obscured by darkness. Eyes that burn with an unearthly light gleam with a hunger for the souls of the living, a morbid appetite that knows no bounds.

The encounter with the phantom truck driver is not one that ends with a mere sighting. No, those who dare to cross his path find themselves ensnared in a web of unfathomable horror.

Misfortune befalls them, calamities that defy explanation and logic. Vehicles stall inexplicably, plunging their occupants into the heart of the desolate night. Unexplained mechanical failures become a sinister norm. And in the most sinister of cases, victims vanish without a trace, their fate forever intertwined with the chilling legend of Route 85.

Whispers among the locals speak of a pact forged with the dark forces of the abyss, a curse laid upon the phantom truck driver that eternally binds him to his infernal journey. Whether he seeks redemption or revels in his malevolence, none can tell. But one thing remains certain: the phantom truck driver of Route 85 is a harbinger of death and despair, a ghastly reminder that some souls are damned to forever haunt the twisted highways of the netherworld.

Travelers be warned, for should you dare to traverse Route 85 under the cloak of night, the phantom truck driver may find you.

Solace at the Barry Goldwater Range

If you are looking for solace, and you are a backpacker, then look no further than the Barry Goldwater Range in southern Arizona. On either side of the road you will see signs that designate that this area is only accessible by permit; however, what many don't know is that these permits are actually remarkably easy to obtain, and thus open up 1.9 million acres of pristine Sonoran Desert to you. Just watch out for bombers.

Figure 77: Gates to the Barry Goldwater Range. Photo by Timothy James Wilson.

Additionally, remember when venturing out into the Sonoran Desert that this land is filled with creatures and plants that seem to have homicidal tendencies, because everything in the desert is competing for resources. This land is truly a place where only the vultures get fat.

Ajo, Arizona

Figure 78: The city of Ajo. Photo taken by Timothy James Wilson.

Ajo is a small town located in the western part of Pima County. At less than 40 miles from the Mexican border the town is heavily influenced by its unique geographic position and has received national attention over the years as its position between the Tohono O'odham Nation, the Cabeza Prieta National Wildlife Refuge, and the Organ Pip Cactus National Monument.

Ajo's history is deeply connected to mining. The town's name is derived from the Spanish word "ajo," which means garlic. It was named after the abundant wild garlic that grew in the area. Ajo's mining history dates to the late 19th century when significant copper deposits were discovered in the nearby Ajo Mountains. This discovery led to the establishment of the New Cornelia Copper Company, which played a vital role in the town's development.

The town grew rapidly as mining operations expanded, and Ajo became a prominent copper mining community. The New Cornelia mine, at one point, was one of the largest open-pit copper mines in the world. Mining operations continued until the mid-1980s when the copper market declined, leading to the closure of the mine.

Ajo is situated in the heart of the Sonoran Desert, surrounded by stunning desert landscapes. The town is known for its unique geography, characterized by rocky outcrops, desert vegetation, and rugged terrain. The Ajo Mountains and the Organ Pipe Cactus National Monument are nearby, offering opportunities for hiking, bird-watching, and outdoor exploration.

Ajo's desert location also means it experiences a hot desert climate with extremely hot summers and mild winters. The area's natural beauty and desert landscapes are significant attractions for visitors.

Ajo has a rich cultural history, influenced by its mining heritage and its location near the Mexican border. The town's architecture reflects its mining past, with many historic buildings made of locally quarried Ajo stone.

Ajo's culture is also influenced by the Tohono O'odham Nation, one of the indigenous groups in the area. The Tohono O'odham have a long history in the region, and their culture and traditions continue to be an integral part of Ajo's identity.

In recent years, Ajo has seen efforts to revitalize the town and promote tourism. The historic Ajo Plaza serves as a focal point for community events and cultural activities. The annual Ajo Fiesta, which celebrates the town's heritage with music, dance, and food, is a significant cultural event.

Art and creativity have also found a place in Ajo's culture, with organizations like the International Sonoran Desert Alliance (ISDA) promoting art and cultural exchange. The Ajo Center for

Sustainable Agriculture supports local agriculture and education on sustainable farming practices.

The Phelps Dodge Hospital
515 West Hospital Road, Ajo, Arizona

Figure 79: The Phelps Dodge Hospital. Photo by Timothy James Wilson.

Perched upon a mountain inf front of the Old Ajo Mine there stands a solemn structure, a testament to pain and sorrow: the Phelps Dodge Hospital, often referred to as the Old Ajo Hospital. Situated within the town's desolate embrace, this deteriorating building exudes an unsettling presence, capable of sending shivers down even the stoutest hearts. It stands as a somber reminder of life's fragility and the enduring echoes of suffering embedded within its walls.

The Phelps Dodge Hospital, a relic of a bygone era, now rests in eerie abandonment. Once a place of healing and hope, it has transformed into a melancholic tomb where whispers from the past mingle with the chilling winds that pass through its shattered windows. Its crumbling exterior, adorned with cracked bricks and fading paint, tells a tale of neglect and decay—a reflection of the torment that once filled its corridors.

Positioned near Route 85, this ominous landmark casts its shadow upon unsuspecting travelers who journey by. The highway becomes a corridor of unease as the hospital's sinister energy seeps into the very essence of the road. It's as though the spirits trapped within the forsaken walls reach out, their ethereal presence extending toward passing vehicles, seeking release from their desolate confinement.

Legends envelop the Phelps Dodge Hospital in a shroud of darkness. Stories of apparitions wandering its dilapidated hallways, their mournful cries echoing through time, reverberate throughout the town. Locals share tales of unexplained phenomena—phantom footsteps in empty corridors, chilling whispers from vacant rooms, and the palpable presence of unseen entities lurking in the shadows.

The tormented spirits of past patients and medical staff are said to haunt the decaying chambers, forever tethered to their tragic past. These restless souls exist between realms, yearning for liberation from their spectral purgatory. Brave visitors who venture into the abandoned hospital speak of cold gusts of wind carrying anguished sighs, while flickering lights cast eerie, dancing shadows upon the crumbling walls.

Deep within the heart of the Phelps Dodge Hospital, a malevolent force lingers—an entity of darkness that thrives on the residual pain and suffering etched into its decaying foundation. Whispers suggest that this malevolent presence feeds on the despair and anguish that stains the very essence of the building, its insatiable hunger unquenched.

Should you dare to step into the shadowed corridors of the Phelps Dodge Hospital? Beware, for the veil between the living and the departed grows thin within its confines. The spirits of the forsaken beckon, their mournful pleas for solace echoing through time. If you heed their call, be prepared to confront the spectral remnants of the hospital's grim history and to acknowledge the chilling truth that certain hauntings persist long after life's doors have closed.

Historic Ajo Plaza
38 North Plaza Street, Ajo, Arizona

Figure 80: The Ajo Plaza. Photo by Timothy James Wilson.

At the heart of Ajo, right along Route 85, a plaza hides under an eerie shroud—a place where the living and the departed become entwined, and the line between reality and the supernatural fades into obscurity. As the sun sets over the town, a peculiar transformation takes over, casting a ghostly veil over the Ajo Plaza and its surroundings.

Local legends tell of a spectral gathering that materializes when night cloaks the town. The spirits of long-past residents, burdened by a restless yearning, converge in this ethereal meeting spot. Their ghostly forms drift along the empty streets, their vacant eyes filled with a longing for a life forever out of reach.

Whispers carried on the evening breeze resound through the melancholic plaza, the voices of days gone by seeking solace in the ears of the living. The chilling wind carries their tales, recounting the hardships and tragedies that befell the town's inhabitants. Unseen hands brush against unsuspecting skin, sending shivers down the spines of those who dare to venture too close to the spectral gathering.

As the midnight hour approaches, a palpable unease descends upon the area. Shadows twist and dance, taking on eerie shapes that seem to mock the living. Eyes peer out from the darkness, following every move, their gaze penetrating the soul, an unspoken warning to steer clear of the cursed plaza.

In the center of the square, an aged fountain stands as a solemn sentinel, its once-clear waters now stagnant and murky. It is said that within its depths resides a malevolent entity—an otherworldly presence that thrives on the lingering anguish that saturates the plaza. The fountain's tainted waters ripple with unseen forces, as if a gateway to the underworld awaits those foolhardy enough to approach.

Beneath the flickering lamplight, ghostly figures manifest, their spectral forms flickering in and out of existence. They are the tormented spirits of miners, forever trapped in a purgatory of labor and despair. Their ethereal appearances bear the marks of suffering and agony, their mournful cries carried on the winds, etching their sorrow deep into the plaza's essence.

Those who dare to explore the Historic Ajo Plaza at night find themselves ensnared in an eerie encounter with the supernatural. The air becomes thick with a foreboding presence, as if unseen hands tighten around their throats, choking the life from their lungs. Desperate pleas for mercy echo through the empty square, only to vanish into the void.

The legend of the Historic Ajo Plaza stands as a haunting reminder that certain places are forever cursed, trapped in a realm where the tormented souls of the past find no rest. It beckons the curious and the daring, tempting them with promises of hidden secrets and otherworldly encounters. But be cautious, for once ensnared in its spectral grasp, escape remains a distant dream, and the boundary between the living and the dead dissolves into a chilling nightmare.

La Siesta Cabins
2561 North Ajo Gila Bend Highway, Ajo, Arizona
Reservations: (602) 975-0106

Within the arid landscape of Ajo, La Siesta Cabins beckon with their rustic charm and tranquil ambiance. This collection of quaint cabins offers travelers a unique desert retreat, where comfort meets the rugged beauty of the surrounding Sonoran Desert.

As you approach La Siesta Cabins, you're greeted by a sense of serenity that emanates from the desert surroundings. The cabins are carefully positioned amidst the native flora, creating an oasis of calm where guests can unwind and reconnect with nature.

The cabins themselves are a blend of classic Southwest design and modern comfort. Each cabin reflects the warmth of adobe-style architecture, offering cozy spaces adorned with desert-inspired décor. Whether you're seeking a solo escape or a romantic getaway, the cabins provide a tranquil haven to rest your head after a day of exploration.

As the sun sets over the desert horizon, La Siesta Cabins come to life in a new way. The clear Arizona skies transform into a mesmerizing canvas of stars, visible from the comfort of your cabin's porch or patio. Immerse yourself in the peaceful symphony of desert sounds—the rustle of palm fronds, the gentle whisper of the wind, and the occasional call of nocturnal creatures.

The location of La Siesta Cabins places you in close proximity to Ajo's attractions. Explore the historic downtown area with its Spanish Colonial Revival architecture and vibrant arts scene. The cabins also provide a convenient base for venturing into the surrounding desert landscape, where natural wonders and outdoor adventures await.

Tacos El Tarasco
15 West Plaza Suite 167, Ajo, Arizona

Really, you can never usually go wrong (in Arizona) with a locally operated taco shop, but Tacos El Tarasco serves some of the best Carne Asada I have ever had. That statement in itself says a lot, since I have lived over 42 years within a three-hour drive to Mexico.

While you're exploring the historic downtown area, I strongly encourage you to stop into this small restaurant for dinner. Their burritos are outstanding, their prices are great, and the service is outstanding.

The Organ Pipe Cactus National Monument
10 Organ Pipe Drive, Ajo, Arizona
Information: (520) 387-6849

In the heart of the sun-drenched Sonoran Desert, the Organ Pipe Cactus National Monument emerges as a breathtaking oasis of natural wonder. Here, the desert landscape reveals its extraordinary beauty through a tapestry of colors, textures, and life forms that have adapted to the harsh yet enchanting environment.

Venturing into the Organ Pipe Cactus National Monument, you find yourself immersed in a living canvas of desert beauty. The sweeping vistas unfold in a panorama of earthy hues, ranging from the soft, golden sands to the vivid greens of hardy desert vegetation. Towering saguaro cacti reach for the sky like nature's sculptures, while ocotillo plants stand sentinel with their vibrant red blooms.

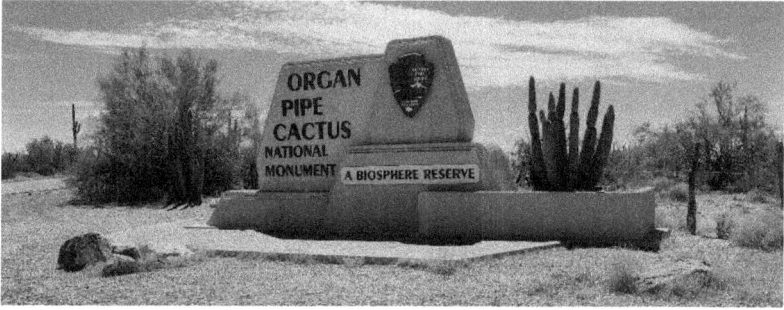

Figure 81: Organ Pipe National Monument. Photo by Timothy James Wilson.

Within the vast expanse of the arid terrain, a botanical marvel stands as a testament to the resilient beauty of the Organ Pipe Cactus National Monument. Named after the iconic organ pipe cacti that grace its landscape, the monument holds a treasure trove of these majestic plants, which are a rarity in the United States outside of this region. Their presence creates an awe-inspiring spectacle that captivates the senses and deepens our understanding of the delicate equilibrium between aesthetics and adaptation that defines life in the desert.

As you wander through the monument, the organ pipe cacti rise like natural sculptures against the canvas of the desert horizon. Their towering frames, adorned with multiple arms reaching skyward, cast intricate shadows in the soft desert light. These silhouettes become more than just plants—they become emblematic of the tenacity of life in a place where water is scarce, and conditions are challenging.

The organ pipe cacti's multi-armed forms are not only a testament to their ability to thrive in the harshest of environments, but also an example of nature's ingenuity. Each arm serves as a reservoir, storing water during rare rainfalls and releasing it gradually during times of drought. This adaptation allows these cacti to survive and flourish where others might falter, creating a living symphony of form and function that harmonizes with the desert's rhythm.

Beyond their utilitarian design, the organ pipe cacti embody an elegance in survival. Their presence is a constant reminder of the tenacious spirit of desert life, where beauty doesn't merely coexist with adversity—it thrives within it. The cacti's flowers, which bloom in hues of white and pink during the summer months, stand as beacons of life in a landscape that often seems barren and unforgiving.

The organ pipe cacti serve as both a botanical wonder and a lesson in resilience. Amidst the extremes of the desert climate, they remind us that survival is an art, and beauty can emerge from the most unlikely places. As you stand before these majestic cacti, let them inspire you to embrace life's challenges with grace and determination, just as they do in the arid embrace of the Organ Pipe Cactus National Monument.

The Organ Pipe Cactus National Monument is a living testament to the remarkable diversity that thrives in this seemingly inhospitable terrain. From the resilient creosote bushes that release a soothing aroma after rain showers to the yucca plants that serve as sources of sustenance for desert-dwelling creatures, every plant and organism plays a vital role in this intricate ecosystem.

The ever-changing weather in this desert realm contributes to the monument's dynamic character. During the day, the sun casts its radiant glow upon the landscape, illuminating the intricacies of the desert flora. When evening descends, a magical transformation occurs as the skies blush with hues of orange and pink, heralding the arrival of the cool desert night.

As you traverse the trails and pathways that wind through the Organ Pipe Cactus National Monument, take a moment to marvel at the exquisite biodiversity that thrives in this unique habitat. The desert's resilience, its ability to support a vast array of life, and its breathtaking natural beauty converge to create an experience that enriches the soul and inspires a deep reverence for the intricate tapestry of life that flourishes in the arid embrace of this remarkable land.

The Devil's Highway

In the haunting and true narrative of *The Devil's Highway* by acclaimed author Luis Alberto Urrea, a chilling true story unfolds against the unforgiving backdrop of the Organ Pipe Cactus National Monument, and the city of Ajo. This gripping tale takes us into the heart of one of the most perilous journeys undertaken by a group of desperate migrants attempting to cross into the United States from Mexico. The very name, "the Devil's Highway" alludes to the treacherous path these individuals faced—a path fraught with danger, suffering, and the relentless pursuit of hope.

In May 2001, a group of twenty-six men left the border town of Altar, Mexico, seeking a new life in the United States. Guided by smugglers, they embarked on a journey across the inhospitable terrain of the Sonoran Desert, through the Organ Pipe Cactus National Monument. However, the desert's scorching temperatures, lack of water, and rugged terrain turned their expedition into a harrowing ordeal. As the days stretched on and resources dwindled, desperation set in, and survival became a test of human endurance.

Haunted Highways

Urrea's masterful storytelling captures the plight of these migrants, vividly painting a picture of their courage, determination, and the tragic consequences of their journey. The group's struggles and ultimate tragedy serve as a powerful metaphor for the broader challenges faced by undocumented migrants seeking a better life in the face of seemingly insurmountable odds.

Luis Alberto Urrea's "The Devil's Highway" is a haunting and poignant account that sheds light on the complexities of immigration and human survival. Drawing from extensive research and firsthand accounts, Urrea crafts a narrative that is both heart-wrenching and deeply insightful. His writing explores themes of desperation, human connection, and the unbreakable will to endure, all set against the backdrop of a harsh and unforgiving landscape.

For those who are captivated by the haunting tale of the Devil's Highway and wish to delve deeper into the personal experiences of those involved, Urrea's book is a must-read. It offers a poignant exploration of the human spirit's capacity to overcome adversity, while also shedding light on the complexities of border politics and immigration policies. Whether seeking to better understand the challenges faced by migrants or simply drawn to a powerful and moving story.

Figure 82: An Organ Pipe Cactus. Photo by Timothy Jam

About The Author

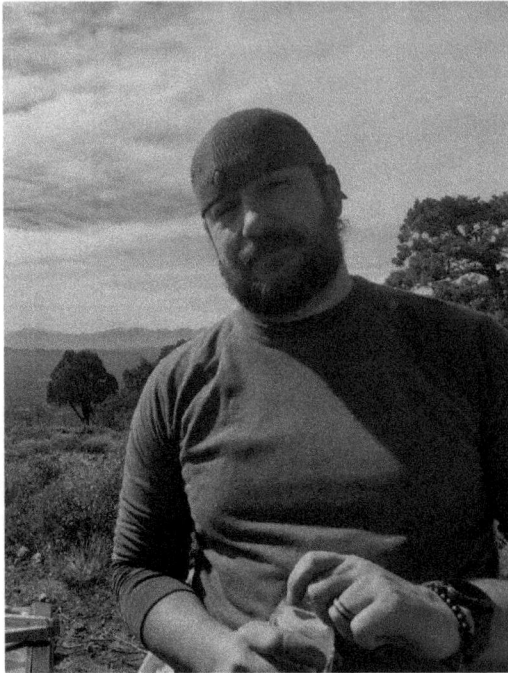

Figure 83: Photo taken by Shirley Marie Wilson.

Timothy James Wilson loves adventure. He grew up in Southern California hiking the many mountains in California. He trekked the John Muir Trail at just 14 years old. When he was 17 years old he moved to Arizona.

Upon graduating from high school, Tim attended the University of Arizona for a few years, before leaving to join the Navy following September 11th. He was an Aircraft Mechanic in the Navy for six years, and worked as an Aircraft mechanic following his enlistment, until 2013 when he decided to finish his degree.

Now living in the Phoenix area, he attended Glendale Community College and Phoenix College, before transferring to Arizona State University where he got his Bachelor of Science in Geography. Tim also holds a Master of Education from Northern Arizona University, and a Master of Business Administration from Grand Canyon University.

Tim spent almost a decade working in higher education and non-profit as a project/program manager, but his true passion is writing, research, and adventure, so in 2023 he decided to write a book, "Spirits Among the Saguaros" about the many adventures there are to be had in Arizona.

Tim is most comfortable near the campfire, telling stories about his many adventures. He loves the outdoors, hiking, backpacking, fishing, and hunting. He's often in front of a barbeque or cooking on the fire for his family.

Tim is married and has three wonderful children. He is also expecting his first granddaughter in early 2024.

Tim is currently working on the following books to come out in the future:

- Spirits Among the Saguaros: Volume 2, expected in 2024
- The Chronicles of Emily Poe, expected in 2024
- Mysteries Among the Saguaros
- Hunting the American Bigfoot
- Ladies Among the Saguaros
- Aliens Among the Saguaros
- Cryptids Among the Saguaros

Tim also is the CEO and President of Midnight Fog Chronicles, LLC, a local micro-publishing company he founded in Peoria, AZ in 2023.

Tim can be found on Instagram @timothyjwilson.mfc.

If You Like This Book, You'll Love What's Coming Next!

Thank you for embarking on this literary journey with me. Your support means the world, and I'm excited to share a special opportunity with you. By joining my exclusive monthly author's newsletter and following me on Instagram, you'll gain access to a world of explorations in the American Southwest and beyond.

Why Should You Join?
Be the First to Know: As a newsletter subscriber and Instagram follower, you'll be among the first to hear about my upcoming releases and projects, giving you the chance to dive into fresh, captivating stories before anyone else. Get ready to lose yourself in exciting new adventures!

Behind-the-Scenes Insights: Delve into the creative process. I'll take you behind the scenes, offering unique insights into my writing journey, as well as my adventures. You'll gain an intimate look at the heart and soul of my work.

Exclusive Content: Subscribers will enjoy exclusive content, including sneak peaks and even short stories that won't be available anywhere else. It's a front-row seat to the literary magic.

Publisher's Insider: Stay in the loop about upcoming projects from my publishing company, Midnight Fog Chronicles. Whether it's a new author, an exciting anthology, or an innovative literary venture, you'll be the first to hear about it.

Special Offers: From time to time, I'll treat my newsletter subscribers and Instagram followers to special discounts, giveaways, and promotions. It's my way of saying thank you for your continued support.

How to Join:
Signing up is easy! To sign up for my newsletter go to https://midnight-fog-chroniclesllc.square.site/
Or follow me on Instagram @timothyjwilson.mfc.

Thank you for your continued support, and I look forward to welcoming you to our exclusive newsletter family.

Happy Reading!
Timothy James Wilson

P.S. Your literary and literal adventure starts here. Don't miss the next chapter—sign up today!

www.ingramcontent.com/pod-product-compliance
Lightning Source LLC
Chambersburg PA
CBHW070053030426
42335CB00016B/1872